C000263866

COSENS OF WEYMOUTH

1918 TO 1996

MONARCH in 1930. AUTHOR'S COLLECTION / SEWARD

For Tom and Beth
who never knew the Cosens steamers but have nonetheless grown up with them.

COSENS
OF WEYMOUTH

1918 to 1996

BY

RICHARD CLAMMER

TWELVEHEADS PRESS

TRURO 2001

CONTENTS

Units of measurement and money used in this book are those which were concurrent with events described. They may be converted as follows:

Money: £1 = 20 shillings (s) = 100 pence (p)
          1 shilling = 12 pence (d)

TWELVEHEADS PRESS

First published 2001 by Twelveheads Press.
Chy Mengleth, Twelveheads, Truro, Cornwall TR4 8SN.
ISBN 0 906294 47 9
British Library Cataloguing-in-Publication Data.
A catalogue record for this book is available from the British Library.

Designed by Alan Kittridge. Printed by The Amadeus Press Ltd., Cleckheaton, West Yorkshire.

INTRODUCTION

With a sharp sound of splintering wood, the crowbar wielded by the skipper of the German tug *Fairplay II* wrenched loose one of the heavy boards sealing the elegant, mahogany main staircase of the Cosens paddle steamer *Embassy*. Accompanied by the ship broker and the author, he wriggled his way through the tiny gap he had created and slid down the stairway onto the vessel's darkened main deck. The date was 24 May 1967 and the tug master was undertaking a final inspection of the vessel, to ensure that she was secure and watertight, before commencing the tow to the breaker's yard. All of her windows and hatchways had been sealed with timber and canvas, so it was by torchlight that we crept around the familiar interior of the old ship. It was a poignant experience to see the beam of the torch settle on the dusty details of the abandoned saloons, illuminate the odd items of ship's equipment left scattered by the departing crew, or pick out the dull brass work and first traces of rust on the steel work of the normally glittering engine room. Gone were the familiar sensations of a pleasure steamer at sea: the heave of the deck underfoot; the warmth and smell of live steam and lubricating oil; and that unique myriad of sounds composed of the rhythmic beat of paddle wheels, hissing of the engines, clanging of telegraphs, tumbling of the wake, whistle of wind in the rigging, clinking of glasses from the bar and the hum of passengers' voices. Instead all was cold, still and silent.

A day later she was gone and, for the first time in 119 years, Weymouth Harbour was without a Cosens paddle steamer. It was the end of a story which had begun on 15 July 1848, when local sea captain, Joseph Cosens, had put the small, chartered paddle steamer *Highland Maid* into service between Weymouth and Portland.

Joseph, together with his younger brother William, had spent his whole career at sea in schooners engaged in the coastal trade between London and Ireland but, as a Weymouthian and entrepreneur, had watched with interest the

A composite postcard, published before the Great War. The MAJESTIC was lost in the Mediterranean in 1916 while serving as a minesweeper.
AUTHOR'S COLLECTION

S.S. "MONARCH"

COSENS & CO'S 2 PLEASURE STEAMERS

COSENS & COMPANYS PLEASURE STEAMERS

BOURNEMOUTH 2 SWANAGE, WEYMOUTH 2 ISLE OF WIGHT ETC.

S.S. "MAJESTIC"

S.S. "EMPRESS"

S.S. EMPEROR OF INDIA.

development of steam navigation from the Dorset port. In 1840 the Post Office packets to the Channel Islands and the long distance coastal packets which called at Weymouth had been joined by the first locally-owned steamer, the 108ft *Rose*, which operated between Weymouth and Southampton to connect

with the railway to London. By 1847, however, the railway had reached Dorchester and the *Rose*'s proprietors, realising that their service would soon be redundant, sold her in January 1848. Joseph Cosens, however, was well aware of plans to build a massive harbour of refuge at Portland. In addition to a vast breakwater, there was to be a citadel, elaborate defences, a convict establishment, barracks, quays and a series of inclined railways designed to move stone from the government quarries to the construction sites. As convicts, soldiers and civilian workmen began to flow onto the island in huge numbers, Cosens reasoned that there was a substantial profit to be made by providing an efficient transport link from the mainland, the only alternative to the twenty-minute steamer crossing being a slow and tedious journey by carrier's waggon across the inhospitable Chesil Beach.

Highland Maid entered service on 15 July 1848 but was soon replaced by the larger *Princess*, whose superior accommodation was appreciated by the increasing number of sightseers who were beginning to flock to Portland to view the works. Despite competition from Philip Dodson's rival steamers *Contractor* and *Ocean Bride*, the service flourished and Cosens entered into a partnership with Joseph Drew, proprietor of the *Southern Times*. In 1852 they introduced the purpose-built steamer *Prince* whose advent stimulated a rapid expansion of excursion sailings along the coast to Lulworth Cove, Portland Bill and more distant destinations as far afield as Dartmouth, Poole and Cherbourg. Excursions were also offered at short notice to view any event or sight of interest from landslips and shipwrecks to captured whales. During this period the Cosens brothers also built up a harmonious relationship with J. T. Leather, the contractor responsible for building the Portland breakwater, which resulted in the steamers becoming heavily and profitably employed in connection with the breakwater works.

By 1858 Cosens had disposed of the opposition from Dodson's vessels, but their relief was short-lived for, in August 1859, local solicitor John Tizard introduced two additional steamers, *Bannockburn* and *Premier* at Weymouth to coincide with the planned arrival of Brunel's leviathan steamship *Great Eastern* on her maiden voyage from the Thames. Whether this was true competition is open to debate, as by January 1860 the two companies had amalgamated to

form the Weymouth & Portland Steam Packet Company with Cosens, Drew and Tizard as the majority shareholders.

During her stay at Portland the *Great Eastern* was thrown open to the public and provided a great boost to the steamers, which provided the only means of reaching her. After her departure the combined fleet settled into a regular pattern of operation with the smaller vessels maintaining a regular service to and from Portland together with trips round the bay and to local destinations, whilst *Premier* and *Prince* were engaged on longer excursions. The arrival of the railway at Weymouth in 1857 brought a welcome influx of potential passengers to the town whilst facilities were greatly improved by the construction of a new pile pier at Weymouth in 1859, jetties at Portland and Swanage and the first pier at the growing resort of Bournemouth in 1861.

The steamers also undertook a great deal of opportunist work. They helped to repair the underwater telegraph cable to the Channel Islands, ferried sailors ashore from the warships of the Channel Fleet which was visiting the new harbour of refuge with increasing frequency, and offered a towage service to sailing ships entering and leaving Weymouth harbour. They also went to the assistance of the many sailing ships which got into distress off the treacherous Dorset coast , and were able to earn sufficient lucrative salvage awards to justify replacing *Contractor* with the purpose-built paddle tug *Commodore* in 1863. Salvage work and the provision of a liberty boat service to the Royal Navy at Portland were to provide a substantial portion of the company's income between the official opening of the breakwater in 1872 and the outbreak of the Great War. Joseph Cosens also added to his personal income by becoming lessee of the Weymouth Harbour dues and operating a successful coal business from his premises on the quay.

Following the deaths of John Tizard in 1873 and Joseph Cosens in 1874, Mr. S. J. Fowler was appointed company secretary and the affairs of the company were managed by a board of directors chaired by Joseph Drew. Two years later, on 10 June 1876, Cosens & Co Ltd, was officially incorporated as a limited company with capital of £12,800 and rapidly went from strength to strength.

During the mid 1870s *Premier* and *Prince* had introduced regular sailings westwards from Weymouth, rounding Portland Bill to call at Bridport, Lyme Regis, Seaton, Sidmouth, Beer and Budleigh Salterton. Initially these trips were advertised to a single destination but, as the years went by, they developed into the once renowned 'Coasting Trip' across Lyme Bay calling at a selection of these places before proceeding to Torquay. At all but Lyme Regis and occasionally Bridport, passengers were landed directly onto the open beaches. The steamer dropped a kedge anchor as she made her approach and grounded her bows on the steeply-shelving shingle. Passengers landed by means of a gangway over the ship's bows.

In the summer of 1880 a new pier with accommodation for four steamers was due to open at Bournemouth. Although the developing resort had been served over the years by a variety of locally-owned steamers, Cosens recognised the potential for further growth in trade provided they could stave off competition from the local companies and the Southampton, Isle of Wight & South of England Royal Mail Steam Packet Company Ltd, (hereafter referred to as the Southampton Company) who were also casting covetous eyes on the station. Accordingly, Cosens rebuilt *Prince* and *Premier* and ordered a brand new steamer *Empress* for delivery during the summer of 1879. At 160ft in length she was the largest and fastest steamer on the South Coast and easily outclassed her rivals. She became the company's flagship and took over the longest excursions, allowing *Prince* to be transferred to Torquay from where she ran excursions along the coast.

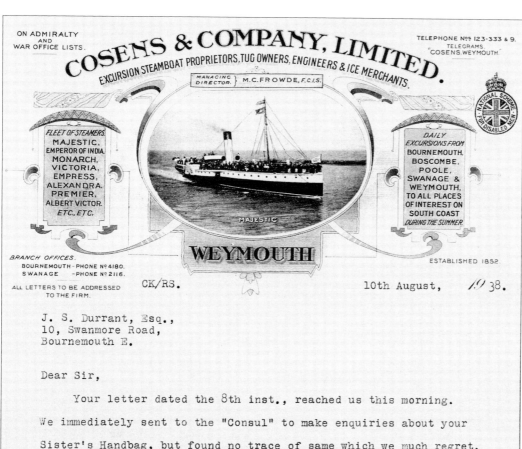

The company's elaborate pre-Great War letterhead survived relatively unchanged until the Second World War and still featured the MAJESTIC, *which was lost in 1916.*
VICTOR GRAY
COLLECTION

The front cover of Cosens & Co Ltd's Official Guide for the 1923 season. AUTHOR'S COLLECTION

Fortuitously for Cosens, the rival Bournemouth Steam Packet Company Ltd was forced to wind up its affairs during the 1880 season and the Weymouth company was able to fill the temporary vacuum by basing *Premier* at Bournemouth from Easter Monday 1881. The arrangement became a permanent one, with one or more Cosens steamers based at Bournemouth in every peace time summer until 1966. Later in 1881, however, the appearance of the newly-formed Bournemouth, Swanage & Poole Steam Packet Company's *Lord Elgin* heralded a period of intense competition at Bournemouth which led to a rapid expansion of both company's fleets.

The Bournemouth Company added three steamers, to which Cosens responded with *Victoria* of 1884, *Monarch* of 1888 and the Weymouth-based paddle tugs *Queen* and *Albert Victor*.

While their steamer services were expanding steadily, Cosens & Co Ltd, had also been busy developing other branches of their activities, and by the 1890s were the largest employer in Weymouth. A well-equipped general and marine engineering works and two modern slipways enabled the company to maintain its own steamers at very low cost in addition to attracting a wide range of outside ship repairing and general engineering work and to proclaim itself as 'shipwrights, general engineers, boiler makers, smiths, millwrights, iron and brass founders, coppersmiths, etc'. Cosens pioneered the installation of electric lighting in their own and several other commercial premises in Weymouth, and developed a brisk trade in maintaining the steam, gas and electrical machinery in numerous local businesses. For many years the company operated a local coal trade and, when this was relinquished in 1884, converted their quayside premises into a cold store and began to import Norwegian block ice. This trade flourished until the Great War when it was replaced by ice manufacturing and cold storage.

The work of ferrying sailors to and from visiting warships in Portland roads has already been alluded to. By 1906 when work on the Portland Breakwaters was finally completed, a major naval dockyard was under construction, a coaling station was well established and the harbour had become a regular base for the fleet. The arrangements for ferrying liberty men by Cosens paddle steamers were formalised in a series of contracts and, until the outbreak of war in 1914, provided a steady source of year-round income which was unique among excursion steamer operators. The new breakwaters were garrisoned and Cosens were also able to obtain a lucrative contract to ferry supplies and personnel to and from the forts, for which purpose a fleet of steam launches and barges was obtained.

One or more of the company's paddle tugs was kept in steam day and night all year round, and a large if irregular income was generated by general towage and salvage work. The latter was dangerous and dramatic work and several of the tug masters became renowned all along the south coast for their daring exploits. A flourishing diving department also developed. This variety of activity made Cosens a quintessential example of Victorian enterprise and of major importance to the economy of Weymouth and south Dorset.

Back at Bournemouth, the next major development in the excursion trade was stimulated by the huge naval review held at Spithead to celebrate Queen Victoria's Diamond Jubilee in 1897. Among the excursion steamer operators from other parts of Britain who sent vessels to take advantage of the event was P.&A. Campbell Ltd of Bristol, who quickly recognised the potential of basing a steamer permanently in the area and sent their splendid

Cambria to Southampton for the 1897 season. This alarmed the local Southampton Company who, seeing their own vessels seriously outclassed, responded by introducing the *Lorna Doone* in 1898 and the *Balmoral* in 1900. The high-speed *Cambria* and *Balmoral* were very evenly matched and frequently crossed from Bournemouth to Cherbourg on the same days, causing intense excitement amongst the public who would often turn out in considerable numbers to watch the two ships racing for the pier at the end of their long day trip to France. Cosens realised that the presence of these two glamorous ships was costing them both prestige and passengers and considered how to respond. Realising that there was little chance of outdoing the speed of their rivals, the Cosens board opted to build a ship of comparable size but greater comfort. The result was their new flagship, *Majestic*, which was delivered in May 1901.

The Bournemouth Company, meanwhile, was in serious financial difficulties and in 1901 was forced to sell their paddle steamer *Brodick Castle* to Cosens. This event, coupled with the arrival of *Majestic* prompted Cosens to abandon their austere black, bell-topped funnels in favour of a new livery of 'buff funnels' with black tops, from which the fleet henceforth derived its 'marketing' name.

The Southampton Company's *Balmoral* and *Lorna Doone* continued to collect passengers from both Bournemouth and Swanage on their long day trips from Southampton and in 1905 the company decided to base a steamer permanently at Bournemouth. By 1907 this had increased to two steamers. In 1908 they introduced the brand new, purpose-built *Bournemouth Queen* and purchased the Bournemouth Company's remaining steamer *Lord Elgin*. Cosens, well aware of these pending developments, countered by purchasing an almost new steamer called *Princess Royal* which, suitably modified and lengthened, entered service as *Emperor of India* in 1908

The next six years represented the zenith of steamer services from Weymouth and Bournemouth. An astonishing variety of excursions ranging from Dartmouth in the west to Brighton in the east and across the channel to Alderney and Cherbourg were available and demand seemed almost limitless. At Weymouth the Admiralty Contract required more and more vessels to be available to tender the anchored warships and in the peak months of the summer the company's resources were severely stretched. *Brodick Castle* was sold at the end of 1909 but, over the next few seasons, Cosens were forced to add *Helper*, *Melcombe Regis*, *Alexandra* and the chartered *Lord Roberts* to their fleet simply to meet all of their commitments.

Thus, the summer of

An example of the crockery used on board the company's steamers throughout the period covered by this book.
AUTHOR'S COLLECTION

1914 found Cosens' steamer fleet and business at an all time high. *Majestic*, *Monarch* and *Empress* were stationed at Bournemouth; *Emperor of India* and *Victoria* were Weymouth-based but came to Bournemouth on several days a week; whilst *Premier*, *Albert Victor*, *Queen*, *Helper*, *Melcombe Regis* and *Alexandra* were on tender, salvage and excursion duties from Weymouth. In addition to these eleven paddle steamers, three large steam launches *Prince George*, *Prince Edward* and *Princess* together with a variety of smaller pinnaces, were on War Office duties at Weymouth.

The outbreak of the Great War brought an abrupt end to this Edwardian idyll. Although a limited Bournemouth-Swanage service and occasional trips to the Isle of Wight were offered until the end of the season, the majority of the steamers were recalled to Weymouth. *Queen*, *Albert Victor* and *Prince George* were immediately requisitioned by the Admiralty for use as examination vessels at Portland, and the salvage tugs together with *Helper* and *Melcombe Regis* were kept busy on a series of dramatic rescues during the winter of 1914-5. As the war progressed more and more of the steamers were taken up for naval service and were gradually dispersed far and wide. *Helper*, *Melcombe Regis* and *Empress* initially became examination vessels at Newhaven after which the latter became a tender at Portsmouth while the others were transferred to minesweeping duties at Belfast; *Alexandra* went as an Admiralty

P.S. VICTORIA.
THIS VESSEL WAS ON
ADMIRALTY SERVICE FROM
1917 TO 1919 INCLUSIVE
UNDER THE NAME OF
H.M.S. VICTORIA IV.

The war service plate carried on board VICTORIA, now on display in Weymouth Museum.
BRIAN JACKSON

ferry to Sheerness and *Victoria* to Plymouth; *Queen* and *Albert Victor* employed as mine layers at Dover; and *Premier* was sent to Harwich. *Monarch* served as a minesweeper in the Bristol Channel and Irish Sea, whilst *Emperor of India* and *Majestic* were sent to the Mediterranean on similar duties.

The only ship the company lost during the war was the splendid flagship *Majestic*, which foundered off Oran whilst on passage between Gibraltar and Malta on 28 July 1916. When the rest of the fleet returned to its peacetime duties it found a world that had changed forever.

This history takes up the story of Cosens' 'Buff Funnel Fleet' in 1918 and follows its fortunes until the disposal of the last steamer, *Embassy*, in 1967. A companion volume is planned, which will expand on this introduction by telling the full story of the formation and growth of the company in the spacious Victorian and Edwardian days before 1914.

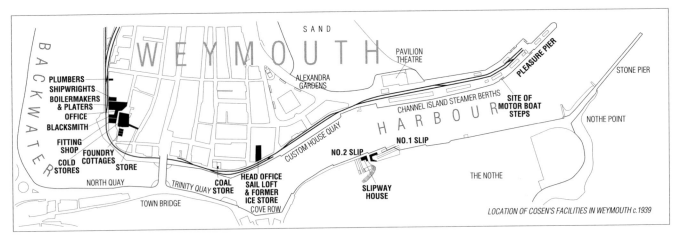

LOCATION OF COSEN'S FACILITIES IN WEYMOUTH c.1939

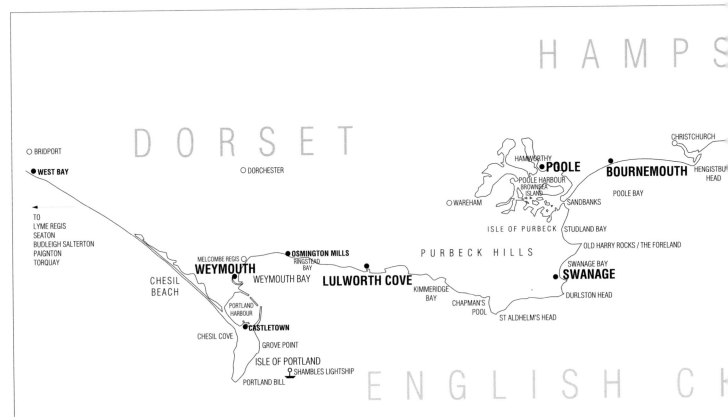

CHAPTER ONE
POST-WAR RECONSTRUCTION

Immediately the armistice was announced on 11 November 1918, Cosens & Co Ltd's thoughts turned to the restoration of peacetime excursion services, if possible for the 1919 season. Their plans hinged on three factors, all outside the company's immediate control, namely the return and reconditioning of the steamers themselves; the recovery from military control of vital facilities at Poole, Swanage and Portland; and the willingness of the Board of Trade (BoT) to issue passenger certificates.

The release of the steamers from war service was extremely unpredictable and made forward planning difficult. Nor was the actual date of release the end of the story, as for each ship there followed a lengthy negotiation over the precise amount to be paid by the government for repair and refurbishment, and where and by whom the work would be carried out. In several cases ships were released into Cosens' hands but lay idle for many months before terms could be agreed and reconditioning could begin.

First to be released was the steam launch *Princess* which left the Tyne shortly after the armistice, arrived in Weymouth in the first week of January 1919 and was immediately reconditioned. Both she and *Prince George*, which had been slightly damaged in collision with the French trawler *Becifique*, were placed in the hands of a London broker 'with view of their disposal if possible.' *Premier* was released from her brief charter at Harwich and steamed as far as Poole where, during December, she was chartered by the Ministry of Shipping as a tug to attend the launch of a large concrete barge. She then returned to Weymouth, was released by the Admiralty during May and by June 1919 was refitting on Cosens' slipway.

Empress arrived home from Portsmouth on 4 January 1919 and news was received that *Helper* had put into Swansea for repairs on her way back from her minesweeping duties at Belfast. She remained there for three months before terms for her reconditioning were agreed and she proceeded to Cardiff where the work was carried out. By the beginning of April work was also in full swing on board *Empress* at Weymouth, and the two ships had been selected to reopen any passenger services which might be permitted during the coming season.

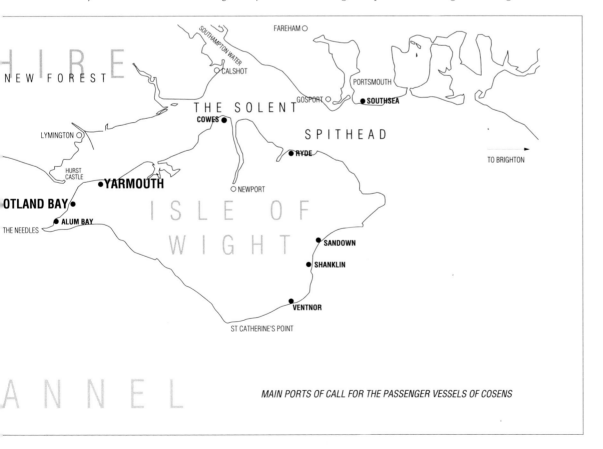

MAIN PORTS OF CALL FOR THE PASSENGER VESSELS OF COSENS

Also during April, *Albert Victor* and *Queen* were released from their work on the controlled minefields at Dover. *Queen* was diverted to act as a liberty boat in Portsmouth Harbour for the rest of the year, while *Albert Victor* returned direct to Weymouth where she lay idle until August when a £3000 settlement for her refit was finally agreed. It is interesting to note that, during January, Cosens had asked J. P. Reynoldson & Sons, the well-known South Shields tug-building company, to quote for a replacement for *Albert Victor* but, due to the immediate post-war shipbuilding boom, they had a full order book and were unable to do so.

Monarch's duties with the Bristol Channel minesweeping flotilla came to an end during May and by mid-July she was lying at Southampton while negotiations proceeded between Cosens and the Director of Ship Repairs over the sum which would be offered in lieu of reconditioning. At their monthly meeting in July the Cosens directors expressed an opinion that in view of the very extensive repairs which would be needed to the 31 year old ship before the BoT would grant a passenger certificate 'if it was possible to sell the vessel it should be done'. By September, however, Cosens had succeeded in

coaxing a generous lump sum of £11,000 from the ministry, so *Monarch* was slipped at Southampton for antifouling and the replacement of four defective hull plates before proceeding to Weymouth during October to undergo full refurbishment during the winter of 1919-20. So delighted was the board with this turn of events that they voted £100 to each of the managers as a reward for their skillful handling of the negotiations.

At the end of 1919 *Victoria* and *Queen* were still under requisition as liberty boats at Plymouth and Portsmouth respectively, but were returned to Weymouth during January 1920. Cosens accepted £5,700 to recondition *Victoria*, but *Queen* was judged to be in such a bad state of repair that they asked the Admiralty to declare her a constructive total loss in return for a compensation payment of £3,500. In a baffling piece of bureaucratic logic, the Admiralty refused Cosens' suggestion but instead returned the ship together with compensation of £4,500 and a brokerage fee of £300. By February *Queen* was back in commission and lying in Weymouth Harbour with banked fires in case she was needed for salvage work. Clearly she had not been in quite such a bad state as Cosens had claimed.

Alexandra, her Medway ferry duties finished, lay at Chatham with a severely corroded, leaking boiler awaiting the outcome of negotiations about her repair. It was eventually agreed that her engines, boilers and paddle wheels would be dealt with by the Naval Dockyard and a £3,000 reconditioning settlement paid before she was steamed back to Weymouth during late February to complete her refit in time for the summer season. *Melcombe Regis* had been transferred to the Medway to take her place and remained at Sheerness until June 1920 when she was reported to be on passage to Weymouth. Cosens, who had been haggling over the reconditioning fee, refused to accept her until a figure was agreed, and she was forced to divert to Portland. She lay there until July when, with a highly satisfactory settlement of £7,436 agreed, the company took delivery and the ship returned to lay up at Weymouth. *Emperor of India*, meanwhile, was still under Admiralty control in the Mediterranean.

The reopening of the Bournemouth station depended partly upon having suitable ships available but equally upon Cosens' ability to obtain overnight mooring and coaling facilities for their steamers. Attempts to revive the pre-war lease on the Hamworthy coal wharf, which had lapsed when the military took over the facility in 1915, met with little success. Despite Cosens' offer of £150 per annum (as compared with the pre-war figure of £30) the Poole Harbour Board finally let the lease to a shipbreaking firm for £200. At Swanage the coal store, catering store and booking office were obtained on a twelve month lease from 31 March 1919 pending the completion of negotiations, which had commenced before war broke out, for their outright purchase by Cosens. It was also discovered that the old Swanage Coal Pier had fallen into a state of serious dereliction and that the Pier Company, realising how little revenue they derived from it, had decided not to undertake repairs. Taken together with the loss of the Hamworthy coaling facility this represented a major threat to the company's interests so consequently, during December, the managers were instructed to make private enquiries to see if the pier could be purchased and, if so, at what price.

To this lack of suitable ships and coaling facilities was added a degree of confusion about whether or not the Board of Trade would be willing to issue Class 3 passenger certificates at all. As late as March 1919 Cosens were being told by BoT head office that they had no objection to the issuing of certificates, but by their local surveyor that none would be issued during the coming season. In view of this high level of uncertainty, Cosens met during early March with their old rivals, the Southampton Company, at Mr Sydenham's steamer office in Bournemouth. Having discussed the situation very fully it was agreed in writing that neither company would run any steamers to or on the Bournemouth and Swanage stations during the 1919 season.

Back at Weymouth, the Admiralty had agreed in March 1919 that they had no objection to the revival of the usual local steamer excursions provided due attention was paid to various restricted areas, and Cosens had obtained a short term lease on Castletown Pier, Portland, which would allow them to assess the post war level of traffic on this traditional service before negotiating a more permanent arrangement. Consequently, on the morning of Monday 9 June, *Empress* made the first post-war public sailing when she took 271 passengers to Lulworth Cove. She was joined a few weeks later by the refurbished *Helper* and, towards the end of the summer, by *Premier*. The three ships, limited somewhat by a shortage of steam coal, maintained the usual pattern of local sailings including Lulworth, Portland Bill, Portland and, from August, visits to warships anchored in the harbour. *Empress* also revived the coasting trip around Portland Bill and into Lyme Bay although, due to the Bridport Harbour Commissioners' attempt to levy a twopenny toll on each passenger landing or embarking from the steamers, Cosens declined to provide calls at West Bay. During July *Empress* stranded briefly at Seaton but was not seriously damaged.

The company's optimism over this gradual return to normality was severely dented on 5 September when a letter was received from the Secretary to the Admiralty confirming that the pre-war Fleet Contract would not be renewed and Cosens' steamers would no longer be required to act as liberty boats at Weymouth. Deprived of this major, year-round source of employment, it was clear that the number of smaller steamers in the fleet would have to be reduced and all were immediately placed on the market. *Helper*, the only suitable vessel so far refurbished, was sold to the Alderney Steam Packet Company at the end of October 1919. Fitted with a derrick on her foremast to assist in cargo handling, she arrived at Guernsey on 8 November and spent the rest of her career maintaining her owner's passenger and cargo service between Guernsey, Sark and Alderney. The last paddle steamer to operate in Channel Island waters, she was badly damaged in a gale at Creux Harbour, Sark, in 1926 and limped

HELPER moored off Creux Harbour, Sark, during her career as an inter-island passenger and cargo steamer. Her cargo-handling derrick is clearly visible while, just aft of the paddle box, passengers can be seen embarking from a small boat.
AUTHOR'S COLLECTION / SEWARD.

13

back to Guernsey where she remained laid up until finally scrapped at Appledore, North Devon, in 1929.

The steam launch *Princess* had been sold to London owners in May for £600, but *Prince George* failed to find a buyer, even when offered at auction by Kellocks, the company's shipbrokers, at the end of 1919. She was steamed very occasionally in order to tow coal barges around the harbour, but began to spend more and more time laid up in Weymouth Backwater.

With their fleet more or less reassembled, reconditioning well under way and the limited Weymouth season completed, the management turned its attention to setting the company on a firm peacetime footing for the decade ahead.

With the sinking of *Majestic* in 1916 the company had lost its premier long distance steamer and consequently ran the risk of being seriously outclassed when the Bournemouth station reopened in 1920. The Southampton Company's *Balmoral* and *Lorna Doone* had both survived the war, and Cosens' short-term disadvantage was heightened by the fact that *Emperor of India* was still under the White Ensign in the Mediterranean and would certainly not be ready for the coming season.

With £20,500 compensation for *Majestic* safely

invested and generous figures rolling into the reconditioning fund, Cosens therefore began to look around for a replacement. In October 1919 they approached both A. & J. Inglis Ltd, *Majestic*'s builders, and the Ailsa Shipbuilding Co to obtain estimates for a new paddle steamer, as well as writing to the Director of Transport and Shipping to enquire whether the paddler *Duchess of Buccleuch* might be for sale. This vessel had been ordered in 1915 from A.& J. Inglis Ltd by the North British Railway for use on the Forth by their subsidiary company, the Galloway Saloon Steam Packet Co. She was never delivered to her owners, but was requisitioned on the stocks and completed as a minesweeper. With a gross tonnage of 450 and measuring 224.5 x 28 x 8.4ft she might have made a very adequate replacement for *Majestic*. Cosens inspected her at Sheerness during January 1920 but, due to the uncertain state of the post war coal and labour markets, it was decided that the probable returns could not justify her purchase. She remained laid up until 1921 when she was scrapped at Llanelly. Inglis declined to quote for a new ship, but Ailsa replied suggesting that a new vessel be designed to incorporate one of the sets of steam engines which they had in stock for installation in the 'Racecourse' class of paddle minesweepers.

In the event Cosens took up none of these options, neither did they consider the purchase and conversion of one of the Racecourse paddle minesweepers themselves, the final batch of which had been completed during the first half of 1918. Two of these fine 245ft ships, HMS *Atherstone* and HMS *Melton* were purchased and converted some years later by the New Medway Steam Packet Company and proved highly successful on coastal and cross-channel excursions as *Queen of Kent* and *Queen of Thanet* respectively, and eventually turned up on the South Coast in 1949 as the Southampton Company's *Lorna Doone* and *Solent Queen*. As each vessel had cost only £55,000 to build and there were over twenty available for disposal, eight of which were brand new, they might have represented a bargain to a firm such as Cosens which was capable of undertaking its own conversion work.

However, it was not to be. Despite a healthy financial position and the apparently pressing need for a fast, modern steamer to represent the company on the long-distance and cross channel trips from Bournemouth, the Board made no immediate move to replace *Majestic*. The topic was regularly revisited at their meetings over the next decade but, despite obtaining updated shipbuilders' estimates on a number of occasions, the board repeatedly put off the decision to build. It would be tempting to interpret

this as over-cautious prevarication, but a closer study of the local and national circumstances at the time illuminates the board's actions in a more kindly light.

1919, the critical year of transition from war to peace and from full mobilization to demobilization was accompanied by a brief economic boom. Whilst this allowed most of the four million men released from the services to be reabsorbed into civilian jobs, it also led to a mania for speculation especially in the engineering, shipping and shipbuilding industries. The scramble to replace war losses meant that demand outstripped the capacity of the shipyards and the price of new ships was forced dramatically upwards. It is therefore not surprising that, faced with a queue of major contracts, some shipyards were reluctant to quote at all for the construction of a relatively minor excursion paddler, nor that the Cosens board found the asking prices unacceptably high.

The brief boom of 1919 was followed by rapid inflation and price rises. By March 1920 the price index stood at 323 as compared with 100 in July 1914, and industrial unrest was rife. There were strikes or threats of strikes in many key industries and, although Cosens managed to avoid any direct action by their own workforce, in January 1920 they were forced to agree to substantial pay rises for all employees. Unrest in the coalmines meant that, by

This view of VICTORIA *speeding out of Weymouth Bay emphasises the lovely sheer of her hull and helps to explain why, despite her lack of covered accommodation, she had such a fine reputation for seaworthiness.*
AUTHOR'S COLLECTION / SEWARD.

Interested passengers line the rails to watch as VICTORIA noses her bows gently onto the beach at Lulworth Cove. After a brief touch astern to bring the ship to a halt, the master on the bridge has just rung stop on the engine room telegraph, and the mate has already left the wheel to make his way forward to supervise the disembarkation of passengers. The seaman in the bows has lowered the landing door in the port bulwark and is preparing to make fast to the wheeled beach landing stage.
AUTHOR'S COLLECTION / SEWARD.

the spring of 1920 and in a number of subsequent years, there were severe difficulties in obtaining adequate supplies of steam coal and prices increased steeply. In these circumstances the older, smaller ships such as *Empress*, *Victoria* and *Premier* with their economical coal consumption and small crews suddenly became a very attractive proposition, and the desire to build a large, coal-eating long distance steamer receded even further.

Locally, the termination of the lucrative Fleet Contract had deprived the company of a major portion of its regular income. Then, as Britain drifted inexorably towards the slump of 1921, the amount of engineering work obtained by the company from the Admiralty, dockyard and other sources dwindled rapidly, raising the spectre of unemployment amongst the shore staff, and adding to the general climate of financial uncertainty. With the Bournemouth station yet to reopen, the directors' report to the AGM in February 1920 contained the restrained but telling statement:

After a lapse of five years, it can be readily understood that all conditions will be considerably altered, in fact the arrangements which previously existed in connection with the excursion steamboat traffic will be drastically affected, and the future is very problematical.

The company's substantial wartime income, together with the large sums received towards reconditioning the ships, had been invested in War Bonds, government securities and other gilt-edged investments, or placed in a very healthy reserve fund, and was earning a useful rate of interest. Faced with an uncertain trading future, the board therefore appears to have repeatedly concluded that it would be imprudent to spend on a new ship but far wiser to retain its investments untouched as insurance against difficult times ahead. Whatever the reasoning, their failure to replace *Majestic* immediately in 1919 represented a turning point in the company's history and the beginning of a gradual decline of its services. Never again was it to order a new ship.

CHAPTER TWO

RETRENCHMENT

1920 TO 1929

1920 opened with a succession of gales and foggy periods which led, within the period of a single week, to several dramatic strandings along the Dorset coast and stirred faint hopes in the Cosens board room that the pre-war days of lucrative salvage awards might be repeated.

On the afternoon of 15 January, the Greek cargo steamer *Preveza* ran aground in thick fog in Chesil Cove, Portland. Being in ballast and riding high in the water, she floated well up the beach where she came to rest broadside on to the sea. The dense fog continued and during the following day, 16 January, the Naval steam trawler *James Fennel* bound from Gibraltar to Portsmouth ran aground on the rocks off Blacknor Point just to the south of the stranded *Preveza*. Fortunately the weather was calm and the crews of both vessels were rescued. *James Fennel* was abandoned and quickly broke up, but strenuous efforts were made to save the *Preveza*. On the morning tide of 16 January the Portland tugs *Petrel* and *Pilot* attempted,unsuccessfully, to tow her off. By the following weekend the salvage contract had been let to a Southampton company and on 25 January their salvage vessel *Ellida* arrived off Chesil Cove. Unfortunately, she managed to foul a wire hawser which became immovably tangled round her own propeller, rendering her completely helpless and tethered by the stern within about 100yds of the shore. Collins' tug, *Petrel*, was summoned from Weymouth and succeeded in passing a tow but was unable to overcome the strength of the tangled hawser which anchored her firmly in place. Throughout the night and the following morning the little tug, rising and falling in the increasing seas off this notoriously dangerous lee shore, held the salvage vessel some distance off shore until she ran so short of coal that she was forced to slip her tow and return to harbour. Early on the morning of 26 January, *Albert Victor*, under the command of Capt Garnett, appeared on the scene, passed a rope to *Ellida* and succeeded in pulling her well offshore but in due course the tow parted and *Ellida* immediately swung round with her bows towards the beach. By 11a.m. the local volunteer coastguard crew had assembled on the beach with their rocket apparatus and fired a line which was attached to *Ellida*'s foremasthead. The 22 crew members were then brought safely ashore by breeches buoy. During the evening the seas abated a little and at high water some Portland fishermen put off in a boat, boarded *Ellida* and succeeded in passing a tow rope to *Albert Victor* which immediately began to pull her out to sea again. Considerable progress was made before the tangled hawser again proved its

strength and the tow parted. *Albert Victor* stood by all night during which time the *Ellida* again drifted ashore and at one point was thought to be in danger of colliding with the beached *Preveza*. At first light the following morning on the next high tide *Albert Victor* passed another tow and this time was successful. The troublesome hawser was finally cut free by the fishermen and *Ellida* was towed around Portland Bill and into the safety of Weymouth Harbour by which time the Cosens tug had been at sea for two days and a night. Her difficult task was achieved in the nick of time, for later that day, Tuesday 27 January, an even more severe gale blew up and conditions on Chesil Beach became appalling. By 11p.m. the shingle had been scooped by the undertow from beneath *Preveza*, 30ft of her stern broke off with a resounding crash and with her interior exposed the sea completed its destruction. The ship was eventually scrapped where she lay and, to this day, the remains of her boilers are occasionally exposed when a gale disturbs the pebbles.

Cosens were awarded £2,500 for *Albert Victor*'s part in the salvage of the *Ellida* and, at about the same time received £1,000 in settlement for their pre-war services to a German liner, the *Bulow*. These useful windfalls could not, however, mask the fact that the company's salvage and towage business was becoming steadily less viable. The inexorable shift from sail to steam in the world's merchant fleets meant a decline in regular towage work in and out of harbour, and less chance of large, valuable sailing vessels getting

The wrecks of the PREVEZA and the salvage vessel ELLIDA being pounded by heavy seas on Chesil Beach, Portland, during the afternoon of 26 January, 1920, shortly before ALBERT VICTOR's second attempt to tow the ELLIDA off.
WEYMOUTH LIBRARY

WRECKS OF SS PREVEZA AND SALVAGE TUG ELLIDA ON THE CHESIL BEACH PORTLAND

The paddle tug QUEEN *entering Lulworth Cove on a sailing from Weymouth. Built in 1883 she was designed to be equally well-suited to towage, salvage or local excursion work and, when employed on the latter, could be fitted with an additional small deckhouse to cover her forward companionway. This structure can be seen in this photograph, situated on the steamer's maindeck just aft of the mast.*
AUTHOR'S COLLECTION / SEWARD.

into difficulty off the Dorset coast. Many small coastal sail traders were fitting auxiliary engines and most steamships now carried the extra safety feature of wireless. In pre-war days the continuous employment provided by the Admiralty liberty-boat contract had subsidised keeping the two tugs, *Queen* and *Albert Victor* in steam night and day all year round, but the loss of the contract and decline in demand for towage now made it difficult to justify keeping even one tug in a state of readiness.

As a consequence of this situation *Queen* was placed on the market and sold on 22 April 1920 to the Ardrossan Harbour Company for £4,250. She sailed from Weymouth immediately, arriving at her new home port, where she was to be used for general berthing duties, on 26 April. Cosens must have been very well pleased with sale price of their faithful old tug which had been in hard and almost continuous use for 37 years, especially since only four months earlier the Admiralty had paid them an extremely

The paddle tug ALBERT VICTOR *was built in 1883 as the* LASS O'GOWRIE *for service on the Tay in Scotland. Purchased and renamed by Cosens in 1889, she was used for both passenger and towage work. This view of her leaving Weymouth on a local passenger sailing, shows the enclosed wheelhouse which was fitted in the early 1920s. Spartan though it was, this structure must have provided a welcome measure of protection to her master and helmsman when the ship was engaged in her winter salvage exploits.*
AUTHOR'S COLLECTION.

S.S. ALBERT VICTOR.

An aerial view of Poole, taken in 1926, showing MONARCH at the Hamworthy coaling berth. The piles of coal stored on the quayside can be seen, as can the narrow gangway across which the coal was carried in baskets to be tipped into the ship's bunkers. The normal overnight berths for the steamers were at Poole Town Quay on the opposite side of the harbour. In the left foreground is Bolson's shipyard with several of the Skylark launches on the slipways, whilst in the extreme top left the new lifting bridge can be seen under construction.
DORCHESTER LIBRARY.

generous £4,500 for her post-war refurbishment. Whether the Ardrossan Harbour Company was as happy with its investment is another matter. Their records show that *Queen* was laid up in January 1922, probably as a result of boiler failure, and replaced by a new tug in August 1922. In March 1923 she was sold for £310 to Lilian Isobel Nelson of South Shields and was broken up shortly afterwards. With *Queen* and *Helper* sold and *Melcombe Regis* laid up *Albert Victor*, by now fitted with the luxury of an enclosed wheelhouse, soldiered on as the company's only tug.

The priority for the 1920 season continued to be the reopening of the Bournemouth station, but substantial difficulties still remained. Negotiations with the Swanage Pier Company proved to be trying, a frustrated minute book entry for February 1920 describing the company as 'in an inanimate state, wanting both directors and funds.' During March an interview with Mr Randall, the secretary of Pier Company was finally obtained, from which it was definitely ascertained that no repairs would be carried out to the old coaling pier, nor would gas and water services be restored to either pier during the coming season. Cosens' enquiries about the possible purchase of the pier had come to nothing and consequently, from 1920 onwards, their steamers no longer coaled nor lay overnight at Swanage. Fortunately negotiations with Poole Harbour Commissioners were more successful, and an agreement for two overnight berths and a coal storage facility at Hamworthy Wharf was reached during the spring. Industrial unrest in the pits meant that coal supplies were both expensive and difficult to obtain and prospects for the coming season looked

precarious until, during May, a reserve of 300 tons was secured and placed in storage at Hamworthy.

By May when the season got underway, the usual running agreements between Cosens and the Southampton Company had been signed and Mr Ward, who had been Cosens' Swanage agent since 1898, (and before that agent for the Bournemouth Steam Packet Company) was now appointed joint agent for both companies. *Monarch* became Cosens' premier Bournemouth steamer, supported during the high season by *Alexandra* on the Swanage run and

Cosens' Swanage agent, Mr. Alfred J. Ward (1869-1941), standing outside the company's local office in High Street, during 1922. Mr. Ward had been the local steamer agent for so many years that, whatever the sign-writing might proclaim, the building was universally known as Ward's Steam Packet Office. When he needed to communicate with the Bournemouth agent or with head office in Weymouth, he would often do so by means of a company postcard sent by care of the purser of the first steamer to depart in the appropriate direction. Many cards have survived, and provide a fascinating insight into the day to day workings of the steamers.
D. HAYSOM COLLECTION.

An official party of directors and invited guests – every one of them wearing a hat – gathering on board ALEXANDRA in Weymouth Harbour for her inaugural post war trip. Note the musicians to the left of the picture. A pianist and flautist can be identified. The mate, Alf Bishop, and an unidentified seaman stand at the gangway to welcome their passenger on board. AUTHOR'S COLLECTION.

other shorter trips. The company's intended deployment of ships for the season is revealed in an application to the Board of Trade to issue Steam 6 passenger certificates to *Premier*, *Empress* and *Victoria* to ply between Weymouth and Lulworth Cove, and for *Alexandra*, *Empress* and *Victoria* to ply between Bournemouth and Swanage. The BoT actually agreed to issue Steam 4 certificates for all of these

vessels allowing a useful increase in passenger numbers, during daylight hours in fine weather. *Alexandra* benefited by 110, *Premier* by 56, *Victoria* by 87 and *Empress* by 71. Thus *Monarch* and *Alexandra* ran from Bournemouth, *Premier* and *Albert Victor* maintained the short trips from Weymouth, whilst *Empress* and *Victoria* were Weymouth based but often steamed to Bournemouth and put in a couple of sailings on the Swanage ferry before returning home in the evening. It is interesting to note that, early in the season, Cosens were approached by the Folkestone Chamber of Commerce and invited to provide a service to and from that port but declined, presumably due to the lack of a suitable steamer.

The season was dogged by poor weather. Passenger figures were not all that had been hoped for, and the steamers experienced a number of mishaps. *Victoria* suffered minor hull damage through being placed in a foul berth at Weymouth during May, and on 4 August was in far worse trouble when she struck rocks whilst leaving Lulworth Cove. The vessel was on her last run of the day and had just embarked 200 passengers who had arrived by earlier sailings to spend a full day or afternoon at the Cove. In backing through the narrow entrance she strayed a little too far to the west, struck the reef known as The Rat, and began to make water. The master very wisely steamed back into the Cove, beached *Victoria*, and sent for a relief steamer. By the time *Premier* arrived on the scene rain was falling in torrents, a heavy mist was hanging over the sea, and the vast majority of the passengers were soaked to the skin. On the short homeward voyage many fell prey to the combined effects of cold, fright and seasickness and,

A short while later, ALEXANDRA, dressed overall for the occasion, heads out of Weymouth on a grey and blustery day. AUTHOR'S COLLECTION / SEWARD.

when *Premier* finally berthed at Weymouth at 10 p.m., many of the bedraggled company had to be carried ashore. *Victoria* followed under her own steam and was quickly repaired on Cosens' slipway. In September *Monarch* broke down off Lulworth whilst on passage to Bournemouth and was forced to return to Weymouth where her passengers were landed and returned home by train. Finally, in November, both *Monarch* and *Victoria* were damaged by Admiralty steam drifters while moored in Weymouth Harbour.

Despite all these misfortunes and the deteriorating national economic situation, the company's large reserve funds and extensive gilt-edged investments built up from war income, reconditioning settlements and the compensation for the loss of the *Majestic*, had generated significant interest and allowed a dividend of 10% to be declared for the year to December 1920. Reconditioning of the fleet had been carried out in the company's own yard at a fraction of the cost received in compensation, and had allowed the workforce to be kept together at a time when the absence of outside contracts would otherwise have led to mass lay-offs.

By September *Emperor of India*, the only unit of the fleet still absent during 1920, was lying at Pembroke Dockyard awaiting survey. In October a lump sum in lieu of reconditioning had been refused and arrangements concluded for the ship to be rebuilt at the Dockyard. In view of the extensive repairs which would probably be required to the existing boiler, Cosens cunningly tried to persuade the Admiralty that consideration should be given to replacing it with a pair of new water tube boilers, for which they would pay a proportion of the cost. The suggestion was declined, but it is interesting to speculate about the effect which a second funnel might have had on improving *Emperor of India*'s profile.

With *Emperor of India* back at Weymouth and the fleet once more at full strength, the 1921 season

MONARCH arriving at Bournemouth Pier.
D. HAYSOM COLLECTION.

should have seen a return to normality but, once again, national circumstances were to intervene. Just as the season was due to commence the national coal strike broke out and all steamer services were suspended until 16 July at Bournemouth and 25 July at Weymouth when the season finally got under way. *Monarch* opened the Bournemouth station, to be joined a week or so later by *Emperor of India*. *Monarch* was employed exclusively on the Swanage service, plus a one way cruise to Poole Quay each evening, leaving *Emperor of India* to carry out the longer runs to Weymouth, the Isle of Wight, Southsea, Ryde and Southampton. On most days *Alexandra* came from Weymouth and was employed either on the Swanage ferry or on an onward trip to Alum and Totland Bays, before returning westwards in the evening. Once a week *Victoria* came from Weymouth via Lulworth and offered a single trip to Swanage, Lulworth and Weymouth during the early evening. At Weymouth the remainder of the fleet provided the familiar mixture of landing trips to Lulworth, Castletown Pier

In this aerial view of Lulworth Cove, EMPRESS can be seen going astern through the narrow entrance, keeping slightly to the east of centre in order to avoid the reef which VICTORIA struck in August 1920. The village of Lulworth nestles in the fold between the limestone and the chalk, whilst to the westwards many of the geological features which made the cruise to Lulworth so popular – Stair Hole, St Oswald's Bay, Man O'War Bay and Durdle Door – are clearly visible.
AUTHOR'S COLLECTION.

*Monarch alongside
Swanage Pier.*
B Jackson collection.

at Portland or one of the 'Super-Dreadnoughts' in Portland Harbour (HMS *Barham* was particularly popular during August) and non-landing cruises to the Shambles Lightship, Pennsylvania Cove, or to view the warships in Portland Harbour. *Alexandra* ran each day to Bournemouth and on Tuesdays, Thursdays and Saturdays *Victoria* was scheduled to leave at 7.30a.m. for the popular coasting trip westwards around Portland Bill to West Bay, Lyme Regis, Seaton and Torquay. Due to the necessity of landing and embarking passengers on the open beaches at West Bay and Seaton this trip was always dependent on settled weather and sadly, during 1921, many sailings were cancelled due to strong winds.

The poor weather, short season and the fact that the coal strike had also led to the partial closure of the company's engineering works from the beginning of May, all contributed to a serious trading loss of £3,417 during 1921. Happily however, the substantial reserves referred to previously more than offset this loss and enabled the Cosens to survive and declare a 6% dividend. The situation cannot have been helped by the fact that, at Bournemouth, Cosens' vessels were certainly outclassed by those of the rival Southampton Company. *Solent Queen* on the Swanage service and *Bournemouth Queen* on the Isle of Wight runs may have been fairly evenly matched with their opposite numbers *Monarch* and *Emperor of India*, but the Southampton Company possessed a trump card in the magnificent *Balmoral*. Refurbished after the

*Capt. Garnett in his first
season in command of
MONARCH, surveys the scene
from the vessels incredibly
narrow and exposed bridge.
Note the way in which the
rails and deck are actually
curved outwards to
accommodate the engine room
telegraphs. The passengers
are looking up in response to
a distinctive whistle from Mr.
Bailey, the Bournemouth
pierhead photographer. The
destination board indicates
that MONARCH is about to
sail for Swanage.*
B. Jackson collection.

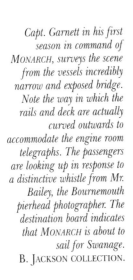

war and still capable of 20 knots, *Balmoral* resumed her programme of long day trips from Southampton and Bournemouth to Weymouth, Torquay, Dartmouth, Brighton, round the Island and, of course, to Cherbourg. The first post war cross-channel sailing from Bournemouth took place on 21 July, the crossing taking 4 hours in each direction at a return fare of 15s. Without a replacement for *Majestic* Cosens were in no position to compete for this prestigious long-distance trade and must, inevitably, have lost passengers to their rivals.

On 25 May 1921 Mr John Geach Rowe JP, the company's Chairman since 1897 and a director since 1883 died, and was replaced as Chairman by Thomas Lynes. He inherited a developing dispute with the Swanage Pier Company who, having recovered from their moribund state of 1920, were now asserting themselves by announcing their intention to levy a charge on each steamer calling at the pier. Cosens and the Southampton Company jointly took counsel's opinion on the matter and awaited the next development which came in March 1922 when the pier company announced that the charge would be 10s.for each ship on each occasion. In April the steamer companies countered that, pending a definite agreement, they would both delete Swanage from their steamer programmes. In May the Pier Company asked for an annual payment of £400 from each company, Cosens offered £50, deadlock ensued and steamer calls were withdrawn. By June the pier company with its main source of revenue removed and, no doubt, under considerable pressure from irate Swanage hoteliers and shopkeepers, withdrew the proposed toll and surrendered. Steamers began calling again on Whit Monday, 5 June 1922.

In addition to these difficulties at Swanage, the 1922 season was complicated by the fact that *Emperor of India* was absent once again, on charter to the Cinque Ports Steam Navigation Company of Brighton, leaving *Monarch* and *Alexandra* to maintain the Bournemouth station as they had in 1920. In pre-war days the Brighton station had been dominated by P. & A. Campbell Ltd's 'White Funnel' steamers *Glen Rosa*, *Albion*, *Ravenswood* and, most notably, their beautiful cross-channel flier *Brighton Queen*. The war, however, had taken its toll on the Campbell fleet with *Brighton Queen* and *Lady Ismay* sunk, and *Waverley*, *Glen Rosa* and *Albion* returned from war service in such a poor state that they were fit only for the scrapyard. 1919 therefore saw Campbells not only short of steamers but also faced with worrying competition in their home waters where Cardiff tug-owner W. H. Tucker had purchased the Furness Railway steamers *Lady Moyra* and *Lady Evelyn* and entered the Bristol Channel trade. Campbells very wisely concentrated all their resources on defeating Tucker, and it was not until the end of 1922 when he eventually bowed to the inevitable and sold his ships to them, that Campbells were able to consider a return to the Sussex coast.

Observing this vacuum, a number of local operators decided to step in and chance their hand.

In 1921 a local syndicate styling itself the South Coast Shipping Company introduced the elderly *Lady Rowena* but found her unsuitable and sold her for breaking up at the end of the season. In 1922 two new operators appeared. The first, Channel Excursions Ltd, introduced *Queen of the South*, formerly the Thames steamer *Woolwich Belle*, whilst the second, the Cinque Ports Steam Navigation Company owned no tonnage but took a five month charter on *Emperor of India*. It appears that this latter concern was, in fact, the South Coast Shipping Co syndicate who, having learned from their disappointing 1921 season with *Lady Rowena*, had decided to try again under a new name and with a more suitable ship.

Capt. Hardy (with his distinguished beard, seated on the steps) and the crew of the MONARCH *at Bournemouth Pier, 1920. The blackboard makes it clear that the stewardess was either forgotten or was regarded as an honorary male. Capt. Hardy transferred to* ALEXANDRA *during the following season, handing command of* MONARCH *to Capt. Garnett who remained with the ship until 1932.*
D. HAYSOM COLLECTION.

Stewardess Hilda Brewer with steward Percy Collins, whom she later married, and two other crew members on board VICTORIA *during the early 1920s. Miss Brewer was a stewardess with Cosens from 1919 until 1928 and served in several different steamers before leaving to work on board the GWR Channel Islands steamers.*
WEYMOUTH MUSEUM

Emperor of India went to Brighton during May under the command of Cosens' commodore, Capt W. C. 'Billy' Read and offered cruises to Eastbourne, Hastings, Newhaven, and westwards to the Isle of Wight and Solent. The weather, however, was not on her side and during the first three weeks of July hardly any trips were run. The charter fee of £1,000 was due to be paid on the first of each month, but the July installment failed to arrive, with the charterers offering £500 and requesting time to find the balance. The August weather was somewhat better than July's and passenger figures must have improved, for the fees were eventually paid and the ship's season was extended well into September. On 12 September, having left Sandown, Isle of Wight, at 4 p.m. on a return sailing to Brighton, *Emperor of India* was caught in a severe storm and took four and half hours to cover nine miles off Selsey Bill. Her upper deck was repeatedly swept by heavy seas and some structural damage was caused. The frightened passengers, most of whom were soaked to the skin, huddled below decks and attempted to keep their spirits up by singing. Capt Read, whose long experience in Cosens salvage tugs had given him enormous experience in dealing with such conditions, passed amongst the passengers offering reassurance, and at 11 p.m., after seven hours at sea, brought the ship safely into Newhaven.

Emperor of India returned to Weymouth to lay up at the end of September. It appears that the charter must at least have broken even for, during November, negotiations were opened for a further charter or outright sale of the ship to the Cinque Ports Company during 1923. In the event these negotiations came to nothing, for P. & A. Campbell Ltd, now the proud owners of the two ex-Tucker ships together with the brand new *Glen Gower*, had announced their intention of returning to the Sussex Coast in 1923. Faced with the prospect of competition from such a popular and established operator, the Cinque Ports

Company decided not to repeat their experiment, and *Emperor of India* did not return to Sussex. With hindsight the decision was clearly a wise one. Campbells returned in force with three large and popular ships, and by the end of the 1923 season had driven Channel Excursions' *Queen of the South* out of business.

July 1922 also saw a flurry of excitement at Weymouth when news was received ashore that the New Zealand Shipping Company's liner *Remuera* had been in collision in the Channel with the Ellerman-Wilson Line steamer *Marengo* and was making for Portland with her starboard bow ripped open and two holds flooded. Fortunately the weather was calm so the damaged liner reached Portland Harbour safely on the morning of 22 July and was beached for emergency repairs. *Victoria* was chartered to land her 563 passengers at Weymouth Quay where they boarded a special train for Southampton, Eastleigh, and London. A large crowd gathered to watch the proceedings and to catch a glimpse of the colourful Mr.'Pussyfoot' Johnson, a well-known temperance propagandist of the time, as he came ashore in his trademark ulster, dark glasses and black, 'wideawake' hat. *Victoria* made two trips to the beached liner and each time she arrived alongside at Weymouth, her decks piled with luggage, was greeted with hearty cheers from the onlookers, to which her relieved passengers responded with equal gusto.

Throughout their long history Cosens had always been strict observers of the Sabbath and, with the exception of vessels engaged on the fleet contract or salvage work, no steamer had ever sailed on a Sunday. Since the war, however, there had been steady trend towards, as the Southern Times explained, enabling 'the toilers of the week to enjoy within proper bounds a certain measure of rational, healthy amusement and recreation.' At many south coast resorts Sunday concerts were now permitted and local char-a-bancs, motorboats and small pleasure craft were reaping their biggest harvests from Sunday trading. The rival Southampton Company had, for some years, been operating Sunday sailings from Southampton and the Isle of Wight piers, but the annual joint running agreement with Cosens continued to stipulate that no Sunday trips would be run from Poole or Swanage. All this was to change on Sunday 31 July 1922, when the Southampton Company suddenly operated a trip from Poole which was so successful that over 200 would-be passengers were left behind on the quay. Faced with this challenge to the status quo, together with the stark possibility of another trading loss for the season, Cosens reluctantly concluded that they must follow suit and, from 6 August 1922, Sunday sailings were advertised from Poole and Weymouth. Although it would appear that the first two week's Sunday sailings called at Swanage, this must have been a short-lived arrangement, for both Bournemouth and Swanage remained opposed to Sunday excursions and refused to accept steamers at their piers until 1928 and 1929 respectively. The Poole excursions, which from 1923 onwards were taken by either *Monarch* or *Emperor of India*, therefore went either to Weymouth or to one of the Isle of Wight piers such as Cowes, Ventnor or Yarmouth. At Weymouth local sailings to Lulworth or to board warships in Portland Harbour were offered in addition to long distance excursions by *Victoria*, *Monarch* or *Alexandra* to destinations including Cowes, Southsea, Torquay or Lyme and Seaton. Between then and the end of the season on 30 September the Poole sailings proved extremely popular, although the financial returns at Weymouth were disappointing. This was a pattern echoed in the passenger returns for the rest of the company's existence: the pre-war situation had been reversed and the Bournemouth station's earnings now far outstripped those at Weymouth.

1922 had been another poor season dogged by bad weather and the early-season loss of earnings due to the Swanage pier dispute. Salvage had contributed very little, with *Albert Victor* only putting to sea on a handful of occasions. On 1 April 1922, with the Weymouth lifeboat in attendance, she towed in the Thames spritsail barge *Savoy* which had been on passage from Cherbourg to Cowes with a cargo of granite when her sails blew out in a gale off Portland Bill. In May 1922, together with Collins' *Petrel* she picked up the five-masted schooner *Jesse Norcross* and towed her in from West Bay and during 1923 she went to the assistance of the schooners *Neta* and *Romanie* and the GWR Channel Island steamer *Lynx*. The financial situation had once again been saved by the company's reserve fund and investment income, together with the charter of the coal-hungry *Emperor of India* and the use of the smaller, more economical

The final sailing bill for the 1922 season shows a typical selection of trips, together with an unusual crew's benefit day which must have provided a welcome boost to their pay packets.
H. A. ALLEN COLLECTION.

Books of Coupons containing 36/- worth of Tickets for 21/-, can be obtained at the Purser's Office on board.

SALOON STEAMER

EMPEROR OF INDIA

(Captain C. W. E. Read).

FARES :

From Brighton to Worthing - - - single 1/6 return 2/6
     ,,   ,,   ,, Eastbourne - - - - ,, 3/- ,, 4/6
     ,,   ,,   ,, Hastings, Southsea, Isle of Wight
            Southampton or Folkestone ,, 5/- ,, 7/6
     ,, Eastbourne to Hastings - - - ,, 2/- ,, 3/6
     ,,   ,,   ,, Dover - - - - ,, 6/- ,, 8/-
     ,, Worthing to Southsea, Isle of Wight or
            Southampton - - - ,, 4/- ,, 6/-
     Channel Cruises 2/-, unless otherwise stated,
     Children under 14 years, half-price (minimum 1/-).

PROGRAMME OF SAILINGS (Weather and circumstances permitting).

TICKETS AT PURSER'S OFFICE ON BOARD.

MONDAY, SEP. 25th. Sailing from West Pier.
11 a.m. **Morning Cruise in Channel**, back at 1 p.m.
3 p.m. **Afternoon Cruise towards Beachy Head,** back at 5 p.m.
7 p.m. **Evening Cruise seawards,** back at 8.15 p.m.

TUESDAY, SEP. 26th. Sailing from West Pier
Grand all day trip to SANDOWN, Isle of Wight,
10.15 a.m. **Brighton to Sandown,** arrive 1.45 p.m.
3.30 p.m. **Sandown to Brighton,** arrive 7 p.m.
7.15 p.m. **Evening Cruise in Channel,** back at 8.15 p.m.

WEDNESDAY, SEP. 27th. Sailing from West Pier
Benefit day for the crew of "Emperor of India."
11 a.m. **Morning Cruise in Channel** to view shipping, back at 1 p.m.
2.45 p.m. **Brighton to Worthing,** arrive at 3.30 p.m.
3.35 p.m. **Cruise off Worthing,** back 4.40 p.m.
4.45 p.m. **Worthing to Brighton,** arrive at 5.30 p.m.
7 p.m. **Evening Cruise seawards,** back 8.30 p.m.

THURSDAY, SEP. 28th. Sailing from West Pier
Grand all day trip to RYDE, Isle of Wight,
10.15 a.m. **Brighton to Ryde,** arrive 1.45 p.m.
3.30 p.m. **Ryde to Brighton,** arrive 7 p.m.
7.15 p.m. **Evening Cruise in Channel,** back 8.15 p.m.

FRIDAY, SEP. 29th. Sailing from West Pier
11 a.m. **Morning Cruise towards Littlehampton,** passing Shoreham and Worthing, back at 1 p.m.
3 p.m. **Afternoon Cruise towards Beachy Head,** back at 5 p.m.
7 p.m. **Evening Cruise in Channel,** back 8.15 p.m.

SATURDAY, SEP. 30th. Sailing from West Pier.
11 a.m. **Morning Cruise towards Beachy Head,** back 1 p.m.
3 p.m. **Afternoon Cruise Westwards,** passing Shoreham and Worthing.
7 p.m. **Evening Cruise in Channel,** back 8.15 p.m.

Refreshments at Popular Prices (Parties catered for).
All passengers are carried subject to the conditions printed on the back of every ticket issued. The Company reserve the right to cancel all or any of the above advertised Sailings without notice.

By order of the Cinque Ports Steam Navigation Co., Ltd.
Registered Offices : 51 Gracechurch Street, London, E.C.3.
J. D. BLAKE MILTON, *Secretary.*
Telephone : BANK 8146.   Telegrams : "JIMMICLE, LONDON."

Frederick C. Jones, Cosens' marine superintendent from 1903 to 1930 and joint manager from the end of the Great War.

The men who maintained the steamers: Blacksmith Charlie Poynton (centre) was typical of the many skilled tradesmen employed by the company in their marine and general engineering workshops. Mr Poyton joined the company as an apprentice blacksmith in 1908 and, with the exception of a ten year gap between 1924 and 1934, served them until his retirement in 1956. Flanked by two 'strikers' he is pictured at his anvil in the blacksmith's shop, c1920.
E. POYNTON

ships in her place.

It was abundantly clear to all concerned that this situation could not be allowed to continue for very long, and at the beginning of 1922 the board had instructed Frederick Jones, the joint manager and marine superintendent, to carry out a detailed survey of the company's fleet, and to present recommendations for the future. His report, presented in March, began by highlighting some key facts in the company's affairs:

1. The Fleet traffic was completely lost and the income on the Portland ferry much reduced due to competition from the railway, motor coaches and char-a-bancs.
2. That income from salvage work, which for the sixteen years prior to the war had averaged £926 per year was now extremely unreliable.

3. That Bournemouth was the only source of profit, due to the existence of the running agreement with the Southampton Company which allowed the pre-war five steamers to be reduced to a more economical two.
4. That Weymouth was making a steady loss due to too many steamers being based there, and that at least three should be sold or broken up.
5. That the price for building a replacement for *Majestic* was currently very high, at £44,000, and rising steadily.
6. That with one exception the fleet were of a great age and that the costs of repairs and maintenance were likely to rise annually.

The report continued by describing the condition of each ship in February 1922, and is worthy of quoting extensively:

Emperor of India Built in 1906 and now 16 years old. Original boiler. Reconditioned by the Admiralty last year and 7 new plates fitted to Hull. Now in good condition. Load line certificate expires May 1925.

Monarch. Built 1888, now 34 years old. Has original boilers - these were retubed in 1916 and have a few years life in them yet. No new plates have been fitted to the hull, though a few have been re-riveted and a few doubling plates fitted. Considerable replating could be demanded at any time now by the BOT as some plates are getting very thin...It may interest you to know that when *Premier* was the same age as the *Monarch* she had 150 new plates fitted. The Load Line Certificate expires May 1924. In the event of new plates being fitted the work would have to be carried out at Southampton entailing extra expense.

Empress. Built 1879, now 43 years old. New boiler in 1903, in good condition. Has had 8 plates renewed in the hull and now requires considerable outlay as her machinery is getting shaky. Load line Certificate expires April 1923.

Alexandra. Built 1879, now 43 years old. New boiler 1892 , now 30 years old but in good condition. Purchased by this company in 1914, previously belonged to the L.&S.W.R. and had considerable plating fitted just before our purchase. Now in good condition considering her age, with the exception of a few plates on the waterline. Load Line Certificate expires July 1923.

Premier. Built 1846, now 76 years old. Up to the year 1895 this vessel had 283 new plates fitted, an average of 5 ³/₄ plates per year. Since 1895 only 17 plates have been fitted, an average of 0.63 per year. It is needless to say that considerable new plating may be demanded at any time. A new boiler was fitted in 1910 and is in good condition. This vessel has no load line certificate.

Albert Victor. Built 1883, now 39 years old. Purchased 1889. New boilers (2) fitted in 1897 and now 25 years old but in good condition. Only one new plate has been fitted to this vessel and considerable new plating may be required at any time. This vessel has no Load Line Certificate.

Victoria. Built 1884, now 38 years old. New boiler in 1912, now six years overdue for lifting which entails breaking up the bridge deck and considerable expense. The hull plating is thin throughout the bottom and a number of plates may be condemned at any time. To replace these it would be necessary to remove the engines - a costly job. 20 new plates have been fitted to this vessel. In addition new main decks are necessary. Load Line Certificate expires May 1924.

Mr. Jones pointed out that it would be possible to save money in the short term by reducing the repair

and maintenance of the ships to the absolute minimum required by the Board of Trade, but that if this course was adopted large sums would need to be spent in order to obtain new certificates when the load line surveys fell due. He counselled against this course of action, recommending instead that it would be cheaper in the long run to continue with a higher level of annual repair combined with some drastic rationalisation of the fleet. He suggested that the slow and uneconomical *Emperor of India*, despite her good condition, should be sold if possible for between £20,000 and £25,000 and replaced by a modern vessel with higher speed and lower fuel consumption. Of the remaining steamers, *Premier*, *Albert Victor* and *Melcombe Regis* should be sold at the best price obtainable, and *Monarch*, *Alexandra*, *Empress* and *Victoria* repaired and replated as necessary. It was also recommended that the company should purchase a motorboat capable of carrying 35 to 45 passengers and operate her from Weymouth Pier on short trips around Portland harbour and for landing passengers on warships which were open to the public.

The board accepted these recommendations unanimously and during the years ahead did its best to implement them. However, in the depressed state of the economy at the time, placing elderly vessels on the market was to prove a very different matter to actually finding buyers.

Between 1922 and 1929, with the exception of basing *Alexandra* at Torquay between 1924 and 1927, the deployment of the steamers and company's excursion programme remained largely unchanged. *Emperor of India* and *Monarch* maintained the

Bournemouth station whilst the rest of the ships were based at Weymouth. There were, of course, many small variations and experiments. Between 1923 and 1927 both *Monarch* and *Emperor of India* offered occasional high-season long distance trips from Bournemouth to Torquay, and in July and August 1925 *Emperor of India* went to Brighton on at least two occasions. Most intriguingly, *Monarch*'s Sunday sailings from Poole Quay on 7 September 1924 and 15 September 1925 took her to Lulworth Cove to land. Since her high foc's'le and lack of beach landing gear rendered it impossible for her to land passengers directly onto the beach, she must either have anchored and ferried her complement ashore in small boats or, more probably, have gone alongside a Weymouth steamer which was already beached at the Cove. *Monarch* always ran the longest season at Bournemouth and, throughout the 1920s, it was usual for her to take a few days off service for bottom cleaning. This was often achieved by beaching her on Weymouth Sands near the Pavilion Theatre and allowing her to dry out on the falling tide, when her crew, assisted by Cosens' workshop staff, could scrape the bottom and apply a new coat of anti-fouling paint.

In response to the 1922 fall in passenger revenue, 1923 fares were reduced in attempt to induce the public to travel. During August 1923 *Albert Victor* went on an eight day charter to Guernsey for a fee of £160, with the possibility of *Alexandra* replacing her for a further three weeks if the trade proved promising. Unfortunately *Albert Victor*'s visit was dogged by poor weather and the option was not taken up, but the charter did have the effect of prompting the board to

ALBERT VICTOR and MELCOMBE REGIS moored just below Weymouth Town Bridge in the summer of 1920 or spring of 1921. MELCOMBE REGIS was never used after the war and lay in the same berth until sold to the ship breakers in 1923. Note her wartime wheelhouse, grey paint and the gun platform fitted to the forward end of the deck saloon. AUTHOR'S COLLECTION / SEWARD.

discuss the possibility of basing a ship either in the Channel Islands or at Torquay on their own account during the 1924 season. The outcome of this discussion, together with the company's diversification into motor boat operations and ice manufacturing is dealt with in subsequent chapters.

The planned major refits went ahead as proposed. During November 1923 *Monarch* was slipped for drill tests at Day Summer's shipyard, Southampton, and the work required agreed with the Board of Trade. Due to a boilermakers' strike the work could not be carried out at Southampton and after tenders were sought the ship was eventually steamed to Willoughby's yard at Plymouth where the work was completed during January and February 1924. *Victoria* underwent similar treatment on Cosens' own slip at Weymouth at a cost of £150, and *Alexandra* was fitted with electric light.

The first vessel to be sold was the *Melcombe Regis* which, since her return from war service, had been lying unused and still in her drab grey paint in a berth outside the Palladium Theatre, just below Weymouth Town Bridge. In November 1923, she was purchased for £780 by the Stanlee Shipbreaking & Salvage Co Ltd of Felixtowe and steam was raised for her final voyage. A Cosens crew led by Capt Marshallsay (master), Tom Pavey (mate) and Frank Bowering (chief engineer) was assembled and the late Sandy Rashleigh, who sailed as seaman/cook, recalled the eventful voyage which followed. No sooner had the ship bidden her farewells to Weymouth and

passed Lulworth Cove than it was discovered that the floorboards in the fore cabin were floating in two or three feet of water and that the level was rising fast. *Melcombe Regis* was immediately turned about and put back into Weymouth where she was beached on the sands beside the pier and allowed to dry out on the falling tide. A cracked plate was discovered and quickly repaired with a patch before the ship set off again next day on her voyage to the breakers. This time all went well until she was off the Isle of Wight, when the weather came in very thick and her exact position became less and less certain. The ship crept onwards through the fog until eventually she came upon some trawlers of whom Capt Marshallsay asked the way to Dover, where *Melcombe Regis* eventually anchored for the night in the eastern corner of the harbour. Next morning she attempted to weigh anchor only to discover that she had fouled an underwater telephone cable, and was eventually forced to slip her anchor. *Melcombe Regis* set off again, this time into strong winds and rising seas. Off the Goodwin Sands alarming noises were heard coming from the port paddle box – two floats had broken loose from the port paddle wheel and were in danger of causing severe damage. The debris was cleared away and the ship limped on her way, but during the next few hours further floats were shed from both wheels and speed was reduced so dramatically that she was making practically no headway. With the prevailing head wind and sea the ship took hours to crawl past the Sunk Light Vessel – 'she was moving

ALBERT VICTOR at Castletown Pier, Portland. This view shows very clearly how Cosens' timber passenger pier was built on to the western face of the massive Castletown stone jetty, from which Portland stone was exported by sea. A string of loaded stone waggons, having recently descended from the top of the island by the famous Merchant's Railway incline, await the arrival of the next coaster. In the background, naval destroyers and a merchant schooner lay at their moorings.
BRIAN JACKSON
COLLECTION

faster than we were and she was anchored.' recalled Mr.Rashleigh – but eventually made it into Felixtowe where she was hailed to go alongside a wharf in the breaker's yard. The steering gear, however, chose this precise moment to disintegrate and, cantankerous to the last, *Melcombe Regis* had to be run ashore on the beach where her crew left her and returned to Weymouth by train.

An arrangement was reached with the Great Western Railway to issue cheap railway return tickets in connection with the coasting trips to Lyme, Seaton and Torquay, enabling passengers to sail in one direction on the steamer and complete the other leg by train. The GWR also agreed to sell tickets for return sailings to Lulworth in connection with their rail excursions to Weymouth. The relationship with the GWR also brought some useful additional trade when a special train brought 88 passengers to Weymouth on 12 July to board the liner *Highland Laddie* at anchor in Portland Harbour. *Albert Victor* took the passengers, their luggage and a quantity of mail out to the liner which sailed immediately for

Buenos Aires. There were problems too: Lyme Regis town council doubled the charges for landing at the Cobb; the Swanage Pier Company still could not be persuaded to permit Sunday sailings; silting at Bournemouth Pier caused difficulties – *Monarch* grounding at the start of the season on Easter Monday; and *Emperor of India* collided with the schooner *Hebe* whilst berthing at Poole. At Weymouth the company suffered from competition from a motorboat service which had begun to operate from a floating landing stage on the esplanade; the price of coal rose again; and the weather was cold and unsettled throughout the season with a particularly depressing August.

In 1924 the weather was even more disastrous, the summer being described as one of the worst on record. The season ran from Easter Saturday until 3 October and was enlivened by the charter of *Monarch* to Messrs. Hicky, Borman, Grant & Co Ltd, to attend a naval review at Spithead on 26 July. The ship operated from Southampton and offered a full day sailing followed by an evening trip to view the

On a sunny spring morning in the 1920s ALBERT VICTOR, PREMIER and EMPEROR OF INDIA slumber in their berths just below Weymouth Town Bridge, while a local fisherman prepares his boat for a day's work on the ferry between Nothe Parade and the ferry steps by Devonshire and Pulteney Buildings. Note the chimney from the coal stove in ALBERT VICTOR's crew's foc's'le and the scars and patches on her well-used hull. PREMIER has been prepared for early season passenger service whilst, in the left background, EMPEROR OF INDIA's foresail has been hoisted to dry.
AUTHOR'S COLLECTION / SEWARD.

Second from the right, Mr. James Halford, Cosens' Bournemouth agent from 1925 onwards, enjoys a joke with a cheerful group of toll collectors on Bournemouth Pier. Agents were key characters in the company's operation, responsible for all local advertising, enquiries, charters, pre-bookings and record-keeping.
D. HAYSOM COLLECTION

illumination, for a charter fee of £350. Both the charter and the company's own sailing to the illuminations required a special dispensation from the BoT to run after dark. In connection with this it is interesting to note that throughout this period the company was actively supporting both the Early Closing Association and the Coastwise Passenger Steamship Owners' Association in their attempt to get the Daylight Saving Bill passed through parliament. This Bill, which later became the Summer Time Act, sought to introduce what we now know as British summer time and offered significant benefits to steamer operators as it would allow them to operate for an hour later each evening without infringing the BoT regulations on sailing after dark.

April 1924 saw the arrival on station of Weymouth's first motor lifeboat, the 40ft *Samuel Oakes*, and with it the cessation of the contract which had existed between Cosens and the RNLI since August 1897, setting out charges for towing the previous pulling/sailing lifeboats. The agreement had been little used for some years, the last recorded payment for a service having been made been on 17 August 1915 when the lifeboat and tug went out to the armed trawler *Kildeer*, but the advent of the motor lifeboat marked a very definite end of an era.

In these circumstances it is not surprising that 1924 was a quiet year for *Albert Victor*, with only two recorded services, the first being the dramatic rescue of the schooner *Fanny Crossfield* during January. Early on the afternoon of 12 January the schooner, her fore and mainmasts broken off and a distress signal flying from her mizzen, was observed about four miles off Portland, drifting rapidly towards Chesil Beach. *Petrel* and *Albert Victor* immediately put to sea but encountered such terrific seas between Grove Point and Portland Bill that they were forced to proceed at dead slow. One exceptionally big sea filled *Albert*

Victor's port lifeboat and did considerable damage on deck, but both tugs eventually reached the casualty. *Petrel* was first on the scene and successfully passed a tow, followed by *Albert Victor* which, after four attempts, also got a tow line on board. The two tugs and their tow arrived off Portland Bill at 4 p.m. just as the spring tide was running at its fiercest against the prevailing gale, causing the notorious Portland Race to spread tremendous seas and broken water for miles around. The severity of the conditions can be judged from the fact that the 5 mile tow from the Bill back to the northern entrance to Portland Harbour took over two hours, the tugs having the added excitement of passing a floating wartime mine along the way.

Albert Victor's second call out during 1924 came during November when, during a severe easterly gale, she raced to the rescue of the SS *Hartley*, which had been abandoned in a sinking condition off Portland Bill. Two months later, on 1 January 1925 *Albert Victor* went to the assistance of the French brigantine *La Servannaise* which, whilst at anchor off Redcliffe Point in Weymouth Bay during a heavy south westerly gale, had dragged across the bows of a steamer and locked their anchor chains together. In the resulting collision she lost her bowsprit and was partially dismasted so the lifeboat stood by whilst *Albert Victor* disentangled the two vessels. On the following day the gale continued and there was a danger that the Frenchman might drive onto the rocks, so the tug went out again and towed her into Weymouth Harbour.

The summer of 1925 brought a happy respite with exceptionally good weather and a consequent upturn in trade. The season was marked by a number of changes in key personnel. At Weymouth the company's long-standing joint manager and secretary, Mark Frowde, resigned with effect from 28

February in order to travel to Australia. Instead of offering a simple leave of absence the board initially insisted upon a curious arrangement whereby Mr Frowde would be required to resign but in return would be paid a grant of £300 on the understanding that should his services be required he would agree to return to his post after a period of twelve months. In his absence Mr F. C. Jones would be promoted to become Works Manager and Marine Superintendent, and Mr. C. 'Charlie' Kaile to the position of secretary. After an exchange of correspondence however, the board shifted its position and decided to create a new post of General Manager, and to offer this to Mr Frowde upon his return from Australia at a salary of £700. Mr. Frowde accepted, withdrew his resignation and Mr Jones was persuaded to adopt the role of acting General Manager during his absence. The new arrangement came into force on 14 March, 1925.

There were changes at Bournemouth too where the company's valued agent Mr Sydenham decided to sell his business and retire due to ill health. This deprived Cosens at a stroke of both an experienced agent and their office accommodation in the Marine Library near the pier. By April new offices had been rented at 1 Arcade Chambers and *Emperor of India*'s former purser, James Halford, appointed as agent. During the winter of 1925-6 Cosens managed to regain a lease on the former offices at the Marine Library and let 1 Arcade Chambers to the Southampton Company. Mr Sydenham attempted to negotiate terms for his re-appointment but was forced to withdraw due to continuing ill health, leaving James Halford to continue what would turn out to be a very long tenure as Cosens' Bournemouth agent. Mr Sydenham eventually died in October 1928.

A small amount of income was generated from salvage work during 1925. On 27 May *Albert Victor* went to Bridport to render assistance to the German three-masted schooner *Margarethe*. The vessel, bound from Gothenburg to Bridport with a cargo of timber had hove to off the harbour mouth to await the tide when a south westerly gale sprang up. Finding herself embayed, she attempted to beat out to sea but was steadily driven towards the surf and eventually dropped both anchors. A message was sent to Weymouth and *Albert Victor*, commanded by the veteran Capt Hardy who had left his sick bed for the rescue, sailed at 9.00 am. Heavy seas and an adverse tide prevented her from arriving off Bridport until 2.30 pm by which time the schooner had lost one anchor and had drifted into the breakers just off the beach. A large crew of spectators had gathered together with the local rocket apparatus crew but, just when a stranding seemed inevitable, the little tug hove into view. Demonstrating his usual superb seamanship, Capt Hardy took the *Albert Victor* straight into the breakers and passed a line at the first attempt. Within minutes a tow-rope had been hauled across and the two vessels began to creep towards the open sea and safety, finally arriving in Portland Harbour at 9pm that evening.

During October 1925 *Alexandra* was on passage from Weymouth to Torquay with passengers when she came upon the steam yacht *Isme* lying helpless some miles north west of Portland Bill. *Alexandra* took her in tow and, on passing Portland Bill, sent signals for a tug. As none was available *Empress* was dispatched and took over the tow somewhere between the Bill and Grove Point and brought the yacht safely into Weymouth while *Alexandra* resumed her voyage to Torquay. Her passengers, although delayed, experienced some unexpected excitement and Cosens eventually received a salvage payment of £150. During November *Albert Victor* was called to the assistance of steamer *Contramaestre Casado* and the schooner *Duchess*, both of which subsequently refused her services, and also to the yacht *Isme* which was successfully salvaged after getting into trouble for a second time.

By July 1925 the board was again discussing the need for a new long distance steamer to undertake Cherbourg, Torquay, Dartmouth and Brighton sailings from Bournemouth which were 'now practically impossible for want of speed.'. Specifications for a vessel not exceeding 215ft in length and 6ft in draft to carry 480 passengers on a No.2 certificate and 850 on a No.3 certificate were drawn up and estimates obtained from a number of leading builders. Consideration was also given to scrapping *Emperor of India* and reusing her engines in a new hull. The results make interesting reading:

BUILDER	SPEED	COAL FUEL	OIL FUEL	TURBINE
Denny Bros.	16¼ knots	£41,450	£1,350 extra	£43,720
J.S .White & Co	17 knots	£40,500	£42,500	
J.S .White & Co	16 knots	£37,500	£39,500	
Fairfield	17¼ knots	£39,000	£40,600	
Fairfield	16¼ knots	£38,500	£40,100	
Inglis Ltd	16 knots	£39,900	£40,800	
Inglis Ltd	17 knots	£41,900	£43,000	
Inglis Ltd	no guarantee	£37,300	£38,200	
Ailsa Shipbuilding	16½ knots	£31,300	£32,820	

Ailsa were subsequently also asked to quote for an 18 knot vessel, not exceeding 220 ft overall, with and without a cruiser stern, but replied that the stipulated speed could not be guaranteed in a cruiser-sterned vessel unless the dimensions were substantially increased.It is interesting to note that, in 1925, oil fired steamers were not only more expensive to build but were also more expensive to run, coal prices still being substantially lower than those for oil fuel. With all the options before them the board again prevaricated, decided that *Emperor of India* must be disposed of before a new steamer could be ordered, and placed her in the hands of a London broker.

In November 1925 a letter was received from a firm of French brokers asking the lowest price for which Cosens would be willing to sell *Emperor of India*. £12,000 was quoted but nothing more was heard and no more potential buyers emerged until November 1929 when representatives from MacBraynes, the well-known Scottish steamer company, came to inspect her. MacBraynes required a guarantee that she was capable of maintaining at least 14 knots but

The souvenir menu for Cosens' first annual dinner to the Employees, 2 January 1926. The seven course meal was followed by an extensive programme of toasts and entertainment which is riddled with well-known names from the company's history. Master S. Davis, for example, went on to become company secretary and a leading light in the local operatic society. One can only speculate about the humorous character songs from the local singing policemen.
AUTHOR'S COLLECTION

COSENS & Co., LIMITED.

WEYMOUTH, BOURNEMOUTH,
SWANAGE, AND TORQUAY.

Dinner to the Employees

at the

QUEEN'S HALL, ROYAL HOTEL,
WEYMOUTH,

SATURDAY, JANUARY 2nd, 1926
at 7.15 p.m.

Chairman - THOS. LYNES, *Esq.*

Sherren, Weymouth.

Cosens felt unable to commit themselves to this and suggested instead that the ship be taken on a month's charter in order that her capabilities might be tested. MacBraynes indicated that they regarded the

suggested purchase price as far too high but nonetheless made a firm offer to charter the ship from June to September 1930. Ironically, Cosens felt unable to spare the ship during their own peak season and declined MacBrayne's offer, thereby allowing the first real chance of ridding themselves of the plodding *Emperor of India* to slip through their fingers.

Not surprisingly, no offers were received for the ancient *Premier* and by the autumn of 1925 the company was faced with a choice between scrapping her or undertaking major repairs. For the past two years she had been used in close co-operation with the company's motor boats which, throughout the day, would carry passengers outwards to land at Portland or onboard visiting warships, leaving the steamer to sweep up the larger numbers of accumulated return passengers at the end of each morning and afternoon. If scrapped it would be necessary to replace *Premier* with either another steamer or a large, new motorboat so, in view of her amazingly economical operating costs and the fact that the repairs could be carried out cheaply by the company's own workforce, it was decided to retain her.

The winter of 1925-6 saw the inauguration of an annual dinner for employees, and the 1926 AGM again raised hopes that a new vessel would be provided at Bournemouth in time for the 1927 season. However, national events during 1926 were once again to thwart the plan. No sooner had the season begun than on 26 April a national miners' strike broke out, halting coal production and causing concern about supplies for the high season. The immediate situation was not too serious as during March the company had taken delivery at Weymouth

EMPEROR OF INDIA lays alongside MONARCH at Bournemouth Pier in 1926. Note the destination board attached to the rails near each steamer's bow. MONARCH's declares 'This steamer for Swanage, 2s' while EMPEROR OF INDIA's certainly includes Totland Bay. EMPEROR is about to depart. A seaman has just slacked away the forward rope while, on the bridge, Capt. Read is about to ring astern on the telegraph.
B. COX COLLECTION

and Poole of a good quantity of coal from their usual supplier, G. Bryer Ash, at 31s 2d and 32s 8d per ton respectively. However, as attitudes hardened on both sides and negotiations faltered, the TUC called a partial national stoppage in support of the miners' cause, to begin at midnight on 3 May.

With an eye to conserving coal stocks for more pressing national needs, the government immediately forbad the bunkering of the pleasure steamers and all services were suspended from 3 May. The General Strike lasted for nine days until 12 May, but the miners' strike dragged on for another six months and the government embargo on bunkering remained in place. During June Cosens appealed for permission to use some of the coal stockpiled at Poole and Weymouth in order to reopen the Bournemouth to Swanage service and to meet a request from the Admiral commanding the 1st Cruiser Squadron to provide liberty boats at Weymouth. Permission was not forthcoming so, in co-operation with the Southampton Company, a supply of foreign coal was obtained at the inflated price of 44s per ton, and a joint Bournemouth to Swanage service reopened on 21 June to be followed by limited sailings on all other routes. The Torquay season did not open until July. Problems were experienced in obtaining further supplies of foreign coal, which in any case was of such poor quality that the steamers could not keep to time. Also during July the government began to requisition the company's stocks of Welsh coal for use in Dorset

hospitals. As the foreign coal was likely to run out by early August, Cosens experimented with burning briquettes in the ships' boilers but very soon these too were controlled and the supply dried up. Fortunately, by late August an agreement was reached whereby the company was permitted to use its remaining stocks of Welsh steam coal for bunkering, in exchange for sending its stocks of poorer foreign coal for use in heating the hospitals.

The company's own bunkering problems were exacerbated by those of the railways who, unable to obtain much coal themselves, suspended their day excursions to the coast and thus starved the steamers of their usual supply of day trippers. Those who did make it to the seaside resorts had little money to spend, and Cosens' income from ticket sales dropped by almost 50% in comparison with the previous season. With coal still scarce and passengers a rare commodity the miserable season was brought to an early close. *Alexandra* returned from Torquay on 8 September while *Victoria* suspended her westward coasting trips and transferred to Bournemouth, permitting *Emperor of India* to be laid up.

With coal supplies fully restored, the 1927 season opened on a relatively optimistic note. The annual running agreement with the Southampton Company contained a small but highly significant variation. In previous seasons each company had advertised only its own outward sailings on the Swanage ferry, but both companies' return times. Then, in 1926, the

A well-laden EMPEROR OF INDIA picks her way through a fleet of racing yachts to berth at Cowes during regatta week. Trips to this fashionable annual event were always in great demand, the excitement of viewing the yacht racing being further enlivened by the prospect of obtaining a glimpse of members of the British and foreign royalty and aristocracy, whose splendid steam yachts were moored in Cowes Roads.
AUTHOR'S COLLECTION.

Capt. William Carey 'Billy' Read, on the bridge of EMPEROR OF INDIA which he commanded from 1921 until 1935.
B. JACKSON COLLECTION

Studland to Sandbanks chain ferry across the entrance to Poole Harbour had come into operation making, for the first time, a bus trip from Bournemouth to Swanage a viable alternative to the steamers. Faced with this potential threat the two companies therefore decided to introduce complete interchangeability of tickets on the Bournemouth to Swanage service and, henceforth, both companies advertised all sailing times. At Weymouth relationships with the GWR were slightly soured by that company's decision to introduce cheap Sunday excursions from Weymouth, but the usual arrangements for circular rail and steamer tours were

unaffected. Cosens also negotiated a joint programme of combined coach and steamer trips with the National Omnibus & Transport Co Ltd, which was to prove a sign of things to come. On 30 May special trips were run to view the French fleet anchored in Spithead and at Weymouth there was some welcome additional work when, on 29 August, the steamers acted as tenders to the liner *Estonia*. The ship called at Portland to collect a party of American students who, having completed a European tour, arrived by train at Weymouth Quay and thence by steamer to the liner which immediately sailed for Halifax, Nova Scotia.

Monday 14 February, 1927 saw *Albert Victor* carry out her last recorded salvage service when, in conjunction with the *Petrel*, she went to the assistance of the oil tanker *Beechwood* which had run aground in thick fog off the entrance to Weymouth Harbour whilst attempting to find her way into Portland Harbour. The grounding excited some interest locally for the 4,285 ton ship had come to grief only 400 yards from the Stone Pier, where previously there had been deep water. An attempt to refloat the tanker on the morning tide failed but, after she had been lightened by pumping some of her cargo into a government oiler, she was successfully towed off during the evening.

1928 proved to be an excellent season, blessed with good weather and a huge increase in visitors to the coastal resorts. At Weymouth the town council announced a major redevelopment plan for the harbour, to include the replacement of the wooden pile pier, the construction of a new town bridge and an extension of the GWR Channel Islands landing stages. This led to some anxiety in the Cosens boardroom that landing facilities for the paddlers would be adversely effected, and discussions with the council continued for several years.

During April Bournemouth Council finally

Photographs of the stokers or firemen who, hidden from the gaze of passengers, laboured to keep the boilers fed with coal are extremely rare. Here, members of EMPEROR OF INDIA's 'black gang' are pictured in 1929. From left to right they are: Percy Fancy, fireman, Charlie Downton, fireman, Bob Wills, apprentice engineer, unknown, Charlie Minton, fireman, unknown and Bill Davis, greaser
AUTHOR'S COLLECTION / BOB WILLS

agreed to allow Sunday afternoon sailings from their pier, and the first trip took place on 29 April. Despite stiff opposition from the local vigilance committee, the Sunday sailings proved so popular that *Emperor of India* and *Bournemouth Queen* were unable to cope with the numbers and *Victoria* had to be brought out to provide extra capacity throughout July. Swanage, however, held firm and despite further negotiations the steamer companies failed to obtain permission for Sunday calls at Swanage pier. Another positive development at Bournemouth was the introduction of combined steamer and motor coach tours round the Isle of Wight. During the spring Cosens and the Southampton Company had been approached by the proprietor of the Totland Bay Hotel, a Mr Anan, with a proposal that passengers landing at Totland Bay should be offered the option of a coach tour around the Island together, no doubt, with lunch or afternoon tea at his hotel. The first trips commenced in June 1928 and proved such a success that the service had to be expanded, and rapidly became permanent feature of the Bournemouth timetable.

At Weymouth, the Holland America Line made arrangements for their liner *Ryndam* to anchor in the bay on Whit-Tuesday 29 May, and for *Alexandra* to bring 980 Dutch passengers ashore for the morning. A special train conveyed the party to Portland to visit the stone quarries and gaze upon such local attractions as Rufus Castle, Church Ope Cove, the Verne Citadel and the Borstal Institution. *Alexandra*

returned the excursionists, together with the Mayor of Weymouth and a party of local dignatories, to the *Ryndam* for an official reception before she sailed again during the evening. During August the GWR experimented with joint rail and steamer excursions from Bristol to Cowes *via* Weymouth, but on the three trips operated a total of only 11 passengers were carried and the arrangement was promptly abandoned. Competition of a new type was experienced when six char-a-bancs began to ply for hire from Devonshire Buildings, adjacent to the entrance to Weymouth Pier. By mid-season these, together with 'the matter of motor car congestion' near the pier gates, were causing the board to complain bitterly to the town clerk and superintendent of police. Finally, the previous owner Mr Ayles having died, the company was able to purchase the freehold of their No 1 slipway at Hooker's Dock for £700, whilst negotiations were opened with the Wilton Estate for the outright purchase of the adjacent No 2 slipway.

Albert Victor soldiered on, employed on short local trips. Her previously exciting life was enlivened only by a few days charter, between December 1927 and March 1928, to the New Era Film Company in connection with the making of the film *Q Ships*. The film told the exciting story of the merchantmen which, during the Great War, had been fitted with concealed armament and set out to lure German U-boats to their destruction. One of the key scenes in

MONARCH backs away from Bournemouth pier shortly after noon on a sparkling summer's day, while one of Bolson's 'Skylark' launches, on a local trip from the beach jetty, passes by in the foreground.
D. HAYSOM COLLECTION.

the film involved the interception and destruction of a merchant ship by a U-boat, played by a submarine of the Royal Navy. For this purpose an elderly West Country topsail schooner named *Amy* was purchased, suitably disguised and packed with a mixture of guncotton, paraffin and high explosives. The scene was due to be filmed in December 1927, with *Albert Victor* acting as the main camera platform, but three times the weather intervened and caused the operation to be cancelled. Eventually, in March 1928, the weather relented and *Albert Victor*, accompanied by a naval tug and the submarine *H22*, set off with *Amy* in tow for the spot south of the Shambles Bank. Unfortunately all did not go according to plan. With the cameras rolling the schooner was stopped and her crew ordered to abandon ship but, before they had time to get clear in their boats, a premature explosion blew her kerosene-soaked masts, spars and deck into the air amid a column of smoke and fire 70 feet high. Burning debris rained down on the *Albert Victor* and two seamen flung themselves overboard from the schooner's boat to save themselves from a falling spar. Remarkably, nobody was seriously hurt. The film crew returned ashore well pleased with some unexpectedly realistic footage while the burning schooner drifted round Portland Bill and into Lyme Bay where she was subsequently sunk by gunfire from the destroyer HMS *Salmon*.

The final blow for *Albert Victor* fell in July 1928 when the Board of Trade made it clear that unless extensive repair work was undertaken they would refuse to renew her passenger certificate for the 1929 season. With no salvage work to justify her retention, the company sold her along with the steam launch *Prince George*, which had lain more or less unused in Weymouth Backwater since the end of the war, for scrap at £335 and £75 respectively. During September *Albert Victor*, a tug to the very last, left Weymouth with the little *Prince George* following astern on the end of a tow rope, bound for Thomas Ward's Briton Ferry breaker's yard.

The decade drew to a relatively successful close, with 1929 again enjoying good weather and passenger figures. During January it was *Premier*'s turn to be chartered to the New Era Film Company for £17 per day. *Monarch* opened the main season at Bournemouth on Good Friday, the first time this had been permitted at Bournemouth. Sunday mornings were still held sacred (and remained so until 1961), with the steamer, usually *Emperor of India*, departing at about 2.30 pm on a sailing around the Isle of Wight with time ashore at Ventnor or to Cowes and Southsea or another Island destination.

On Sunday 14 July the battleship HMS *Emperor of India* was open to the public in Swanage Bay and the Swanage Pier Company made an exception to their general rule by allowing *Alexandra* from Weymouth to call at the pier on her way to the warship, and then to run a shuttle service between Swanage and the ship for the rest of the day. Visits to warships in Portland Harbour continued to be regular events, highlights of the season being visits by H.M.Ships *Iron Duke* and

Tiger. On each occasion 3d. of the 1s 9d fare was donated to naval charity. This event clearly set a precedent for, less than a month later on 4 August, a regular Sunday service between Bournemouth and Swanage began for the first time. For many years, however, the service operated only in the high season and after morning church services had finished. September's revenue received a welcome boost from the Schneider Cup air races, which took place in the Solent on 7 September. *Emperor of India* was fully booked from Bournemouth, *Monarch* was chartered to the Supermarine Aviation Company from Southampton, while *Victoria* and *Alexandra* brought a good crowd from Weymouth. *Emperor of India* as usual was the first to finish on 15 September, followed by *Victoria* and *Alexandra* a week later, while the rest of the fleet soldiered on until 5 October when the weather eventually broke.

During October 1929 the Board of Trade informed the company that extensive repairs would be required to *Monarch*'s boilers and that in order to carry out the work they would need to be removed from the vessel. This, of course, raised the perennial debate about replacement versus repair, and invitations to tender for a new steamer were again sent to a selection of shipyards. Fairfield, Denny, John Brown and Inglis all declined to quote due to full order books, but the Ailsa Shipbuilding Company and J. Samuel White of Cowes quoted £31,000 and £29,500 respectively for a 15 knot steamer somewhat similar in design to the Southampton Company's *Bournemouth Queen*. Quotes were also sought for the repair of *Monarch* and the replacement of her boilers and, true to form, it was this course of action which the board decided to take. The contract was let to Messrs J. Thornycroft & Company of Southampton and by December the old boilers had been lifted out and condemned, and price of £5,250 agreed to cover the cost of replacements together with all necessary hull plating and work began.

Although there had been several seasons of good weather the 1920s, viewed overall, represented a depressing period of decline and retrenchment for the company. The combination of national economic depression, industrial strife, poor weather, changed trading conditions and the loss of the lucrative salvage and fleet tender businesses led to an unprecedented fall in trading revenue. Although it is easy to be critical of the board's failure to build a new ship, their conservative attitude was probably responsible for allowing the company to survive this difficult decade. By controlling expenditure, following Mr Jones' plan of 1922 and retaining the company's extensive wartime investments, they found it possible not only to keep on the bulk of their workforce, but to declare a healthy dividend throughout the period. Their conservatism was, however, tempered by the certain knowledge that the business could not be allowed to stand still and the decade was marked by diversification into motor boat operation, ice manufacturing and the introduction of Torquay as a steamer base.

CHAPTER THREE
MOTORBOATS & SPEEDBOATS

In addition to their paddle steamers Cosens had, for many years, owned three smaller steam launches together with a mixed fleet of harbour craft including several coal barges, a lifting barge and a 30ft motor boat. The steam launches *Prince George*, *Princess* and *Prince Edward* had originally been acquired to meet the requirements of contracts with the War Office and the Admiralty to carry water, supplies and personnel to and from the breakwater forts, and to carry out a variety of other tasks in connection with coastal defences around Weymouth and Portland. They were also used for towing coal barges within Weymouth harbour in connection with the company's salvage and shipyard work, and on a multitude of other jobs.

Prince George, the largest of the three at 67ft 7ins overall, had been designed by Cosens and built during 1898 on their No2 slipway at Weymouth. Little used after the Great War, she languished in Weymouth Backwater until dispatched to the breaker's yard along with the tug *Albert Victor* in 1928.

Princess, the next largest, measured 55ft x 9ft 4ins x 4ft 6ins and had been built as the *Lady Bird* in Hull in 1873. A wooden vessel with carvel planking, a square stern, and small cabins fore and aft, she originally had two lug-rigged masts and was fitted with a compound condensing steam engine (cylinder 13ins and 8½ins diameter x 9ins stroke) by C. D. Holmes of Hull. Cosens purchased her from John William Shepherd, a merchant of Royal Chambers,

Hull, on 16 October 1876 for the sum of £550. During her life at Weymouth she was refitted several times, was reboiled in 1886, retubed in 1895 and completely refurbished upon her return from war service on the Tyne in January 1919. She was immediately offered for sale and, during May 1919, was purchased by new owners in London.

Prince Edward, the baby of the trio, measured only 28ft x 7ft 6ins and was an open launch with short planked decks fore and aft and a large open cockpit surrounded by wooden combings. The cockpit was divided into two sections, the aft one having bench seats on all four sides. The forward cockpit had seats along each side and housed the vertical compound steam engine (4½ins and 7½ins diameter x 6ins stroke) and the vertical boiler, 3ft 6ins high and 3ft in diameter.

For many years it was the practice to use *Prince Edward* at Weymouth during the summer months, but to dispatch her to Poole each autumn to act as tender and workboat for the larger steamers laid up for the winter on buoys in the Wareham Channel. *Monarch*, *Emperor of India* and *Majestic* all took turns at Poole, leaving in rotation for refit at Weymouth and (in the case of the largest ships) drydocking at Southampton or elsewhere. A skeleton crew, often consisting of master or mate and the chief engineer, remained on board each ship to carry out maintenance work and act as watchmen and the little *Prince Edward* represented their vital link to the outside world. Early

The little steam launch PRINCE EDWARD, *her open cockpit sheeted over, lies at her mooring in the Backwater. The scene in the background is now but a memory, the open-fronted timber stores and the tall block of Burdon's Buildings all having been swept away by redevelopment. The loaded coal trucks are awaiting discharge into Cosens' or GWR barges which will be towed down-harbour to bunker the steamers. The small local steam tug* ST.KEVERNE *lays alongside an ancient yawl at the quayside.*
AUTHOR'S COLLECTION.

Motorboat 466 in Weymouth Backwater. The fact that she is flying an ensign and crewed by a smartly-dressed coxswain suggests that the photo may have been taken when she was pressed into service to inaugurate Cosens' motorboat service on Whit Monday, 1922.
AUTHOR'S COLLECTION

in the 1930s her steam engine was lifted out and replaced by a Wolseley car engine but shortly afterwards she sank in Poole harbour and never returned to Weymouth. Her place as winter tender was taken by the passenger launch *Weymouth Queen*.

In addition to the steam launches, Cosens also had a 30ft clinker built, wooden motor launch often referred to as *No 466*. Little is known about the boat but it is assumed that she too was a workboat and not used on a regular basis for passenger carrying.

The company's original decision to become involved with passenger motor launch operation was taken at the board meeting held on 13 March 1922, when it was resolved to purchase a motor boat capable of carrying between 35 and 45 passengers, and to run her from Weymouth Pier in conjunction with *Premier* on the short trips to Portland and visiting warships. During April a boat was inspected at Southend but was judged to be too expensive, so an order for a brand new hull was placed with a Portland boatbuilder named Watson, for delivery in time for the 1922 season. The completed hull would be fitted

with a Parsons engine by Cosens themselves, the total cost not exceeding £700. Unfortunately, the boatbuilder failed to meet the delivery date and when the new service commenced on Whit Monday the 30ft workboat, No.466, had to be pressed into service, carrying 120 passengers on her first day of operation. The new boat, named *Weymouth Queen*, was eventually delivered in time for the start of the 1923 season, the completion of her hull having been passed from Watson to two other boatbuilders named Roberts and Hinde.

While Cosens were establishing their new service from the pier some worrying competition appeared on Weymouth seafront. A syndicate of local boatmen – Louis Basso, Charlie Monger, Norman Pratt, James Newell and Percy Rule – known collectively as the Weymouth Motorboat Service, began operating a fleet of launches from a floating landing stage on Weymouth beach near the Jubilee Clock. At first Cosens were not unduly disturbed but it soon became evident that the opposition, located at precisely the point where day trippers would emerge from Weymouth station onto the seafront, had the potential to cream off a great deal of casual trade. To catch a steamer required a conscious effort to walk the length of the seafront to the harbour whilst the new floating stage formed a natural focus on the beach, and the motorboat's lower fares and shorter trips offered an attractive alternative to Cosens' traditional, longer excursions.

In 1923 Cosens sought the council's permission to operate from the pier and the beach but when they discovered that the annual charge for using the latter was to be £2 for every passenger on *Weymouth Queen*'s certificate, they quickly decided to concentrate on the service from the pier. By the end of the season however the competition had begun to bite and by September 1924 the board had concluded that there was no choice but to take the war into the enemy's camp and erect a Cosens' landing stage on Weymouth beach. The council's approval was obtained and a

Cosens' first purpose-built motor launch, WEYMOUTH QUEEN, sweeps past Weymouth Pierhead very early in her career. She had significantly higher freeboard than the other motorboats and was unusual in being steered from the bows. Coxswain Jack Moggeridge is at the wheel while engineering apprentice Reginald Fry, who served as engineer, stands amidships. The warships in the background are dressed overall.
COURTESY R. FRY.

JUBILEE CLOCK TOWER AND MOTOR BOATS, WEYMOUTH

The beach landing stage and Jubilee Clock on Weymouth seafront in the mid 1920s. The tide is high, allowing three of the four motorboats at the stage to moor close to the beach.
AUTHOR'S COLLECTION

search started for a suitable fleet of motor launches.

Negotiations were opened with Messrs Basso and Monger regarding the possibility of both companies sharing their existing landing stage, but this was felt to be impractical. A discussion ensued on the proposed competition for the beach trade which resulted, somewhat to Cosens' surprise, in the Weymouth Motor Boat Company offering to sell the whole of their property, rights and goodwill as a going concern for the sum of £7,000. As an alternative, the motorboat company offered £2000 for the purchase of *Weymouth Queen* together with Cosens' undertaking to withdraw permanently from motorboat operations and confine their operations to steamers only.

The board declined the second offer, but resolved to undertake a detailed survey of the motorboat company and its assets. The property on offer consisted of:

Motorboats	
Pearl	£650
Ruby	£550
Diamond	£550
Laurel Leaf	£525
Weymouth Belle	£550
Southern Maid	£550
Sleuthound	£100
plus a bare hull belonging to Mr. Basso.	£400
Total	£3,875

4 Tenders	£ 70
5 Rafts	£1,400
Moorings	£275
Landing Stages	
(3 big, 10 small, including one at Osmington)	£115

Sundries: Goodwill, existing agreements and licences with Weymouth Town Council and the BoT, and the undertaking not to run motorboats at Weymouth for a period of 10 years. £1,250

Grand Total £7,000

On 31 January an agreement was signed for a purchase price of £5,400. Louis Basso retained ownership of the hull and the small motorboat *Sleuthound* which had no passenger certificate, and was paid £112 to refit the landing rafts in readiness for the coming season which opened, under Cosens' ownership, on 23 May 1925.

The rafts themselves were hefty affairs, constructed of solid baulks of timber which are said to have formed the boom defences across the entrances to Portland Harbour during the Great War. A planked decking was provided well above water level, and the square, wooden stanchions were joined by detachable wire handrails to ease embarkation. The individual rafts were held end to end with lashings or shackles passed through strong metal rings, and the joints were covered by specially designed flexible flaps. At the beginning of each season the rafts were towed into position and moored securely. At the landward end the rafts were linked to the beach by staging and the whole affair was positioned by the knuckle which used to exist in the promenade just to the north of the Jubilee Clock. Needless to say, it was extremely prone to damage in easterly winds, and Cosens had their first of many such experiences on 15 September when the rafts broke adrift in an easterly gale. It was also discovered that the five existing rafts did not reach far enough out to sea to allow the boats to berth at low spring tides, and urgent consideration was given to providing an extension.

Each boat carried about 53 passengers and was operated by a crew of two, coxswain and engineer. The coxswains were all experienced local boatmen, many of them ex - Royal Navy and several formerly in the employ of the Weymouth Motorboat Service. Some were employed by Cosens throughout the year, spending the winter months as riggers or boiler-cleaners, whilst others were seasonal and found other forms of employment during the winter. Some well-

This photo, taken during the summer of 1925, reveals a wealth of fascinating detail about mooring arrangements in Weymouth Harbour. RUBY and WEYMOUTH QUEEN are moored at the steps always used by the pier-based motorboats, close beside the wooden landing stage from which EMPRESS has just departed. The staging in the foregound was also used by Cosens' steamers, as was the curved wooden Pile Pier itself. Passengers and onlookers made good use of the covered shelters to the right. The GWR Channel Islands steamer REINDEER is moored at the passenger stage while, in the distance, either LYNX or GAZELLE lies at the cargo stage. Cosens' No1 slipway is clearly visible above EMPRESS's bow. AUTHOR'S COLLECTION / SEWARD

RUBY, pictured here, PEARL and DIAMOND were ex-Admiralty boats and could always be distinguished from the other launches by the distinctive, heavy rubbing-bands around their hulls.
AUTHOR'S COLLECTION.

RUBY, pictured here, PEARL and DIAMOND were ex-Admiralty boats and could always be distinguished from the other launches by the distinctive, heavy rubbing-bands around their hulls.
AUTHOR'S COLLECTION.

known pre-war coxswains included Jack Moggeridge, Capt Thomas, Frank James the landlord of the Chaplehay Tavern, George Rix, Horace Pearson, Robbie Robinson and Peter Jackson. Since the summer months were relatively quiet in the company's engineering works, engineering apprentices were frequently sent to the motorboats as engineers, usually gaining promotion to coxswain once they had obtained their local boatman's ticket. Into this category fell Reginald Fry, Bob Wills, Reg Willshire, Bill Morris, Harry Larkham and John Guy. The boat engines were a varied collection and must have posed quite a challenge to the young apprentices. *Sapphire*, *Ruby*, *Weymouth Queen* and *Pearl*

were the most straightforward, all being equipped with 28 h.p. Parsons engines. *Southern Maid* was fitted with a sleeve valve Kelvin, whilst *Weymouth Belle*'s 4 cylinder Atlantic petrol/paraffin engine earned her the affectionate nick-name 'Daisy' - some days she goes and some days she won't! During the 1930s Freddie Wells was in overall charge of the operation and sold tickets, initially from a small hand cart which doubled as an advertising hoarding, and later from a small wooden booth. He was assisted by Frank 'Arduna' Greetham, who acted as berthing master on the pontoons.

The motor boats soon established themselves as a major part of the Weymouth operation. Throughout

DIAMOND, with a full load of passengers on board, sets course for Portland Harbour.
AUTHOR'S COLLECTION

the 1930s they regularly carried between 20,000 and 25,000 passengers per year to Portland Harbour, figures which were almost identical to those for the steamers running to Portland from the harbour, or for either the Lulworth service or the longer day excursions from Weymouth. In a typical year they accounted for a very useful 20% of the Weymouth passenger figures and 10% of the company's total.

Needless to say there were small incidents to enliven the daily round. During the summer of 1926 the *Diamond* ran down and sank a small boat in the bay, resulting in Coxswain James' dismissal from the company's service. In July 1927 the Admiralty began test-firing torpedoes in circles in the bay and the motorboats had a few near misses, or were delayed for long periods. Following Cosens' complaints the Admiralty produced a chart showing the danger area and agreed to limit test firings to before 10am and between 1pm and 2 pm. On Whit Monday 1928 a number of intending passengers were thrown into water from the beach landing stage when of one of the motor boats made an over-vigorous approach. Perhaps the new apprentice on the engine controls had not yet mastered the art of engaging astern gear. A claim for damages was quickly settled.

During September 1927 Louis Basso approached the company, offering to sell them a large motorboat of similar design to *Ruby* and *Diamond*. This was almost certainly the boat described as 'Mr.Basso's Hull' in the original sale documents, and his offer came at a timely moment. Although Cosens had

enough boats to maintain the beach service under normal conditions, a series of minor breakdowns during the previous season had convinced them of the need for a standby boat. A deal was struck and the new boat, named *Sapphire*, was purchased during October for the sum of £420.

The next major development came during the winter of 1928-9 when Mark Frowde, the managing director, urged the board to cash in on the contemporary craze for speed and purchase two speedboats to run from Weymouth. Cosens immediately applied to the council for permission, only to discover that two other firms had already lodged similar requests and that the Harbour Committee had recommended that sole rights be granted to the Speed Boat Supply Company. Some quiet lobbying persuaded the full council to express a preference for local enterprise and to refer the recommendation back for reconsideration. An agreement was finally reached that the rights to run speedboats would be let to the highest bidder.

Cosens were informed that their bid had been successful early in February 1929 and were granted exclusive rights to run two speedboats from the pier for the 1929 and 1930 seasons for a fee of £100 per annum. This welcome news came too late for the company to carry out its original plan of building the new boats in their own yard so instead they were forced to look elsewhere.

The most favourable terms were obtained from the British Power Boat Company of Hythe and an

Frozen in time, passengers on board WEYMOUTH BELLE stare into the lens of a Weymouth beach photographer's camera before setting off on a trip to Portland. The photographs were processed immediately and, later in the day, could be purchased from the display board outside the photographer's booth on the seafront. This picture shows interesting detail of the sturdy floating landing stage, as well as the triangular version Cosens's houseflag which the motorboats always flew from their bows.
AUTHOR'S COLLECTION / BOB WILLS

SOUTHERN MAID in the act of 'springing off' the windward side of the beach stage. Coxwain Frank James is at the wheel while apprentice Bob Wills bends to put the engine into gear. Frank James spent the winter months as as shipwright with Cosens, while Bob Wills went on to serve as engineer in several of the paddle steamers. Later in life both men were well known as local publicans, Frank at the Chapelhay Tavern and Bob at the Swan in St. Thomas Street. RUBY is moored at the seaward end of the stage. AUTHOR'S COLLECTION / BOB WILLS

The brand new speedboat MISS WEYMOUTH *at the British Power Boat Co's Hythe boatyard shortly before her delivery to Cosens in May 1929.*
AUTHOR'S COLLECTION

agreement was signed for one boat, *Miss Weymouth*, to be delivered on 1 May and the second, *Miss Dorset*, on 21 May. The choice of names and builder was certainly influenced by the fact that, during the late twenties, the British Power Boat Company was seldom out of the news. Already well-known for their innovative and highly-successful racing hydroplanes, the company rose to great prominence in 1929 when

it built the 900 h.p. *Miss England* for Major Henry Seagrave. Seagrave, who had already broken the world land-speed record and was an archetypal 'Boy's Own' hero, piloted *Miss England* to success in the 1930 world powerboat championships at speeds of over 90 m.p.h. The yard's owner, Hubert Scott-Payne, became famous in his own right as designer and pilot of a succession of record breaking boats named *Miss Britain* and frequently appeared in the newsreels. With their choice of *Miss Weymouth* and *Miss Dorset* as names for their new speedboats Cosens clearly intended to create a link in the public mind with Seagrave and Scott-Payne's stirring deeds and bask in a little free, reflected glory.

The builders were as good as their word and both boats were delivered on time, although *Miss Weymouth* was then delayed in the Solent for some days by bad weather which made it impossible for her to proceed to Weymouth. Both boats measured 23ft x 6ft x 1ft 10inches and were constructed of mahogany with single skin sides and double skin bottoms. They could carry eight passengers in three separate cockpits and, with their names emblazoned in large white letters along their glittering hulls, caused quite a stir as they sped around Weymouth Bay at 25 knots.

In keeping with their glamorous image the new boats were driven by 'pilots' instead of coxswains. Two dashing gentlemen, Lieutenant Evans and Captain Lees, were engaged for the task but managed to cause so much unspecified 'trouble' that both were instantly dismissed on 31 May. They were replaced by reliable local men Sid Windsor and Andy Hancock. After their

retirement in the early thirties, the company reverted to using engineering apprentices as 'pilots' for the speedboats and for several years before and after the Second World War *Miss Weymouth* was driven by Bob Wills who was also responsible for the care and maintenance of both boats. After the war *Miss Dorset* was driven by Reg Willshire. The two friends developed a routine of approaching each other head on before sheering off at the last moment and passing at a combined speed of 50 knots, each boat's wash soaking the occupants of the other craft. Possibly as a result of this practice all passengers were issued with protective oilskin coats before putting to sea.

The speedboats ran from the pier during 1929 and 1930 but transferred to the beach pontoons for the 1931 season. Cosens' agreement with the council permitted a maximum of five motorboats and two speedboats to operate from the pontoons in exchange for an annual payment of 10% of gross takings. It was renewed on alternate years until 1935 when the council agreed to a four year lease, taking the company through until the end of 1939. Terms and conditions remained the same throughout the period, except in 1932 when it was agreed that Cosens should extend the pontoons to 325ft in length. Due to her deep draft, *Weymouth Queen* was unable to use the pontoons except at high water and consequently operated from Weymouth Pier throughout her career.

Every Wednesday throughout the pre-war period one of the motorboats, usually *Sapphire*, would run an afternoon trip across Weymouth Bay to Osmington Mills. A dinghy was towed astern and on arrival one of the crew would row ashore and push a small wheeled landing stage into the water from the pebble

beach for the launch to come alongside. Passengers and crew would walk up to the Picnic Inn to enjoy a lobster or cream tea before returning to the boat. Although in those days there was an iron marker to assist with navigation through the off-lying rocks, Osmington was never an easy place to approach from the sea and one can only wonder at the skill of the coxswains who thought so little of taking loaded passenger boats in on a regular basis.

When war was declared on 3 September 1939 all motorboat services ceased immediately and shortly afterwards Weymouth was declared an examination and contraband control base. The involvement of the Cosens fleet in this and other aspects of the war is

Miss Weymouth shows her paces in Weymouth Bay. AUTHOR'S COLLECTION.

Miss Dorset approaching the beach stage in about 1950. Note the massive engine casing. B. JACKSON COLLECTION / KESTIN

A group of motorboat crewmen pose for the camera on Weymouth seafront in the 1930s. They are, back row, left to right: Harry Larcombe, Bob Wills, Bill Morris (apprentice), and John Guy (apprentice). Front row, left to right: Capt. Thomas, George Rex, Freddie Wells (ticket seller), Harris Pearson, 'Robbie' Roberts and Frank 'Arduna' Greetham.
AUTHOR'S COLLECTION / BOB WILLS

fully described in a later chapter and at this point it is sufficient to summarise the involvement of the motorboats. The examination of the papers and cargoes of neutral ships directed to anchor in Weymouth Bay involved a great deal of ship to shore work, and for this purpose the Admiralty announced that they would requisition any six of the motorboats. It was recognised that Cosens themselves required access to several launches to carry workmen and materials to and from the many ships which were putting into Weymouth and Portland for repair by the company. In the event, only two of the boats were initially taken up for contraband patrol work.

In February 1940 two of the motorboats were again requisitioned by the Admiralty for general ship to shore work in connection with a degaussing establishment which had been set up at Portland. The boats were in constant use servicing the needs of a wiping unit fitted into one of Cosens' coal barges until both she and her attendant tug were sunk by bombs late in June. Deprived of their employment the two launches were immediately derequisitioned and returned to Cosens.

During May 1940 small craft from ports all over the south of England were requisitioned and despatched to join the armada which succeeded in rescuing the bulk of the retreating British Expeditionary Force from the harbour and beaches of Dunkirk. At Weymouth, *Weymouth Queen*, *Pearl* and *Laurel Leaf* were requisitioned and set off towards Dover, but received orders to return before reaching their destination. We know that *Weymouth Queen* was officially released on 3 June and, although for many years a story circulated amongst Cosens staff that the boats had broken down en route for Dover due to

their naval crews being unfamiliar with the idiosyncrasies of their engines, it would appear that the boats simply set off too late to be of any help.

Throughout the remainder of 1940 and 1941 several of the launches were requisitioned for short periods. In November 1940 *Weymouth Queen* was badly damaged whilst moored in Portland Dockyard. Bob Wills recalled that she had been crushed by a warship and that 'her engine was returned to Cosens in a bucket'. Whatever the true facts, she was obviously beyond economic repair as, after protracted negotiations with the Admiralty, Cosens accepted £450 in compensation and the boat was broken up towards the end of 1941.

In August 1941 *Diamond* and *Weymouth Belle* were both requisitioned, followed by the *Laurel Leaf* in December. Also in December the *Southern Maid* was sold for £450 to Mr. J.W. Hitchins of Bristol.

Up until the beginning of 1942 all requisitioned vessels had been taken by the government on a charter basis which meant that a monthly hire fee was payable to the owner, together with a lump sum to meet the cost of reconditioning upon the vessel's return. This arrangement, whilst very attractive to the owners, was uneconomic for the government who announced that henceforth they would purchase vessels outright. At the end of the war, provided they were no longer required by the government, vessels would be offered back to their owners at the original purchase price. On this basis *Diamond* and *Laurel Leaf* were sold in February for £465 and £480 respectively, followed by *Weymouth Belle* in May and *Sapphire* in June at £500 each. The beach landing rafts were also taken by the Admiralty on hire.

In addition to work on the contraband patrol,

Weymouth Belle spent much of the war as a fireboat in Weymouth Harbour. She was fitted with a large motor-powered fire pump and Bob Wills recalled that by directing the fire hoses over the stern she could be propelled as fast as her own main engine would drive her. *Sapphire* was also used as a fireboat at Harwich until 1943 and may subsequently have returned to Portland and Portsmouth in a similar role. At some stage she was shipped overseas, probably to Ceylon, and was never offered back to the company. *Pearl* and *Ruby* were retained by Cosens as workboats.

Thus, at the end of the war *Weymouth Queen*, *Southern Maid* and *Sapphire* had gone for ever, *Ruby* and *Pearl* were still in Cosens' possession, and remaining boats were offered to the company for repurchase. *Diamond* and *Weymouth Belle* were rejected as unsuitable, but *Laurel Leaf* was purchased on 6 June 1946 for £100. Following an engine overhaul and a small amount of work to her keel, she was soon ready for further service. The speedboats *Miss Weymouth* and *Miss Dorset* had been carefully stored throughout the war with their engines removed, and were found to be in first class condition and capable of returning to work within a few days.

In order to re-establish the service from the beach it was necessary to recover the landing rafts, negotiate a new lease with Weymouth council and then bring the fleet back up to strength by obtaining suitable additional boats. In July 1946 the Ministry of Transport agreed to return the five rafts together with a lump sum payment of £1,665 plus a hire fee of £60 per annum from the date of requisition, but no attempt was made to refurbish them until a firm agreement had been reached with the council.

In November 1946 the council announced that it was contemplating supplying its own beach landing stage, but soon changed its mind and offered Cosens a three year lease for the compay's own stage, five motor boats and two speedboats in return for a payment of 10% of gross takings. significantly, the council reserved the right to allow other boats to use the beach as well. With the 1947 summer season approaching Cosens agreed to the council's terms and immediately set to work on repairing their rafts.

The requirement for additional boats was met on 1 March 1947 when two 36ft harbour service launches were purchased from the Admiralty Small Craft Disposal Unit for £625 each. Launch No 42770 became *Topaz* and No 42971 *Emerald*, both arriving in Weymouth by road during April. At the same time, four new Perkins diesel engines were ordered and installed in *Ruby*, *Pearl*, *Topaz* and *Emerald*. *Laurel Leaf* retained her original Parsons petrol/paraffin unit.

At the same time it was decided to modernise the appearance of the launches by fitting streamlined central cabins and short funnels on what was fancifully described as 'miniature liner lines'. *Laurel Leaf* was the prototype but was never fitted with a funnel and somehow always managed to look ungainly. The other boats were far more successful. Their cabin sides were elegantly curved and fitted with large windows together with a central entrance

TOPAZ at the beach stage on 2 September, 1950 in post-war guise with funnel and streamlined cabin.
G. E. LANGMUIR

amidships in each side. The well-proportioned oval funnels were painted in company colours and carried the exhaust from the engine box upwards through the after end of the cabin roof. *Pearl*, although regularly used on the passenger service, was also the company's main workboat and was used on a wide variety of towage and harbour tasks. Having a large towing post installed amidships, she was never fitted with a cabin.

The speedboats provided a limited service during 1946, but the rest of the refurbished fleet re-entered service at the start of the 1947 season and continued until 29 September. Peter Jackson, the company's chief rigger and sailmaker, took charge of the shore side of operation and passenger figures proved most encouraging. 35,873 people travelled in the motorboats and 17,847 in the speedboats, a substantial increase on pre-war days.

The post war SAPPHIRE (ex. VICTORY), purchased in 1948, was significantly smaller than the other launches.
AUTHOR'S COLLECTION / KESTIN.

Weymouth Beach and Seafront in about 1950. Cosens' beach staging is in the foreground while behind it, close beside the Pier Bandstand of 1939, is the rival staging owned by White Motorboats. Both landing stages and the Pier Bandstand have now disappeared and even the traditional rowing boats have gone from Weymouth beach.
AUTHOR'S COLLECTION.

As a result of these encouraging statistics and because *Pearl* was frequently required as a workboat, it was decided to purchase an additional boat for the 1948 season. In July 1948 an open launch named *Victory* together with 100ft of pontoon 'as used on Weymouth beach' were purchased for £1,775 from local boatman C.A. Barlow. From this wording it can be assumed that Barlow had started running from the beach in the Spring of 1948 and that high price paid by Cosens reflected their desire to buy off any competition. *Victory*, renamed *Sapphire* (II), was much smaller than the other boats and was never fitted with a cabin. She was powered by a two-cylinder Lister diesel engine.

Cosens' attempt to dispose of any competition was ultimately unsuccessful for Weymouth council seemed determined to exercise their right to allow other boatmen to trade from the beach. As the years passed a syndicate known as White Motor Boats was established and ran five launches from their own beach landing.

The post-war operation settled into a regular and fairly unremarkable pattern. Throughout the 1940s and 50s Portland was busy with warships of all shapes and sizes together with a range of laid up merchant shipping, a trip round the harbour in one of the motorboats was a fascinating and impressive experience. During the winter months the boats, apart from *Pearl* and any other in use as workboats, were lifted out of the water and stored on the quay in front of the company's engineering works.

The speedboats continued in operation until 1952, when the decision was made to dispose of them. Although passenger figures continued to be sound, they had dropped from a 1947 peak of 17,847 to an average of about 7,000 between 1950 and 1952. The speedboats no longer appeared as fast or glamorous as they had back in 1929, and public tastes seemed to be changing. Their high speed running had always been heavy on fuel and engines and in 1939 their original 105 h.p. Power-Meadows units were reported to be worn out. A new, 135 h.p. Chris Craft Type M engine was purchased and installed in *Miss Weymouth*, whilst the redundant engine was cannibalized for spares for *Miss Dorset*. By 1946 the Chris Craft had been superseded by a 136h.p. 8 cylinder Chrysler. In November 1947 a unused Gray 6-cylinder Firebowl engine was bought to replace the old Power-Meadows but this solution was clearly less than satisfactory for, in early 1949 a Perkins diesel engine was installed. Attempts to obtain a second engine for the other boat were unsuccessful which was just as well since the Perkins proved to be far too slow and *Miss Dorset* became very unpopular with her coxswains.

The weather during 1951 was disastrous, with over 26 days lost on the Weymouth station and passenger figures fell sharply. At around this time it was also discovered that the speedboats were suffering from nail rot and that their hulls would need refastening in the near future. The decision was therefore made to withdraw them at the end of the 1952 season. After languishing in the backwater for some months, both boats were sold. *Miss Weymouth*'s hull and engines were sold separately during 1954, but the fate of *Miss Dorset* is unclear. There are unconfirmed reports that she was wrecked on Chesil beach whilst on passage to new owners in the west country but, as the sale of another engine is also recorded, it is equally likely that her hull was broken up by Cosens.

The motor boat service continued through the 1950s with the winters being enlivened by the regular wranglings with the council over the terms of the lease. From 1951 the 10% charge was altered to a lump sum of £500 per annum and this arrangement was continued until 1956.

At about midnight on 25 May 1951 the Weymouth berthing master noticed a passenger launch slipping out of the harbour without lights. The police were informed and the *Emerald* was soon discovered to be missing from her moorings. The naval authorities at Portland were informed and a number of small naval craft put to sea whilst the searchlights of the battleship HMS *Vanguard* played over the area in a vain attempt to locate the missing

48

boat. Nothing was seen or heard of *Emerald* until, later next day, she was discovered drifting off the Isle of Wight and towed into Yarmouth. On board was a young seaman named Rive who had recently left Cosens' employment. It emerged later that he was desperately unhappy with life at sea and had decided to return to his family in Guernsey. Being without the money to pay his fare he had stolen the *Emerald* to get himself home, but had got off course and run out of fuel. When *Emerald* was returned to Weymouth it was discovered that the engine had also run out of oil and caught fire. Rive was returned to Guernsey and put on probation.

During the night of 23-24 October 1954 it was the turn of *Topaz* to catch fire. The night was exceptionally wet and the official explanation was that rainwater had caused a short circuit in her battery cables. However, since she was laid up ashore with her battery removed, the workshop staff preferred the theory that the blaze had been the result of cigarette end dropped by a courting couple who had been sheltering in the boat's cabin. Fortunately the damage was not too extensive, and she was quickly repaired.

By 1955 the boats and pontoons were beginning to cost more and more each year in repairs. Wage and fuel costs had risen, competition from White Motor Boats had intensified and, although passenger figures remained good, the board decided to review the situation. In January 1956 Mr Brookes, the marine superintendent, was asked to prepare a full statement of running and maintenance costs for the past two years and on the strength of these a decision was reached to stop running at the end of the 1956 season.

The boats made their last trips in mid September and *Topaz*, *Emerald*, *Sapphire* and *Laurel Leaf* were immediately placed on the market, together with the landing stages. *Ruby* and *Pearl* were retained as workboats. By December no offers had been received by either of the brokers so the boats were advertised in both the Western Gazette and 'Motor Boat' magazine. This approach bore more fruit and gradually the boats were sold.

Topaz was sold to a gentleman named Stallard who used her in the Totland and Alum Bay area of the Isle of Wight, and to deliver supplies to the Needles lighthouse. Because of her central cabin she proved unsuitable for this purpose so was exchanged for the open *Sapphire (II)* which had been purchased by ex-Cosens skipper Capt 'Pony' Moore who ran her from the steps on the landward side of the pleasure pier. Both parties were delighted with the deal. *Sapphire* went to the Isle of Wight whilst *Topaz* returned to her old haunts at Weymouth.

After Pony Moore died in 1960, *Topaz* was operated by his sons Ken and Rory until sold at the end of 1961 to Bob Wills, an ex-Cosens chief engineer, former coxswain of both motor and speedboats and at that time the landlord of the Swan Inn in St Thomas Street. Bob restored and re-engined the boat and continued to work her on the traditional trips around Portland Harbour. From 1967 she ran in partnership with the motor vessel *Weymouth Belle* (ex-*Bournemouth Belle*) which revived the longer sailings to Lulworth but in 1969 was the victim of her own success when Bob Wills replaced her with the larger launch *New Britannic* from Ramsgate and sold her to new owners at Poole. *Sapphire* returned to Weymouth many years later where, restored to her original name of *Victory* and fitted with a small forward cabin, she was used as a fishing boat. She was last seen by the author moored in Weymouth backwater in about 1992.

Laurel Leaf, always the 'ugly duckling' of the fleet, languished at her moorings until 1959 when she was eventually sold to a new owner in Swanage. *Emerald* is thought to have gone to Eastbourne together with the old beach landing stages.

With the passenger launches dispersed, *Ruby* and *Pearl* soldiered on as workboats at Weymouth. They were employed during the season in towing the oil barge *Melway* to and from the backwater to refuel the paddle steamers moored below the Town Bridge, as well as general towage duties with vessels coming for repairs in the backwater or onto the company's slipway. *Pearl* was often used as a diving boat, when a 3-cylinder, hand-operated air pump would be lifted on board by crane and operated by a couple of apprentices borrowed from the workshops. The divers, who were volunteers from among the workshop staff, included Fudge Hanger and foreman shipwright Des Townsend during the 1950s and, before them, Bob Groves.

Between May 1958 and December 1960 a number of large BP and Shell oil tankers were laid up at buoys in Portland harbour. Cosens mothballed the ships, carried out repairs and routine maintenance. *Pearl* provided a regular twice-daily, year-round tendering service to these ships to change over the day and night shipkeepers, who were also employed by Cosens. It was during this period that the resources and skills of the motorboat crews were tested to the limit. The daily service was maintained in all but the most severe weather conditions. On black winter nights, difficulties were sometimes experienced in avoiding the unlit mooring buoys in Portland Harbour, and in fog finding the correct tanker often proved a challenge. *Ruby* had always been considered the best sea boat in the fleet and it was upon her that the brunt of the work fell. At the start of the contract she was fitted with a factory-reconditioned Perkins engine, given a thorough refit and fitted with navigation, interior and searchlights to allow her to work around the clock.

Thus, two of the original ex-naval boats purchased from the Weymouth Motorboat Service back in 1925 were destined to become the last in Cosens' service. Both lasted until the mid 1960s when first *Ruby* and then *Pearl* were sold, the latter to an ex-Cosens carpenter called Bobby Kinder. Both boats lingered on for some years as fishing or workboats in Weymouth harbour, but then disappeared. *Pearl* is believed to have moved to Poole but their final fate is unknown.

CHAPTER FOUR

ICE MAKING & COLD STORAGE

The company's second attempt at diversification during the 1920s involved the expansion of its cold storage facilities and the development of an ice making plant.

Cosens had originally entered the ice trade back in 1884, from which date regular cargoes of Norwegian block ice arrived in sailing ships to be landed at Custom House Quay and stored in the cork-lined ice rooms or 'wells' beneath the company's first-floor head office. The ice was swung out of the ships' holds by the Norwegian crews and once on the quay was dragged along planks by gangs of Cosens' workmen using large metal tongs. Inside the ice rooms chain tackles were used to stack the blocks of ice four or five high to maximise storage capacity and reduce melting.

This trade continued until 1914 when the outbreak of the Great War threatened to disrupt the supply of ice from the Baltic. The company therefore decided to change its emphasis to the storage of manufactured ice and the cold storage of meat. In February 1915 the rented premises on Custom House Quay were purchased for £1,300 and £1,676 was immediately spent on modifications. Some vacant ground floor spaces were converted into cold-storage rooms, the ice wells were relined and a Lightfoot/British Lindie double-acting ammonia compressor installed. This belt-driven machine was capable of maintaining the temperatures in the cold rooms at about 15°F during the summer months.

Manufactured ice was purchased in regular 300 ton loads from Messrs Gough of Southampton.

Unfortunately, for the next ten years, both of these new trades proved extremely marginal. Both the price of electricity and that of wholesale ice rose remorselessly (the latter by 33% in 1916-7 alone), whilst in 1917 leaking water from the ice store seeped into adjoining warehouses, damaging goods and leading to a costly dispute. Trading losses were made in several years and matters were brought to a head during 1921 by a series of misfortunes including an electricity strike and a series of problems with the refrigeration plant which caused a large quantity of meat to go bad. Following an expensive legal dispute, the beleaguered board decided to close the cold storage facility from 18 February 1922.

Ice sales fared a little better although, in 1920, these too were threatened when Messrs Gough declined to guarantee the normal summer supply and Cosens were forced to purchase from manufacturers in Bristol and Bath. In April 1921 it was once again able possible to obtain a cargo of high quality Norwegian block ice but it is believed that this was the last cargo of ice ever to be landed at Weymouth, since by the winter of 1922 regular supplies of Gough's manufactured ice had once again been restored.

While all these problems were occurring at Custom House Quay, the company had negotiated the purchase of a large foundry situated between St

Adorned with Christmas Trees and blocks of ice, the Ford T truck purchased by Cosens in June 1921 from Messrs. Tilleys for £266.10s.8d., prepares to take part in the Weymouth carnival.
BILL MACEY

Nicholas Street and West Street, and backing onto their main engineering works on the Backwater. For several years Cosens had rented and used the building as a foundry but, in November 1923, discovered that Bristol Industries Ltd were attempting to obtain the property and convert it into a cold store. This news galvanised the board into action and by January 1924 they had purchased the foundry together with a narrow adjoining strip of land.

Plans were immediately laid for the conversion of the building into a modern ice-making plant and cold store. The contract for the refrigeration machinery was let to J. & E. Hall Ltd who, for £3,280, installed a horizontal, double-acting ammonia compressor together with all associated machinery. The Lightfoot British Lindie compressor was relocated from Custom House Quay to give extra capacity and act as a reserve machine. The Lightfoot was of smaller capacity than the Hall plant, but was capable of maintaining low temperatures between October and April. With continuous running the Hall plant was theoretically capable of producing six tons of ice per day and maintaining the cold stores at about 15°F. However, in practice, when ice making in the summer months, both machines were run in tandem to keep temperatures down to an acceptable level. The meat was stored in cork-insulated chambers on two floors. Some chambers were cooled by having refrigeration pipes running round the walls whilst others received cold air forced through trunkings from an air-cooling plant.

The new plant was officially opened for business on Thursday 23 April 1925, but ice manufacturing did not begin until 1 May 1927, by which time various teething difficulties with both machinery and staff had been overcome. From then on the plant settled into a steady and profitable trade with large quantities of meat being stored for three major wholesalers, the most important of which was the Sansinena Meat Company. Manufactured ice was supplied to local hospitals, butchers, fishmongers and hotels and Cosens' little, open-backed Ford lorry was delivering ice to Bridport and Swanage three times each week. Further improvements were made during 1935 when the loading bay was extended and a new office constructed on adjacent land in West Street. In 1939 a new air cooler was installed and the lift replaced by the splendidly named Hoisting Appliance Co.

Upon the outbreak of war the cold stores continued much as before, except that their contents were more and more carefully monitored and controlled by the government. From April 1942, all cold store employees came under Ministry wages and conditions, which forced the disgruntled management to issue wage rises of 33% simply to meet the national minimum wage rate. Due to post-war rationing the cold stores were not deregulated until 1954, but as early as 1946 plans were being made to demolish three dilapidated cottages adjoining the cold stores and establish an ice cream factory on the site. In 1948 there was talk of

extending and modifying the cold stores to accept frozen fish, fruit and vegetables and there was even an enigmatic reference to the possibility of an ice skating rink.

While initial investigations were underway word was received from the National Federation of Cold Storage and Ice Trades, of which Cosens was a member, that a new national association was to be formed to which only those cold stores in possession of a Lloyd's certificate would be eligible. To obtain such a certificate would almost certainly require modification to be made to the ice plant and cold stores so, from August 1947, the quest for certification was pushed forward hand-in-hand with a feasibility study for a possible ice cream factory.

By February 1950 the plans were finalised and Cosens wrote to the Ministry of Food to apply for the necessary allocation of fats and sugars, which in austere, post-war Britain were still in short supply, for the making of the ice cream. Unfortunately, the argument that the demand for ice cream on board their own and the parent company's pleasure steamers would justify the license did not impress the ministry and the application was turned down. In 1952 it was suggested that the problem might be overcome by co-operating with a company which already held a license, but approaches to the Clover Leaf Ice Cream Company were quickly rebuffed

By May 1954 ideas of ice rinks, ice cream and frozen foods had all been set aside and the ice manufacturing trade was in decline. It was therefore decided that the alterations should go ahead on a slightly different basis. The old ice plant was cut up and a large, additional cold store, which became known as Towers' Lamb Room, was installed in its place. A new, high-speed twin cylinder Douglas compressor and air cooling plant was installed, followed in October 1955 by a new, roof-mounted condenser. The old condenser together with the Lightfoot and Hall compressors were retained as

Cosens' cold stores seen from West Street. The cold rooms were behind and above the loading bay. The building on the left with large, slatted refrigerant condensers on its roof housed the original ice making plant and was later converted into the No.1 cold store room, known as 'Tower's Room' as it was used to contain that company's supply of lamb. On the extreme right of the photograph is the back of the boilermakers' shop. The ground floor where bulky items were kept was known as the works under store, while the main stores were situated above.
COLIN CADDY COLLECTION.

Shift engineer Brian Jackson oils the Hall compressor, 1962. Looking very like a steam engine, the machine was driven by a DC electric motor with a belt to the flywheel on the left of the picture. Note the Cosens' house flag painted on the front guard.
B. JACKSON COLLECTION

spares. A new air lock entrance was added to the building in March 1956. The main clients for the extended cold stores were the meat importers Armour, Towers, the Sansinena Meat Company and Swifts.

Unfortunately, the long-awaited improvements had really come too late. By the late 1950s improvements in refrigeration meant that most butchers were able to install their own cold rooms and no longer needed daily deliveries of meat from their local cold stores. Refrigerated lorries made it possible for the large wholesalers to cut out the middle man

and deliver direct to individual butchers' shops. The writing was already on the wall for the large commercial cold stores and, with the age of domestic refrigerator ownership, supermarkets and pre-packed food just around the corner, the end could not be long in coming.

Cosens did their best to fight off the inevitable. By 1959 revenue was falling steadily and during the next two years the company advertised extensively in an attempt to reverse the trend. 1960 saw a slight, temporary increase in earnings due partly to the release of large quantities of Argentine beef onto the British market and partly to the Admiralty using the cold stores while their own facility at Portland dockyard was closed for rebuilding.

During 1962 Cosens received £1,197 compensation for the disruption caused during the conversion of Weymouth's remaining DC electrical supply to AC and used the income to replace the Hall and Lightfoot compressors with a second Douglas plant, giving the company two identical modern machines which could be used alternately. During May the Lightfoot was dismantled but the disused Hall machine was left in situ because a large part of the engine room pipe work was supported by its cylinder block.

The downward spiral in trade continued, assisted by a steady round of wage and price increases which hastened the loss of several valued customers, and a decision was finally reached to close the cold stores on 30 November 1964. The date was postponed until 31 December to meet demand from wholesalers who wished to store chickens and turkeys over the Christmas period and during this period a vain attempt was made to sell the cold stores as a going concern to the Western Ice & Cold Storage Co Ltd. More significantly, news was received from the Town Clerk of development plans regarding the lower end of the town, which might affect the site and it was decided that it would be unwise to proceed with negotiations for the sale until the council had announced more details. These, of course, were slow in arriving, so Cosens increased their rates by another 20% and continued trading while negotiations proceeded behind the scenes.

In January 1965 Cosens realised that the cold store site might represent a very valuable bargaining chip. Most of the company's main engineering works site on the Backwater was held on leasehold from the council, and the plan was made to exchange the unwanted cold store for the freehold on that property. This was particularly timely in view of the fact that the company was planning a major modernisaton of its works, which would involve much rebuilding. In view of this it was decided to postpone any notice of closure in order to retain maximum bargaining power with the council. The final agreement was signed during the winter of 1967-8 and the properties exchanged. After standing empty for some months the ice stores were demolished in May 1968.

Left to right. Edward Fourguard, Cosens' clerk; Sam Macey, Cosens' storeman; Tony the office boy; Jack Stride, manager for Swift of Bournemouth; 'Tilly', clerk for the Sansinena Meat Company; and Bill Skidmore, manager for Armour Star, outside the Cold Store offices.
BILL MACEY

CHAPTER FIVE
THE TORQUAY EXPERIMENT
1924 TO 1927

The brief charter of *Albert Victor* to run from Guernsey in August 1923, together with the possibility that *Alexandra* might have replaced her for a longer period had the weather proved more favourable, prompted the board to consider a third possibility for diversification: placing a ship either in the Channel Islands or at Torquay on their own account during the 1924 season.

The Channel Islands, with their swift tides, physical isolation from the mainland and uncertain passenger patterns, were an area of which the company had little practical experience or knowledge. Torquay, by contrast, was practically a home-from-home for Cosens' steamers, having been a regular destination for both the coasting trip and direct sailings from Weymouth and Bournemouth for most of the company's history. All the piers which might be visited from Torquay were well known to their masters who also had the expertise required to undertake the beach landings required at some of the smaller West Bay resorts. Easily accessible by rail and only four hours steaming away from the company's

workshop facilities at Weymouth, Torquay certainly seemed the safer option. The only drawback was the fact that the area was already served by the Devon Dock, Pier and Steam Ship Co Ltd's (DDP&SS Co Ltd) two paddle steamers *Duke of Devonshire* and *Duchess of Devonshire*, and that Cosens would be therefore be entering into direct competition with an established and popular operator in its own home waters.

By January 1924 it had been decided, notwithstanding the risk that the trade might prove insufficient for two companies, that Torquay should be tried for the 1924 season. It should be remembered that, at this time Cosens owned more steamers than they actually required and that *Premier*, *Albert Victor* and *Emperor of India* were still advertised for sale. The board reasoned that the Torquay experiment might yield a useful profit but that, even if it failed to do so, one steamer and her crew which would otherwise have to be paid off, would be kept in gainful employment.

In April an agreement was reached with Messrs

ALEXANDRA arriving at Weymouth, her regular Wednesday destination. Note the 'C' on the funnel, intended to distinguish the Cosens ship from the rival Devon Dock, Pier and Steamship Company Ltd's similar ships, DUKE OF DEVONSHIRE and DUCHESS OF DEVONSHIRE.
AUTHOR'S COLLECTION / SEWARD

S.S. ALEXANDRA.

ALEXANDRA berthed at
Victoria Pier in the entrance
to Lyme Regis harbour. In the
background the soft clay
cliffs, with Golden Cap
prominent in the centre of the
picture, stretch eastwards
towards Bridport.
H. A. ALLEN COLLECTION

Parkes who ran a coal business from 20, Fleet Street, Torquay to act as district agents and supply bunkers to the ship. G. H. Collins & Co and G. Player, coal merchant, were engaged as local agents at Paignton and Teignmouth respectively. Cosens also wrote to the DDP&SS Co Ltd announcing their intentions and suggesting an agreement between the two companies as to fares and programmes. The DDP&SS Co Ltd replied in non-committal tones and meanwhile rushed to prepare *Duke of Devonshire* for an early entry into service on Monday 5 May.

Alexandra, under the command of Capt W. J. S. Carter, entered service on Saturday 31 May 1924. She was almost identical in size to the opposition steamers and shared a similar profile and livery. In order to avoid confusion amongst potential passengers, each side of *Alexandra*'s buff funnel was therefore adorned with a large, black letter 'C' to distinguish her as the Cosens vessel.

Neither company could afford to become involved in a destructive fare-cutting war, especially in view of the atrocious weather throughout May and June which led to many cancellations and depressed passenger figures severely. Towards the end of June the managers met and signed a working agreement that both companies should charge the same fares and would meet once per fortnight to draw up a programme of sailings. The DDP&SS Co Ltd which owned both Exmouth and Teignmouth piers had originally planned to abolish pier tolls for passengers using their own ships, but now decided that such a move would be counter-productive. Instead the pier toll at Exmouth was raised by 2d. and the *Alexandra* was charged 10s per day for each pier used.

Alexandra's sailings settled into a fairly regular weekly pattern. At least once a week, initially on Mondays, she went to Plymouth, leaving Brixham at 10am, Paignton at 10.25am, Princes Pier Torquay at 10.45am and arriving alongside the GWR's Princess Royal Pontoon in Millbay Docks at 2 pm. After about two hours ashore in Plymouth, passengers were back on board for a 4.15 pm departure, and were back in Torquay by 8.20 pm. Combined rail and steamer tickets were available for all Plymouth sailings, allowing passengers to travel in one direction only by steamer, or to undertake a circular tour from any of the calling points or other inland locations such as Newton Abbot or Exeter.

Once a week, usually on Wednesdays, she went to Weymouth 'The English Naples' taking about four hours in each direction and allowing two hours ashore. Dartmouth, only an hour away from Torbay by sea, was a frequent destination for morning or afternoon cruises. Except at low tide when passengers were landed by boat, *Alexandra* would berth alongside the South Embankment at Dartmouth, where her passengers could either enjoy time ashore or transfer

*Pictured from the end of the
famous stone Cobb,
ALEXANDRA is seen leaving
Victoria Pier, Lyme Regis,
with the elegant little resort in
the background.*
H. A. ALLEN COLLECTION

to one of the River Dart Steamboat Co's little paddle steamers for the trip up the beautiful River Dart to Totnes or, at low water, as far as the picturesque village of Dittisham. Combined tickets for the sea and river trips were sold on board *Alexandra*.

Salcombe, in the next estuary to the west, was a popular but less regular destination. Due to the notorious bar across its entrance, the Salcombe estuary was only accessible for a few hours either side of high water which made timetabling more difficult and tended to dictate half day trips only. Once inside the estuary the steamer anchored off the town and landed her passengers by small boats, a slow process which was another factor in limiting visits to a maximum of once per week. An alternative destination when the tides were unsuitable for Salcombe was Lyme Regis in Dorset, where the steamer would berth alongside Victoria Pier.

A full day coasting trip would leave Brixham at 10.15 am, Paignton at 10.40 am. and Torquay at 11 am, arriving at Teignmouth pier at 11.50 am. From there the steamer would take about forty five minutes to Budleigh Salterton and another hour and a quarter to Seaton at both of which she would land passengers over her bows directly onto the beach. Whilst her passengers enjoyed two hours ashore at Seaton, *Alexandra* would offer a one hour trip round the bay to local passengers, before sailing at 4 pm to retrace her course back to Brixham where she would arrive at 7.20 pm. Shorter half day and afternoon trips were also offered to Budleigh Salterton or Budleigh and Seaton according to the tides and other constraints of the week's schedule. Needless to say, the beach landing trips were the most prone to disruption by the weather and many were cancelled during the dreadful summer of 1924.

Considering the exceptionally poor weather, the earnings on the Torquay station were not as disappointing as might have been expected and the board resolved to continue the operation for the 1925 and 1926 seasons at least, after which the question reviewed again.

In February 1925 the managers met to discuss arrangements for the coming season. Anxious to cut expenditure and maximise income, Cosens tabled a number of suggestions which were eventually agreed by both companies. Fares on all trips were increased by 6d, the cost of the combined steamer and rail tour to Plymouth rose by 1s and the number of advertisements printed and complimentary tickets issued was reduced. Cosens changed their Plymouth trips from Mondays to Thursdays, and suggested that each company should run only one trip per week, alternating between Tuesdays and Thursdays. The DDP&SS Co Ltd would have none of this, however, and insisted that their previous arrangements of three trips per week be adhered to.

Alexandra opened the 1925 season for Cosens on 29 May and, in July, introduced the first Sunday afternoon trips from Torquay. The DDP&SS Co Ltd immediately called a special meeting to decide whether they should break with tradition and follow

suit but, in the event, resolved that 'no steps should be taken for the present'. They managed to stick to their principles for another year and it was not until 8 August 1926 that they finally succumbed to commercial pressures and followed Cosens' sabbath-breaking lead.

Despite the excellent weather throughout the summer of 1925, trade still did not come up to expectations and the chairman's report at the AGM in February 1926 revealed that 'Torquay was not a paying proposition at the moment, but that the company was nursing the station in anticipation of future developments'.

1926 is remembered chiefly for the nine-day General Strike. Far more damaging to the steamer operators however was the national miners' strike, which lasted from April until November and led to a severe shortage of bunker coal. *Alexandra* was unable to enter service until mid July and lasted only until 8 September when both she and the opposition retreated to winter lay up. It had been the shortest season on record and, even when the ships had managed to operate, lack of rail excursions to the coast and the air of general economic uncertainty ensured that very few passengers came up the gangways.

It was clear that this loss-making situation could not be endured for much longer so, during the winter of 1926-7, unofficial overtures were made to the DDP&SS Co Ltd with a view to their taking over the *Alexandra* and Cosens' goodwill at Torquay. Not surprisingly the Devon company showed little interest and arrangements for the 1927 proceeded much as before.

During April the two steamer companies agreed with the GWR to issue a joint poster and handbills for the circular trips to Plymouth, the cost of which would be shared equally between the three parties. A number of proofs were inspected over the next few weeks but, owing to the railway company's insistence on advertising the return leg specifically by train - which would mean running the return steamer from Plymouth empty - the scheme was dropped and each

ALEXANDRA making her approach to the open beach at Seaton to collect the group of passengers who can be seen gathered on the shingle. A kedge anchor has been dropped over the steamer's stern, the hinged gangway over the bows has already been lowered into position and Capt Carter has just rung astern on the engines to bring the ship to a halt with her bow grounded gently on the beach. This was a highly skilled operation and even with the moderate surf shown in this photo must have provided some tense moments for crew and passengers alike.
B. JACKSON COLLECTION

company continued to advertise independently as before. Cosens trips to Plymouth were now advertised for Tuesdays and Thursdays.

As the season progressed and profits failed to rise, the relationship between the two steamer companies became more strained. In June Cosens complained that the opposition had broken the annual agreement by advertising season tickets from Torquay at £4 instead of 4 guineas (£4. 4s) and by undercutting Seaton fares by 6d. The Devon company pleaded clerical error but then responded by refusing to entertain Cosens' proposal for joint advertising of the Plymouth service.

The weather throughout the summer was atrocious. August was the wettest on record with the South West receiving more than twice its normal

precipitation, and rain falling on 25 days in the month. This unprecedented weather had a devastating effect on the passenger figures and income of both companies. *Alexandra* made her last sailing from Torquay on 24 September 1927 and retired to Weymouth. An analysis of her earnings and expenditure for the seasons 1924-7 revealed a loss of £3,000 that the board quickly resolved could not be allowed to continue.

Accordingly, in October 1927, Cosens wrote to the DDP&SS Co Ltd asking whether they would be willing either to sell the *Duke of Devonshire* and *Duchess of Devonshire* or to purchase the *Alexandra*. The Devon company responded that they could find no employment for a third steamer at Torquay and had no intention of selling their own steamers separately. They would, however, consider an offer for their entire business which, in addition to the steamer services, included Exmouth Dock with its slipway and repair facilities, Exmouth and Teignmouth piers, ferry services from Exmouth to Starcross and Brixham to Torquay, together with extensive mortgage and property services. Cosens replied that they could not entertain the purchase the whole business, so a state of temporary stalemate persisted throughout the winter.

In February 1928 a new solution began to emerge. The Cosens' board discussed the idea that the Devon company might be willing to pay an annual grant if Cosens refrained from running out of Torquay. The manager was instructed to open negotiations and a series of meetings took place resulting in an opening bid from the Devon company of £300 for 1928 only, to be increased to £350 if

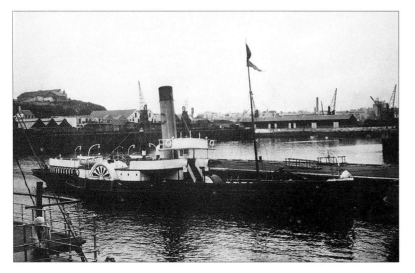

passenger receipts exceeded the 1927 figures by more than 30% and that no further competition was forthcoming. Cosens countered with a quite unreasonable demand that the arrangement be permanent, which succeeded in forcing the Devon company's offer up from a one to a four year term.

By March 1928 a provisional agreement had been reached for an annual payment of £350 over five years, and Cosens felt sufficiently confident of the outcome to declare their abandonment of the Torquay station and to specify the use of *Alexandra* 'on additional intermediate trips from Bournemouth during the month of August in particular' in their annual agreement with the Southampton Company.

Various drafts passed to and fro between the companies' solicitors during the summer of 1928 and eventually on 2 October the final agreement, backdated to 1 March 1928, was signed. The DDP&SS Co Ltd agreed to pay Cosens a sum of £350 on 30 November each year until 1932, after which the arrangement would be renewed annually until such time as either party gave six months notice of its cancellation. In return, Cosens agreed not to operate or assist anyone else in operating sea excursions from Torquay, nor to compete in any way with the Devon company's steamers in the area between Exmouth and Dartmouth. The only exception to this was any Cosens steamer starting from Weymouth and plying from ports and beaches en route to Torquay, as had happened prior to the competition in 1924. In this way Cosens' traditional coasting service around Lyme Bay was protected.

Thus, from the 1928 season, the status quo was restored at Torquay. The *Duke of Devonshire* and *Duchess of Devonshire* had clear seas once again and Cosens, instead of operating a loss-making service, could enjoy a small but steady income without even putting *Alexandra* to sea. Indeed they must have derived considerable satisfaction from the fact that, even after *Alexandra* was sold out of the company's fleet in February 1931, her ghost continued to generate revenue.

Following Cosens' departure, the *Duke of Devonshire* and *Duchess of Devonshire* continued as usual, but it is apparent that times were hard. In April 1931 the Devon company offered to sell their steamers to Cosens but the offer was declined and throughout the 1931 season *Duchess of Devonshire* remained laid up, leaving *Duke of Devonshire* to soldier on alone. In 1932, *Duke of Devonshire* faced unwelcome opposition at Torquay from P. & A. Campbell Ltd's larger and faster *Westward Ho* whilst *Duchess of Devonshire* was chartered to Capt E. R. F. Colberd who based her at Lyme Regis.

In 1933 *Duke of Devonshire* was sold to P. & A. Campbell Ltd who left her laid up in Exmouth Dock, while *Duchess of Devonshire* passed into Colberd's ownership, marking the end of the DDP&SS Co Ltd as excursion steamer operators. *Duchess of Devonshire* continued to serve the Devon Coast until, on 27 August 1934 she dragged her kedge anchor whilst landing passengers on Sidmouth beach and was

wrecked. *Duke of Devonshire* left the area in 1934 to new owners in Cork, but returned to her traditional south Devon routes for the seasons of 1936 and 1937 under the ownership of Mr Alexander Taylor of Torquay. In December 1937, as if finally submitting to the inevitable, she was sold to Cosens and moved to Weymouth where she was renamed *Consul*.

A sailing bill, issued on 24 August1927, provides details of ALEXANDRA's movements.
H. A. ALLEN COLLECTION

No. 14.   **Pleasure Sailings from Torquay, Paignton, Teignmouth, Budleigh Salterton, Sidmouth, Seaton, Lyme Regis, etc.**

STEAMER TRIPS

BY THE "C" FUNNEL

SALOON STEAMER 'ALEXANDRA'

(Captain W. J. S. CARTER).

This Speedy Saloon Steamer will (weather and other circumstances permitting) carry out Excursions as below.

The Company will not be responsible for any accident, or injury to, or loss of life, or loss or damage to property of the passenger, of whatever nature, and whether caused by perils of the sea, accidents incidental to navigation or defects latent or otherwise in Hull tackle, machinery or staging pier gangways or other property of the Company, or by any act, neglect or default of the Company, Pilots, Master, Engineers, Officers or Mariner or any other person in the Company's employ or otherwise howsoever.

Hot and Cold Luncheons, Teas, Wines, Spirits, etc. provided at Moderate Prices

Saturday, Aug. 27th H.W. 7.42 p.m. MORNING TRIP	**To Dartmouth** (for the River Trip to the picturesque Village of Dittisham), leaving Paignton 10-30 a.m., Torquay (Princess Pier) 10-50 a.m. Returning from Dartmouth at 1-20 p.m. or 7 p.m. Fare 3/6, or to include Trip to Dittisham 4/6.
CHEAP AFTERNOON RIVER TRIP Dartmouth Regatta this day	1-20 p.m., **Dartmouth to Torquay**, returning 2-25 p.m. Fare 2/- **To Dartmouth** (for the famous River Dart Trip or up and down the English Rhine), leaving Torquay (Princess Pier) 2.25 p.m., Paignton 2-45 p.m. Returning from Dartmouth 7 p.m. Home 8 p.m. Return Fare 2/6, or to include River Dart Trip 4/-
Sunday, Aug. 28th H.W. 8.17 p.m. CHARMING AFTERNOON TRIP	**To Salcombe**, leaving Paignton 2-40 p.m., Torquay (Princess Pier) 3 p.m. Returning at 6-30 p.m. Due back Paignton 8.40 p.m., Torquay 9 p.m. Return Fare 4/-.
Monday, Aug. 29th H.W. 8.45 p.m. A FINE DAY TRIP ABOUT TWO HOURS ASHORE	• **To PLYMOUTH** leaving Brixham 10 a.m., Paignton 10-25 a.m., Torquay (Princess Pier) 10-45 a.m. Due Plymouth 2 p.m. Returning from Plymouth 4-15 p.m. Due Brixham 7-45 p.m., Paignton 8-5 p.m., Torquay 8-20 p.m. Return Fare 6/6. Passengers returning by Rail must ask for Circular Rail Tickets when booking on Board. The G.W.R. issue combined Rail and Steamer Tickets at reduced fares from Exeter, Dawlish, Teignmouth, Newton Abbot, Kingskerswell, Torre, Paignton, Brixham, Kingswear and Dartmouth in connection with this Trip. For particulars, see Company's handbills, obtainable at Stations and Receiving Offices
Tuesday, Aug. 30th H.W. 9.14 p.m. COASTING TRIP	**To Teignmouth, Budleigh Salterton, and Seaton**, leaving Brixham 10-15 a.m., Paignton 10-40 a.m. Torquay (Princess Pier) 11 a.m., Budleigh Salterton 12-35 p.m. Due Seaton 1.30 p.m. Returning from Seaton 4 p.m., Budleigh Salterton 5-5 p.m., Teignmouth 5-50 p.m. Due Torquay 6-40 p.m., Paignton 7 p.m., Brixham 7-20 p.m. Return Fares: Brixham to Teignmouth 3/-, Budleigh Salterton 5/6, Seaton 6/6. Torquay to Teignmouth 2/6, Budleigh Salterton 5/-, Seaton 6/-. Teignmouth to Budleigh Salterton 3/-, Seaton 4/6. Budleigh Salterton to Seaton 2/6. 2-30 p.m., **Trip in the Bay at Seaton.** Fare 9d.
Wednesday, Aug. 31 H.W. 9.43 p.m. GRAND DAY TRIP TO LOVELY DORSET	**To Weymouth** (Dorset—the English Naples) leaving Brixham 9-15 a.m., Paignton 9-40 a.m. Torquay (Princess Pier) 10 a.m. Returning from Weymouth at 4-15 p.m. Due Torquay 8-30 p.m. Return Fares from Brixham 8/-, Torquay or Paignton 7/6
Thursday, Sept. 1st H.W. 10.12 p.m. A FINE DAY TRIP ABOUT TWO HOURS ASHORE	**To PLYMOUTH**, leaving Brixham 10 a.m., Paignton 10-25 a.m., Torquay (Princess Pier) 10-45 a.m. Due Plymouth 2 p.m. Returning from Plymouth 4-15 p.m. Due Brixham 7-45 p.m., Paignton 8-5 p.m., Torquay 8-20 p.m. Return Fare 6/6. Passengers returning by Rail must ask for Circular Rail Tickets when booking on Board. The G.W.R. issue combined Rail and Steamer Tickets at reduced fares from Exeter, Dawlish, Teignmouth, Newton Abb t, Kingskerswell, Torre, Paignton, Brixham, Kingswear and Dartmouth in connection with this Trip. For particulars, see Company's handbills, obtainable at Stations and Receiving Offices
Friday, Sept. 2nd H.W. 10.42 p.m. MORNING RIVER TRIP AFTERNOON	**To Dartmouth** (for the famous River Dart Trip, or up and down the English Rhine), leaving Paignton at 10-10 a.m., Torquay (Princess Pier) 10-30 a.m. Returning from Dartmouth 2-30 p.m. Fare 3/6, or to include River Dart Trip 6/-. **To Budleigh Salterton**, leaving Torquay (Princess Pier) 3-30 p.m. Due Budleigh Salterton 4-45 p.m., returning at 6 p.m. Home 7-15 p.m. Return Fare 3/-.
Saturday, Sept. 3rd H.W. 11.18 p.m. MORNING RIVER TRIP	**To Dartmouth** (for the famous River Dart Trip, up and down the English Rhine), leaving Paignton 10-10 a.m., Torquay (Princess Pier) 10-30 a.m. Returning from Dartmouth 2-30 p.m. or 6-30 p.m. Fare 3/6, or to include River Dart Trip 5/-.
AFTERNOON TRIP TO DITTISHAM	2-30 p.m., **Dartmouth to Torquay.** Returning 3-30 p.m. Fare 2/- **To Dartmouth** (for the River Trip to the picturesque Village of Dittisham), leaving Torquay (Princess Pier) 3-30 p.m. Returning at 6-30 p.m. Home 7-30 p.m. Fare 2/6, or to include Dittisham Trip 3/6.
Sunday, Sept. 4th H.W. 12 p.m. GRAND COASTING TRIP	**To Budleigh Salterton** and **Seaton**, leaving Paignton 2-40 p.m., Torquay (Princess Pier) 3 p.m., Budleigh Salterton 4-15 p.m. Due Seaton 5-30 p.m. Returning from Seaton 6-30 p.m. Due back Torquay only 9 p.m. Return Fares: Torquay to Budleigh Salterton 3/-, Seaton 3/6 Budleigh Salterton to Seaton 1/9

The Catering Department is fully Up-to-date and combines perfect administration with moderate charges.

NO EXTRA CHARGE FOR USE OF PROMENADE BRIDGE DECK.

SEASON TICKETS, £4 4s. 0d.   Available for all Trips, including Sundays when running.
Weekly Tickets, 16/6 (commencing any day).   Children under 12, half-fare.   2/- charged for dogs.

When the tide does not answer for going alongside the Quay at Dartmouth, Passengers must land and embark in boats. The landing or embarking of Passengers at all Piers or Beaches is to be at the sole discretion of the Captain, and the Company further stipulates that they reserve to themselves the right of making any alteration in their PROGRAMMES which the exigencies of the weather, traffic, number of Passengers, special events, or other circumstances may require, with the further condition that the Company is not responsible for any loss, inconvenience, or expense arising from any aforesaid conditions. The Return Trips advertised are based upon the supposition that the Steamer performs the Day Trip contemplated, and that no occasion has arisen to necessitate any alteration, and that the Company is not responsible to any Passenger for any loss or expense in case they are unable to complete such Return Trip.

Should any Trip be postponed a large Ensign will be hoisted at the foremost head of the Steamer at Torquay for an hour before advertised time of Starting.

The Great Western Railway issue cheap third class return tickets, at about a single fare for the double journeys, from Exeter, Dawlish, Teignmouth, Newton Abbot, Torquay, Paignton, Dartmouth, Brixham, etc., to Teignmouth, Torquay and Dartmouth in connection with the above Steamer Trips. For particulars of fares and trains by which tickets are available see the G.W.R. Company's pamphlets and bills, obtainable at the stations, or from W. T. PARKES & Co.

Bicycles 1/6 single journey.   Tickets available on day of issue only and are not transferable.   Deck Chairs 2d. each single journey.

Further information may be obtained from the District Agents, PARKES' COAL OFFICE, 20 Fleet Street, Torquay (Phone 2343); or from the Owners, Messrs. COSENS & Co., Ltd, Custom House Quay, Weymouth (Phone 333 and 175). Dartmouth Agents: G. H. COLLINS & Co., Ltd. (Phone 7). Paignton Agents: PLEASURE GROUNDS & ENTERTAINMENTS OFFICE, The Esplanade, (Phone, Paignton 5203). Teignmouth: G. PLAYER, Coal Offices, Wellington Street (Phone 7)

PARKES "QUALITY" COALS

By Order,
M. C. FROWDE } Managing Director
Cosens & Co, Ltd.

Torquay, 24th August, 1927.

GREGORY & SCOTT, PRINTERS, 28 FLEET STREET, TORQUAY.

CHAPTER SIX

PROBLEMS ASHORE & AFLOAT

1930 TO 1932

Captain H. J. Hardy.
B. JACKSON COLLECTION

Captain J. J. Marshallsay,
seated on the steps, with the
crew of VICTORIA.
AUTHOR'S COLLECTION /
M. PROWSE.

Although relatively stable in terms of the services operated, the early nineteen thirties were characterised by a series of problems with piers and other shore facilities, the loss of several familiar company servants and by some dramatic incidents afloat.

1930 opened with the sad news of the death of Captain Harbin John Hardy on 5 January. Capt Hardy had served his apprenticeship in sail, and had sailed in a variety of fishing trawlers and coastal sailing ships before joining the Weymouth & Channel Islands Steam Packet Co Ltd as a deckhand in their early paddle steamers *Aquila* and *Cygnus*. In 1881 he joined Cosens & Co as a seaman, rising quickly to the rank of mate and then captain. During his time with the firm thousands of day-trippers knew him as a genial skipper, but it was as a tugmaster that he really excelled. He was a superb seaman, an instinctive navigator and, as senior master of the *Albert Victor*, his salvage exploits made him famous amongst the seagoing fraternity all along the south coast. Capt Hardy officially retired in 1919 but continued to take command of one or other of the paddlers during the summer months for several more years. On the day of his funeral flags were flown at half-mast from all of the company's ships in Weymouth Harbour. Capts Read, Garnett, Leddy, Carter, Rawle, Hope and Bowering acted as pall bearers and a floral anchor was presented by the company. Speaking at the funeral, one of his friends recalled, 'No weather was too bad for him. Sometimes he would be missing for two or three days at a time; but he always brought his ship safely back to port, and usually with a wreck in tow'.

Capt Hardy's death was followed in March by that of Capt Marshallsay, for many years master of the *Empress*, and in April by Capt John Cox. Then, following a long illness, the company's marine superintendent and works manager Frederick Jones passed away in June. Over 300 applications were received for the vacant post and a Mr. J.M. Ward was appointed to begin a three month probationary period on 22 July. Mr Ward, who was a qualified chief engineer and marine surveyor, had his permanent appointment confirmed in October. Universally known as 'Sharky', he was to become a familiar figure on Weymouth harbourside for the next thirty years.

On 11 April 1930, *Monarch* arrived back at Weymouth from her reboilering looking somewhat different. When the new boilers had been lifted on board during March, a decision had been taken to modernise her appearance by fitting larger outer funnels with a diameter of 5ft 3 inches as compared with the 4ft originals. In either 1930 or 1931 a wheelhouse was also fitted to the bridge. With one or two minor problems ironed out and her refit completed, *Monarch* opened the season at Bournemouth on Good Friday. Unfortunately the weather was very poor and the trade scarcely justified keeping her in steam.

No sooner had the season begun than a series of problems arose with piers and ports of call. Castletown Pier at Portland was in very poor condition and estimates for its repair had been submitted to the landlords back in February. The work required was so extensive that, by July, the Admiralty was threatening to demolish the pier completely unless Cosens would commit themselves to a minimum of another seven year's tenancy. As the Portland traffic still represented a major portion of the company's Weymouth income, Cosens readily agreed to this suggestion and a seven year lease was signed on 10 October. In return for a rent of £100 per annum the Admiralty undertook to refurbish the pier in time for the 1931 season.

The next difficulty arose at Swanage. High winds on Good Friday had caused problems with berthing, and several steamers had fallen heavily against the landing stages. On April 19 the Swanage Pier Company wrote to both Cosens and the Southampton Company holding them responsible for the damage and declaring the pier unfit for further use. An urgent meeting was held with Major Burt of the pier company but, as no firm date for reopening could be obtained, both steamer companies arranged to substitute Totland Bay for Swanage on their timetables.

EMPRESS making the last passage through the old Weymouth Town Bridge on 29 September 1929 AUTHOR'S COLLECTION

A few moments later, EMPRESS edges her way carefully through the temporary footbridge which was erected across Weymouth Harbour during the reconstruction of the Town Bridge. AUTHOR'S COLLECTION

This decision generated its own problems for, within one week of the alternative service beginning, Capt Garnett of the *Monarch* had reported that the piles of Totland Bay Pier were in a very bad state and that, in his opinion, it was unsafe to go alongside. Negotiations were immediately opened with the owner of the pier, Mr Anan, who gambled on the unexpected boost to his income outweighing the likely cost of repairs and released the steamer companies from any liability for damage caused by steamers berthing at pier.

The northern berth of Swanage pier reopened to traffic on 5 June but the steamers' masters reported that the new piles were most unsatisfactory. Completion of the southern berth was delayed until August when that too was discovered to be unsuitable for passenger trade. Negotiations between the solicitors of the pier and steamer companies were to drag on for several years to follow. Strained relationships were not improved when, during July, *Emperor of India* approached the pier at excessive speed and struck it a heavy blow. The mate who had been on the bridge at the time was immediately replaced.

Things were little better at Weymouth. By the spring of 1930 work on the construction of the new Town Bridge was nearing completion. This must have been a great source of relief to Cosens as, for the previous two years, access to their Backwater berths outside the workshops had been severely limited.

Having made the first passage of the new Town Bridge EMPRESS, closely followed by the Weymouth lifeboat, heads down the harbour on 4 July 1930. Like ALEXANDRA (left) and VICTORIA (right) she is packed with local children, who had been given time off school to attend the historic event. AUTHOR'S COLLECTION / SEWARD

Before...The old steamer landing, passenger shelters and the curved, wooden pile pier at Weymouth, c. 1930
WEYMOUTH LIBRARY

After...Reconstruction work underway at Weymouth. In the foreground are the berths, cranes, platforms and sidings used by the Channel Islands passenger steamers. Beyond, the building work terminates at the new Pleasure Pier. Access to the new pier which, from 1933 onwards was Cosens' principal departure point, was by way of a footpath running parallel to the railings on the left hand side of the photo.
WEYMOUTH LIBRARY

During the demolition of the old swing bridge and the construction of its twin-bascule replacement, cofferdams and a temporary wooden footbridge with a single lifting span had been placed across the harbour at the foot of St Nicholas Street. Manoeuvring the steamers through these obstructions had proved a slow and ticklish business. In June *Empress* had broken off a wooden pile belonging to the bridge construction company, and its removal proved an expensive exercise. Embedded 15ft into the harbour mud, the pile refused to submit to the efforts of lifting barges and cranes and was eventually blown out with explosives.

The new Town Bridge was officially opened on 4 July by HRH the Duke of York amidst great celebrations. *Alexandra* and *Victoria* were moored just below the bridge to act as floating grandstands for hundreds of local school children who had been marched down to the harbour to witness the historic event. *Empress*, her decks also crowded with cheering schoolchildren, was given the honour of being the first vessel to steam through. Dressed overall and closely followed by the Weymouth lifeboat, she paddled slowly between the raised bascules and dipped her ensign to the watching Duke. The whole event was filmed by a Pathé newsreel team and the resulting publicity and goodwill must have far outweighed the fact that the three steamers had been provided free of charge.

Any celebration of an end to disruption was, however, premature. In August 1930 Weymouth Corporation announced that the long-awaited major reconstruction of Weymouth Pier would go ahead immediately. The plans involved the complete reconstruction of the quayside to accommodate two full-length rail tracks, modern cranes and additional quayside buildings. The old Cosens and GWR timber landing stages would be incorporated into the new structure and the pile pier would be demolished and replaced by a larger remodelled pleasure pier.

Between the initial announcement and the start of work in February 1931, Cosens had to negotiate hard to ensure that the final specification required the contractor to provide adequate public access and berths for the steamers and motorboats during the period of construction. They were quite reasonably concerned at the possible effects on passenger figures of running their excursion steamers from the middle of a major building site.

Another worry reared its head during September when the GWR announced a plan to widen and extend the Backwater quays outside Cosens' engineering works in order to realign the curve of the railway line around Ferry's Corner. Such a development could deprive the company of its winter lay-up berths and would almost certainly render their fixed sheerleg crane redundant. Negotiations were immediately opened with the GWR and Weymouth Corporation and were to continue until the work was eventually completed in 1938.

All these problems were compounded by the weather and the general economic state of the country. The summer of 1930 was wet and windy, keeping passengers away and leading to the cancellation of many sailings. Over a third of all *Victoria*'s coasting trips westward from Weymouth were cancelled and only nine out of twenty-six broke even. The Depression hung like a pall over the country. Unemployment was rife and, responding to the general lack of disposable income, the railway companies cancelled many of their day excursions to the coast. Starved of passengers and short of orders for the engineering department, Cosens' trading income fell sharply.

During November *Alexandra* was slipped for her BoT survey but was refused a further certificate unless extensive repairs were undertaken. Following a brief inspection the managers decided that the condition of the 52-year-old ship did not justify the expense of repairs, so she was advertised for sale. During January 1931 she was sold for £335 to Pollock Brown & Co Ltd, to whose Southampton shipbreaking yard she was delivered a few days later.

Remarkably, however, the old ship was destined to escape the shipbreaker's hammer for a few more years. After lying at the breaker's yard for just over a year she was sold again on 8 February 1932 to Capt Alfred Hawkes of Littlehampton. Hawkes promptly raised £900 by mortgaging the ship to Clifford Whitley of the Hotel Metropole, London, and James Rhodes, a mercantile marine officer also of London. In May the ship was sold to Whitley who became

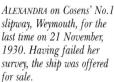

managing owner and immediately re-mortgaged the ship to Sir Malcolm McAlpine, the well-known public works contractor, in order to raise a further £2500.

The new owners' intention was to put her into service on the Thames in London as a floating dancehall and cabaret in imitation of the famous Mississippi showboats. The old ship was slipped and repainted at Southampton. Her tall funnel and masts were replaced by shorter ones, all hinged to allow the ship to pass beneath the Thames bridges. The navigating bridge was removed and replaced by a wheel and two bridge cabs on the forward end of the promenade deck. Her decks were relaid to be suitable for dancing, the foredeck was covered by an awning and a huge theatre-cum-dance hall was erected on top of the after saloon. Although still registered at Weymouth as *Alexandra*, huge illuminated signs along the deck rails proclaimed her as the *Show Boat*.

Various difficulties arose with the Board of Trade

ALEXANDRA on Cosens' No.1 slipway, Weymouth, for the last time on 21 November, 1930. Having failed her survey, the ship was offered for sale.
WEYMOUTH LIBRARY

ALEXANDRA, complete with dance hall on the promenade deck, in use as 'The Show Boat' on the River Thames in central London, during the summer of 1932.
B. JACKSON COLLECTION.

and the London County Council but eventually these were overcome and the ship made her first sailing from Westminster Pier in June 1932. Painted in a gaudy livery and festooned with coloured lights, she offered evening dance cruises upstream to Richmond and downstream as far as Greenwich. Various popular artistes of the day were engaged to add to her attractions but, in spite of this, she failed to make a profit and was withdrawn at the end of the season.

The next summer found her anchored off Margate as a stationary showboat but, not surprisingly, this experiment proved even more of a failure and after a few weeks she was transferred to Shoreham Harbour. There, her night club activities soon brought her into disgrace and she was closed down before the end of the season. Throughout the winter she lay deteriorating in a mud berth.

Meanwhile, in Manchester, a master mariner from Aberdeen named Capt Andrew Hardie had hatched a plan to introduce dance cruises on the Manchester Ship Canal and *Alexandra*, lying for sale at Shoreham, came to his attention. His offer was accepted, a deposit paid and a party of ship repairers were sent from London to prepare the vessel for sea. A captain and crew of five were engaged and steam was raised for the voyage round to Manchester. At this point Capt Hardie's funds ran out. The ship repairing firm was unable to obtain payment, the crew were left without wages and the grand plan for the Manchester Ship Canal sank quietly from sight.

Repossessed by Clifford Whitely, *Alexandra* was quickly sold to T. W. Ward Ltd for breaking up on the Thames at Grays. Towards the end of November 1934 many Shoreham residents turned out to watch the old *Show Boat* leave harbour under tow on her last voyage. H. A. Allen recalled that 'Coastal steamers in port saluted her with their whistles as she passed silently on her way. As she reached the open sea, she dipped gracefully in the moderate swell as if paying her courteous respects to the harbour that had sheltered her in her final years.'

Unsettled by the sudden though not unexpected demise of *Alexandra*, Cosens looked about for a replacement. On 29 December 1930 a small deputation travelled to Bristol to inspect P. & A. Campbell Ltd's *Brighton Belle*, which had been offered for sale for £10,000. It seems probable that the inspection was instigated by Cosens as something of a knee-jerk reaction. *Brighton Belle* would undoubtedly have made a very satisfactory replacement for *Alexandra* as she was 21 years younger, 29ft longer, of a similar speed and, with her full-length promenade deck, offered superior accommodation and a far more modern appearance. She was very similar in size and specification to the Southampton Company's *Bournemouth Queen* and it may have been in Cosens' mind to pair the two ships on the Bournemouth station.

Campbells, for their part, do not appear to have been desperate to sell the *Brighton Belle*, despite the fact that the depression was beginning to bite deep into the Bristol Channel trade. 1929 and 1930 had been indifferent years and the burgeoning unemployment in the valleys of South Wales had led to a dramatic fall in passenger figures. *Brighton Belle* was the most expendable of their fleet and Campbells, with few financial reserves to draw upon, would undoubtedly have welcomed the boost to their funds had it been possible to sell her at a sufficiently high price. Accordingly they settled on an optimistically inflated asking price, and sat back to await Cosens' reaction.

As no further reference to the transaction is contained in either company's minute books it is clear that, upon mature reflection, Cosens thought better of the deal and decided not to proceed.

During the winter of 1930-1 major defects were discovered in the main steam pipe of the *Emperor of India* and in one of *Victoria*'s crank shaft webs. A new web was ordered from Harland & Wolff at Southampton but this too was found to be flawed and had to be replaced. The Board of Trade insisted on major repairs to the *Premier*. *Monarch*, lying at her winter mooring in Poole Harbour, grounded on an exceptionally low tide and damaged one of her paddle wheels.

The 1931 season proved to be no better than the last. The weather was poor, especially in August, and passenger figures did not improve. Severe competition from motor coaches did not help matters, and the company responded by offering more combined steamer and coach tours, which were well received by the public. Shanklin Pier on the Isle of Wight reopened to steamer traffic at Easter and, from Whitsun, became a welcome addition to the Bournemouth programme. This good news was offset by the serious damage to Poole Quay which made overnight berthing of the steamers extremely difficult and led Cosens to investigate the possibility of one steamer laying overnight at Swanage. At Weymouth the harbour improvements were in full swing and the Company was offered temporary facilities at the new Naval Steps, in place of its normal landing stage.

Victoria replaced *Alexandra* on all long trips from Weymouth and was fitted with a radio gramophone at a cost of £52 10s 0d. Since *Victoria* lacked a deck saloon and offered only limited covered accommodation, the return leg of many full-day excursions must have been cold, wet and tedious. Any means of entertaining passengers and distracting them from the outdated facilities on offer represented a very good investment.

During the wet and windy August, repairs to Swanage pier were eventually completed, but *Premier* managed to collide with Portland Pier and *Monarch* sustained damage whilst landing passengers on board the battle cruiser HMS *Hood* in Swanage Bay.

The Schneider Cup air race was again scheduled to take place in the Solent on 12 September and offered the possibility of a welcome boost to late season income. Plans were laid to charter *Monarch* to the Supermarine Aviation Company, to run *Emperor of India* from Bournemouth at a fare of £1 1s. to include luncheon, and to bring *Victoria* from

EMPEROR OF INDIA at Yarmouth's attractive wooden pier.
H. A. ALLEN COLLECTION

Weymouth. In the event the French and Italian competitors withdrew from the race forcing Cosens to reduce all their fares and, although *Emperor of India* and *Monarch* both made their trips, the race itself was cancelled due to poor weather conditions.

During September the *Monarch* was in collision with the French ketch *Marcel Rene* and steps were taken to have the latter arrested on her next visit to England in order to enforce payment for the damages. A few days later *Monarch* picked up a small boat off Old Harry Rocks and took her into Poole where a salvage claim was filed. During the same week *Emperor of India* collided with Bournemouth Pier and sustained some damage. As usual she was the first to finish her season on 13 September, to be followed by *Empress*, *Premier* and *Victoria* on 19, 20 and 26 September respectively.

Monarch was last to finish on 3 October and proceeded straight to the Naval Floating Dock at Portland. Together with *Victoria* and *Empress* she was due to undergo a load line survey during the winter and, notwithstanding her recent reboilering, it was apparent that much work would need to be carried out. An appeal to postpone the survey by one year fell on deaf ears and by November the surveyor had confirmed the worst. Tenders were obtained from Harland & Wolff of Southampton, Philip & Sons of Dartmouth and J. S.White & Co Ltd of Cowes. Whites' quotation of £560 was accepted and *Monarch* sailed for Cowes on 21 November to undergo a major refit.

The surveyor also decided that the boiler of the *Empress* would have to come out in order that the interior of the ship could be thoroughly examined. Accordingly she was towed to Portland where the boiler was lifted out by one of the large dockyard cranes. The ship and boiler were then towed back to Weymouth where extensive replating was undertaken on Cosens' slipway. *Victoria*, which had escaped from her survey more lightly, was also repaired by the company's own staff.

In an attempt to halt the steady decline in passengers during the dismal summers of 1930 and 1931 and to counter the increased competition from motor coaches, Cosens and the Southampton Company agreed to reduce fares between Bournemouth, Southampton and the Isle of Wight for the coming season. Joint arrangements were also agreed with Mr Anan of Totland Bay Pier for combined steamer and coach tour of the island to begin at Easter.

No sooner had these arrangements been finalised than an engineer's report declared Totland Bay Pier unfit for further use. Mr Anan suggested that the steamers should call instead at the nearby Victoria Pier, but this was found to be impractical owing to the strong tidal streams running at that point. Instead, the steamers were diverted to Yarmouth Pier, the arrangement with Mr Anan was cancelled and the two companies co-operated to offer connecting coach tours on their own account. The fare from Bournemouth was 10s 6d, of which 5s 6d was paid to the coach operators. Mr. Anan prevaricated about undertaking the necessary repairs to the pier, which were estimated at over £1,000, and at the same time toyed with the idea of introducing a ferry service between Victoria Pier and the mainland. In the event he went ahead with neither scheme, and Totland Bay Pier lay derelict until finally reopened to steamer traffic on 17 June 1951.

VICTORIA landing passengers over her bows at West Bay during one of her regular westward coasting trips. The ship very occasionally moored between the piers but the company preferred to avoid paying harbour dues by using beach landings whenever possible. AUTHOR'S COLLECTION

VICTORIA at Lyme Regis showing detail of the hinging gangway used to land passengers on the open beaches along the Dorset coast. This extraordinary contraption was raised and lowered by a system of ropes and pulleys passing through a sheave on the top of the forward anchor davit and down to the capstan. H. A. ALLEN COLLECTION

Victoria, together with the Southampton Company's *Princess Elizabeth*, opened the 1932 Bournemouth season on Good Friday but earnings were disappointing. The Swanage Pier Company still refused to allow Sunday sailings from their pier, but did allow *Victoria* to land passengers there on an Easter Sunday trip from Bournemouth to Lulworth Cove. *Monarch* returned from Cowes during April and re-entered service in early May. Cosens expressed themselves well pleased with the both the quality of the repairs carried out by Whites, and with the final bill of £922.

The substitution of Yarmouth for Totland Bay was not the only major timetable change during the 1932 season. At Weymouth, in June, the momentous decision was taken to abandon *Victoria*'s coasting trips around West Bay due to falling income and increased competition. Henceforth *Victoria* was employed on alternative direct sailings from Weymouth.

On Tuesday 28 June *Premier* with 150 passengers on board sailed from Weymouth on her usual 2.30pm trip to Portland. Instead of heading directly for the northern entrance to Portland Harbour her master, Capt A. R.'Pony' Moore, followed his usual practice of swinging to starboard and following the line of the coast past the Nothe Fort and Newton's Cove before turning to run parallel with the breakwater and towards the entrance.

Inside the harbour, meanwhile, the submarine HMS *Rainbow*, commanded by Lt Com Thomas

Yeoman, R.N., had weighed anchor at 2. 41pm. and was heading at 7 knots towards the same entrance. At 2.44pm *Premier* was spotted on the opposite side of the breakwater and a long blast was sounded on the *Rainbow*'s syren. Two minutes later, as both vessels cleared the breakwater head and came into full view of one another on a steady bearing, it became apparent that a collision was inevitable. Both ships rang down full astern and *Premier* whose passengers, blissfully unaware of the impending disaster, were gazing in delight at the approaching submarine, came to a halt in the centre of the Northern Entrance. *Rainbow*, with her helm hard over and still travelling at about 3 knots began to swing to starboard, but too late to avoid the paddle steamer.

The submarine's stem and net cutter ploughed into *Premier*'s starboard bow at angle of about 70 degrees from the stern, carrying away her bulwarks and a tearing a massive hole in the hull plating. By sheer good fortune the impact was some 5ft forward of the old steamer's only collision bulkhead, for there can be little doubt that had it been further aft the outcome would have been very different indeed. As it was the forepeak flooded rapidly but the bulkhead held. Although many passengers were knocked off their feet and severely frightened there was little real panic on board. The stewardess, Miss Down, was below in the refreshment bar at the time of the collision and recalled; 'My first thought was for the cash till. The floor of the saloon suddenly lifted. I

PREMIER at Trinity Quay, Weymouth, following her collision with HMS RAINBOW, 28 June 1932. The extensive damage to the starboard bow is clearly visible. Cosens' motorboat WEYMOUTH QUEEN lies alongside.

Entrance to Poole Harbour.   W.13.

heard shouting and next felt a crash which shook *Premier* from stem to stern. Some of the women and children were terribly frightened but they soon pulled themselves together. One of the pipes from the boiler burst, filling the place with steam. I groped for the till and then ran up on deck.'

Having assured himself that his ship was not in imminent danger of sinking, Capt Moore ordered his passengers aft and got lines on board the *Rainbow*. *Premier* was hauled round so that her stern and starboard sponson rested along the submarine's port side, gangways were improvised and passengers were rapidly transferred. One passenger recalled, 'Then a hatch opened and we went below, packed together like sardines. It was very hot and sailors brought water. Some children were crying because they had lost their mothers and husbands their wives, but the alarm was only temporary'. The sight of rescue craft dashing to the scene from the torpedo range and depots, the breakwater and Weymouth Bay was a source of great relief, and there was only one more moment of fear when the two ships began to drift apart and some thought that the *Premier* was sinking. Within a short while all of the passengers had been transferred into motorboats and landed at Weymouth. *Rainbow* retired to Portland Dockyard and *Premier* limped slowly back to Weymouth where, moored at Trinity Steps, she became a source of great interest to press and public alike.

The next day she was hauled onto Cosens' slipway for repairs to begin. Hull plates, frames, bulwarks and decking all had to be replaced and it was assumed locally that the 86 year old ship would be out of service for a considerable time. However, by working day and night Cosens' engineering staff completed the work in remarkably short order and only one week later, on the evening of Wednesday 5 July, a large crowd gathered to cheer her back into the water. The next morning she ran trials in the bay before departing on her first public sailing, an afternoon trip around Portland Harbour, where one of the first ships she passed was HMS *Rainbow* which was anchored close to the spot where the collision had occurred. That evening the Fleet arrived to be inspected by the King and *Premier* took out a large group of passengers who, in addition to 'obtaining fine views of the grand assemblage of warships, saw Weymouth's beautiful illuminations and enjoyed dancing on board'. Together with her fleet mates, *Premier* was busy with similar afternoon and evening trips throughout the Fleet's stay, and Capt Moore expressed himself well satisfied with the repairs. 'The vessel is going as well as ever. In fact she seems all the better for her rest. She is going to run for a great many years yet.'

An Admiralty Court of Enquiry was convened on board HMS *Titania* at Portland on 6 July and cleared Lt Com Yeoman of any responsibility for the collision. Cosens responded to this judgement the following day by issuing a writ on Lt Com Yeoman. Their statement of claim maintained that *Rainbow* had kept a bad look out, had improperly entered the harbour entrance at excessive speed, had failed to keep to the starboard side of the channel, warn of her manoeuvres by proper sound signals, slow down in time or port her helm. She was clearly in breach of the regulations and therefore responsible for the collision.

The High Court hearing was held in London on 12 December before Mr Justice Langton and two Elder Bretheren of Trinity House. In opening his summing up he exercised a little judicial wit by mentioning that the case was remarkable not only for *Premier*'s great age, but also because it was 'the first time that a submarine had "come to the surface" in an Admiralty Court.'

The court upheld the fact that Capt Moore had been on the bridge all the time and that his prompt actions had brought *Premier* to a stop before the collision occurred. It concluded, in direct contradiction to the previous Admiralty hearing, that Yeoman must be regarded as the greater offender since he had failed to keep an adequate lookout or judge *Premier*'s movements in time. He was judged to be in clear breach of the rule forbidding any outgoing vessel to leave harbour when another was about to enter.

Capt Moore did not escape criticism either. The judge continued: '*Premier*, with what I can only class as a very careless look-out, never became aware of the fact that *Rainbow* was in the vicinity at all until she got quite close to the piers. *Premier* was approaching what I may call perhaps a semi-blind corner at full speed with a bad look out, preparatory to making a sharp turn. The Elder Bretheren advise me that, although Capt Moore was entitled to approach the harbour at a fine angle, to do so at that time at that speed was bad seamanship.'

Thus, two thirds of the blame was allocated to *Rainbow* and one third to *Premier*. The matter, however, was not quite closed. The Admiralty objected to the damages awarded against them and claimed that, in view of her great age, *Premier* should have been declared a constructive total loss. A second hearing was held at the Admiralty Court on 14 March 1933 at which the Admiralty were unable to sustain their claim, but did manage to get Cosens' repair bill reduced from £945 to £691. A final result of the collision came four months later when, on 24 July 1933 after strong lobbying from the Admiralty, the rule of entry to Portland Harbour was reversed, henceforth giving priority to outgoing vessels.

The second major drama of the season occurred when *Emperor of India* went to the rescue of the Southern Railway paddle steamer *Southsea* on the afternoon of 7 September 1932. *Emperor of India* was on an afternoon sailing from Bournemouth to Ventnor and around the Isle of Wight and had just passed the Needles when she spotted the *Southsea* flying distress signals and lying at anchor broadside to the seas about three miles off Brook Chine. Capt Read took the *Emperor* as close to the casualty as he

dared when, using a megaphone, the master of the *Southsea* explained that his ship's port paddlewheel was completely disabled due to a fractured shaft and requested a tow.

Emperor of India did not have a single rope long enough for the job, so the crew was instructed to shackle four together before Capt Read began the difficult task of passing the tow. There was a stiff breeze with a heavy sea running and it took half an hour and several attempts before *Emperor* could be manoeuvered close enough to the rolling *Southsea* for a line to be thrown and the heavy tow rope hauled across. *Southsea*'s anchor was weighed and very slowly the two ships set off towards St. Catherine's Point. All went well until at 6.30pm off Blackgang the tow suddenly parted and *Southsea* began to drift rapidly towards the rocky ledges of the shore. Both ships were now within three-quarters of a mile of the coast but Capt Read, drawing on his long experience in Cosens' salvage tugs, acted very swiftly and had the *Southsea* back under tow within five minutes. As soon as news of the casualty reached Portsmouth the Admiralty tug *Resolve* had been dispatched to the aid of the *Southsea* and both the Yarmouth and Brook

A 1931 sailing bill for a Sunday trip to Cowes
H. A. ALLEN COLLECTION

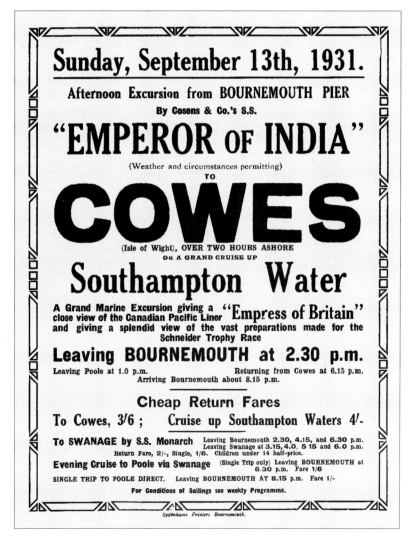

EMPEROR OF INDIA's 210 H.P. compound diagonal engine was by far the most powerful in the post-1918 Cosens fleet. DORCHESTER LIBRARY.

10.45pm to be greeted by a crowd of relieved friends and relatives. One passenger explained to a *Bournemouth Daily Echo* reporter that during the rescue and subsequent tow the vast majority of passengers on both ships had been terribly seasick but had born their ordeal with patience. He went on to add, 'I should like to say that the Captain and crew of the *Emperor of India* did exceedingly well. The boat was manoeuvered in a very heavy sea with the utmost skill and fine seamanship. The captain and crew are to be very much congratulated on what they did.' The assessors at the subsequent High Court salvage hearing in London obviously agreed, for *Emperor of India* was awarded a handsome £1,000 in salvage fees whilst the tug *Resolve* received £250.

lifeboats had been placed on standby. The tug eventually arrived and took over the tow from *Emperor of India* just to the east of St Catherine's Point. It was not until the early hours of the next morning that *Southsea* arrived back in Portsmouth where special trains and ferries awaited to rush her 500 weary passengers onwards to their destinations

Emperor of India's passengers fared a little better. The ship, which should have arrived alongside Bournemouth pier at 9.00pm, finally berthed at

This unexpected windfall represented a welcome bonus to a remarkably successful season. The weather had been a great improvement on 1931 and the presence of the King and his fleet at Weymouth during a period of exceptionally fine weather in July had given the passenger figures a tremendous boost. The Weymouth steamers, motor launches and speedboats had all been extremely busy and many special trips had been operated from Bournemouth. Ashore there had been an upturn in outside work at the engineering works and the company had been successful in purchasing the freehold of their No 2 slipway from the Wilton Estate for the sum of £1,350. There was general optimism that the worst effects of the depression may have passed.

With the harbour reconstruction works completed in 1933, VICTORIA is seen moored in the principal berth at the new Weymouth Pleasure Pier. Less frequently Cosens used the other side of the pier while at busy times two steamers could easily be accommodated on the harbour side. AUTHOR'S COLLECTION / SEWARD

CHAPTER SEVEN
THE TIDE BEGINS TO TURN
1933 TO 1938

If the years 1930-2 had been generally difficult for Cosens, the remainder of the decade was marked by a steady improvement in the company's fortunes, improved weather and passenger figures, and by some significant fleet changes.

During the winter of 1932-3 a conference was held in London between Cosens, the Southampton Company and the Swanage Pier Company, at which the steamer companies submitted a scheme to minimise the risk of steamers damaging the pier and offered to pay half the costs. During the autumn of 1932 the pier had again suffered from the over-enthusiastic attentions of the *Emperor of India*, and it was clear that something had to be done to reduce the monotonous frequency of insurance claims. The new proposals, which involved building dolphins close beside the landing stages, were initially rejected by the pier company but continued protests from the steamer companies brought about a change of heart and the plans were eventually agreed in March 1933. Work began in April and by June the new dolphins had been completed, tested and declared satisfactory.

Emperor of India had undergone a load line survey in the Admiralty dry dock at Portland during November 1932, and the surveyor produced a formidable list of renewals and repairs which would be necessary before a new passenger certificate could be granted. Having sought tenders from a variety of shipyards, Cosens awarded the contract to J. Samuel White & Co Ltd of Cowes, where *Emperor of India*

spent most of the winter. The Board of Trade were obviously impressed with the quality of the completed work for, when the ship emerged in March, they agreed to grant a load line certificate for five instead of the usual four years.

Monarch, in company with the Southampton Company's *Princess Elizabeth* opened the 1933 Bournemouth season on Good Friday, 14 April and continued to run for nine days after which she laid up again to await the start of the main season on 8 May. Regular passengers noted with sadness the absence of her long-standing master, Cap. Garnett, who had been confined to his sick bed throughout the winter and finally died on 16 May. His place on *Monarch*'s bridge was taken by Capt Carter. The deployment of steamers followed the usual pattern with *Monarch* and *Emperor of India* at Bournemouth, *Premier* on the short runs from Weymouth to Portland, *Empress* on the Weymouth to Lulworth service and *Victoria* maintaining the long distance sailings from Weymouth to Swanage , Bournemouth and the Isle of Wight.

The season turned out to be refreshingly successful. The weather was good, no mishaps to steamers or piers were recorded, passenger figures showed a welcome increase and the works department was busy with outside work. The Weymouth trade received a welcome boost on 13 July when a visit by H.R.H. The Prince of Wales kept two steamers and three launches fully occupied. Only two

MONARCH and EMPEROR OF INDIA alongside Bournemouth Pier with VICTORIA and the Southampton Company's BOURNEMOUTH QUEEN off to seaward.
D. HAYSOM COLLECTION

The dummy submarine for use in the film 'Jack Ahoy' under construction at Weymouth during the autumn of 1933. In the background EMPEROR OF INDIA is laid up for the winter while a horse and cart make their way across the Town Bridge.
THE SUBMARINE MUSEUM, GOSPORT.

VICTORIA undergoing her annual refit on Cosens' slipway during the 1930s. The boat with her sail hoisted on the Weymouth Sailing Club moorings is OSPREY, the second of the famous Weymouth Falcons, several of which can still be seen on the moorings today.
AUTHOR'S COLLECTION / SEWARD

clouds appeared on the horizon, and both of these proved to be of minor importance. The first came in June when the police questioned the legality of the 'automatic machines' which had been carried onboard the steamers for the past two seasons. Despite negotiations carried out through the Coastwise Passenger Steamship Owners Association a prosecution followed in December and the company was fined £20 plus costs. The second presented itself during August when P. & A. Campbell Ltd wrote to announce that their Devon-based steamer *Westward Ho* would be calling at Weymouth to pick up passengers on her sailings from Torquay to

Bournemouth. Since *Westward Ho* was a large, fast and relatively glamorous steamer she had the potential to steal significant numbers of passenger from the older and ill-equipped *Victoria*. Cosens immediately wrote a strong letter of protest and, to everyone's surprise, Campbells withdrew their proposal. No more was ever heard of the matter.

A bonus to a very encouraging season came in the form of a lucrative contract with the Gaumont Picture Corporation, who were making a film called '*Jack Ahoy*!'. Starring Jack Hulbert as an accident-prone tar who saves the admiral's daughter (played by co-star Nancy O'Neil) from the clutches of marauding

VICTORIA *at Bournemouth Pier on a day trip from Weymouth.*
H. A. ALLEN COLLECTION

Chinese bandits, the film involved several sequences where the characters were pictured on board a submarine at sea. Cosens were commissioned to create a dummy submarine for the purpose. A plywood and timber conning tower and section of hull was constructed on top of an old ship's boiler and given a very passable appearance by the addition of imitation rivet heads, periscopes and a coat of battleship grey paint. The whole contraption could be raised and lowered in the water by pumping air in or out of the boiler to give the impression of the submarine surfacing or diving.

The seagoing sequences were filmed during November 1933 in Newton's Cove where the dummy submarine was towed each day by the *Premier*. In one scene Jack Hulbert was seen clinging to the conning tower as the submarine submerged and in another the vessel was attacked by Chinese pirates in a gunboat, which was actually one of Cosens' speedboats with a dummy gun fitted to her bows. During the making of the film many of Weymouth's unemployed found themselves dressed in naval uniforms and marching around Castletown Pier and Bincleaves as film extras, whilst the domestic requirements of the film crew gave a welcome out-of-season boost to local boarding house proprietors. The arrival of a large group of Chinese extras added an exotic oriental touch, and the town must have seemed strangely dull when the filming was completed in mid November and normality returned to the harbour.

During October it was *Victoria*'s turn for her load line survey, when it was discovered that fifteen bottom plates would have to be renewed. To do this the engine and boilers would need to be lifted, so tenders were sought from various shipyards. In the end it was decided to do the work on the company's own slipway

at Weymouth and extra hands were engaged for the purpose. Thus the year ended with yet another boost for Cosens' own engineering staff and to Weymouth's employment statistics.

1934 was an uneventful but successful season. Profits were down by £3500 on the exceptionally good 1933 results, but a comfortable surplus was recorded in all departments and a 15% dividend declared.

In July 1934 the Portland Publicity Committee approached the company with a request that steamers should once again call at Church Ope Cove below Pennsylvania Castle. The committee offered to lend all possible assistance to facilitate the landing and embarkation of passengers, but is unclear whether any calls actually took place.

One day during July rumours began to circulate in Weymouth that *Victoria* had narrowly escaped being struck by a torpedo in Weymouth Bay, and it was not until the ship's return in the evening that the truth was discovered. *Victoria* had been on passage from Weymouth to Bournemouth and was abeam Arish Mell Gap near Lulworth when the bow lookout had reported a torpedo approaching from the starboard bow. The master had immediately rung down 'standby engines' and *Victoria* took quite a list to starboard as the cameras of two hundred or so holiday makers clicked at the rare and exciting site of torpedo gliding at shallow depth across her bows approximately 100 yards ahead. A further thrill followed a few minutes later when a submarine suddenly broke surface on *Victoria*'s starboard quarter and steamed alongside for some while. The conning tower hatch opened and some naval personnel popped up and waved to the passengers before the submarine submerged again as quickly and silently as she had arrived. Putting a positive gloss on what could have been quite a serious incident the ship's purser, Sydney Davis, commented 'We in *Victoria* continued our pleasurable way to Bournemouth with the comforting and reassuring thought that the Navy is always keeping an eye on us.'.

All other significant developments took place at Bournemouth. In February 1934, Capt Robinson, the town's well-known pier master, died. In July Cosens were served with notice that their Bournemouth office, which was leased from a Mr Nelson Jennings, was to be demolished in the autumn and a hunt was started for new premises. A suitable office was soon located at number 8 Bath Road and a lease signed from 1 November.

During November Cosens and the Southampton Company both received letters from the Town clerk of Bournemouth asking whether they would be prepared to run excursions from Boscombe Pier in the event of a new landing stage being provided there. During December soundings were taken around the pier and, by January 1935 both companies had agreed in principle to provide a service when and if the necessary work was carried out. It was emphasised however that due to the shallow water off the pier any service would be irregular and tide-dependent. In the event, Bournemouth Council voted during March not to provide a landing stage during 1935, but to leave the matter in abeyance until the following season.

The major event of 1935 was the King's Jubilee Review, held at Spithead on 16 July. As early as March it had been resolved to mark the event by granting all shore staff a day's holiday with full pay, and to compensate the steamer crews with an extra day's pay in lieu. A series of meetings were held with the Southampton Company at which it was agreed to co-operate in the provision of excursions to the review

Ticket for trip by EMPEROR OF INDIA to view the Review.
AUTHOR'S COLLECTION

COSENS & CO., LTD.

No. 121   No. 121

Royal Naval Review

at SPITHEAD by

T.M. THE KING AND QUEEN

Tuesday, 16th July, 1935

Special Excursion from Poole or Swanage by the P.S. "EMPEROR OF INDIA," leaving Poole Quay at 8.0
Swanage Pier at 8.30 a.m. (by Queen)

CHILD 10/6   CHILD 10/6

N.B. A LIMITED NUMBER OF LUNCHEONS WILL BE PROVIDED TICKETS FOR WHICH MUST BE BOOKED BEFOREHAND. [P.T.O.

and to pool all earnings on this station for the Jubilee Bank Holiday weekend on 5 and 6 May.

As all vessels proceeding to the review were required to be in their designated anchorages by 1pm and would not be permitted to weigh until after 6pm. It was agreed that each company should run one steamer to the review itself at a cost of 17s 6d and a second to the evening illuminations at 6s 6d. Cosens designated *Emperor of India* and *Monarch* respectively. *Victoria* and *Empress* were both let on private charter for £250 and £150 respectively, the latter to take a party of Bournemouth errand boys from Poole Quay. An application to charter *Monarch* was turned down as this would have left no vessel available to provide the evening public sailing to the illuminations. During June it emerged that there was public demand for a trip which combined the review and the evening illuminations and it was agreed that the Southampton Company's *Queen* should make the trip at a fare of £1 1s 0d while *Monarch* maintained a restricted service between Bournemouth and Swanage before proceeding to the illuminations during the evening. The two ships' receipts were pooled.

The review, which attracted excursion steamers from as far afield as the Thames and Bristol Channel, was a great success and provided a significant boost to the company's income for 1935. Despite poor weather in May, June, the last week of August and all of September, the peak weeks of July and early August were blessed with fine weather and the steamers were frequently filled to capacity.

On 30 August 1935 both *Emperor of India* and *Victoria* were caught at sea in an exceptionally heavy gale and letters of appreciation were sent to Captains Read and Rawle by the board, congratulating them on their fine seamanship in landing their passengers safely. The windy conditions continued into September and managed to disrupt the end of the season. *Emperor of India* and *Empress* were due to finish on 14 September, followed by *Premier* on 21 September, *Monarch* on 29 September and *Victoria* on 5 October. However, on the night of 17 September during a heavy gale and an abnormally high spring tide, *Monarch* was thrown against Poole quay and suffered extensive damage. A survey was carried out and temporary repairs effected to allow her to be taken to Weymouth, where the underwriters agreed that she should be docked and repaired at Portland. *Emperor of India* took *Monarch*'s place at Bournemouth until 29 September when she too sustained damage from heavy seas whilst on passage to Weymouth for winter lay up.

A few weeks later, during November, the directors and employees of the company gathered on board *Emperor of India* to bid farewell to her master, Capt William Carey Read, who was retiring at the age of seventy. Capt Read, affectionately known as 'Billy', had first gone to sea in 1879 in the Weymouth-registered sailing ships *Harmon* and *Kate* trading to the Baltic. He then went deep-sea in the square-riggers *Holmsdale* and *Diamond* sailing to the Far East,

Cosens directors and staff gather on the deck of the EMPEROR OF INDIA *to mark the retirement of Capt. W. C. 'Billy' Read after 40 year's service with the company. In the front row, left to right are: C. H. J. 'Charlie' Kaile, company secretary; Commander A. H. Dunn and Col. C. P. Symes, directors; Capt Read, Thomas Lynes, Chairman; Mark C. Frowde, Managing Director and J. Vincent, director.*
AUTHOR'S COLLECTION

before spending an exciting interlude ashore in Australia. In 1885 he joined the Royal Navy and served in *HMS Revenge* before returning to Weymouth in 1895 when he joined Cosens. After a brief period as a rigger and boatswain at the slipway he was appointed to command the tug *Queen* where he soon became famous for his exploits as a salvage skipper. Later he moved to *Melcombe Regis* where he spent part of the war before moving to command *Alexandra* on Admiralty duties at Chatham. In 1921 he was posted to *Monarch* but the coal strike prevented him from taking her into service, and by later that season he had been appointed to *Emperor of India* where he spent the rest of his career.

At a ceremony in the ship's dining saloon the company Chairman, Thomas Lynes, spoke of Capt Read's forty years loyal service to the company, the twenty-six ships he had rescued whilst in command of the salvage tugs, his superb seamanship and of his popularity with passengers and crew alike. After a wallet containing a cheque had been presented the assembled company drank his health and then adjourned to the promenade deck where a charmingly informal group photograph was taken to record the occasion.

1936 was another season of very poor weather, remembered chiefly for the entry into service of the new Cunard liner *Queen Mary*. The huge ship, fresh from her builders on the Clyde, made her first visit to Southampton on 27 March. After a period in dry dock she returned to the Clyde for speed trials before undertaking a brief inaugural cruise from

Southampton on 14-15 May and sailing on her maiden voyage to New York on 27 May, 1936. The ship caused a sensation with the public and hundreds of thousands packed the shores of Southampton Water to watch her stately progress. The pleasure steamers which went to witness the maiden departure

A poster for one of MONARCH'S *special Sunday excursions from Swanage Pier to view the liner* QUEEN MARY *at Southampton.*
H. A. ALLEN COLLECTION

An advertising bill for two of Cosens' trips to the 1937 Coronation Review at Spithead. The original was printed in patriotic red, white and blue.
VICTOR GRAY COLLECTION.

Channel Islands steamers. This innovation quite obviously cut into Cosens' earnings, but the company could do little but protest and watch developments carefully.

During September the *Emperor of India* was returning to Bournemouth from the Isle of Wight when one of her wheels struck some submerged wreckage and was seriously damaged. Capt Carter, who had replaced Capt Read, managed to bring the ship to anchor and transfer his passengers to *Monarch*. *Emperor of India* eventually limped into Poole where temporary repairs were effected which allowed her to carry on until the end of the season, when more permanent work could be carried out at Weymouth. Capt Carter received the formal thanks of the board for his skill and seamanship which had prevented the breakdown developing into a potential stranding.

As the season drew to a close it was announced that the new King Edward VIII would be visiting Portland on 12-13 November 1936 and consideration was given to operating a special excursion. However, in view of uncertainty as to his His Majesty's precise movements and the precarious nature of the weather, it was decided not to proceed. Instead, one steamer and two motor launches were offered on charter to anyone interested in organising a trip, but no interest was expressed.

In contrast to the previous year, 1937 proved to be a highly significant one in the company's history. The year opened with the announcement that, following King Edward VIII's abdication, King George VI and Queen Elizabeth's Coronation Review would be held at Spithead on 20 May and discussions were immediately opened with the Southampton Company regarding joint arrangements. Initial agreements were modified as bookings developed and it was eventually decided that *Bournemouth Queen*, *Mauretania* (*Queen* renamed at the request of the Cunard company to retain the famous name for their future use), *Emperor of India* and *Monarch* would provide a selection of combined and separate trips to the review and evening illuminations, and that their earnings would be pooled. *Victoria* was chartered on behalf of the Admiralty for £350, and *Monarch* received an additional £500 charter to act as tender to a liner belonging to the Rotterdam Lloyd company. It was planned to use *Empress* to maintain a restricted Bournemouth-Swanage service but, in the event, she too was chartered by the RAF Yacht Club. With no steamers available, the 'ferry' was maintained on review day by a fleet of hired motor coaches.

Cosens took out substantial insurance against cancellation of the review due to bad weather, but need not have worried. The day was blessed with good weather and passengers were rewarded with a fine view of the majestic Royal Yacht *Victoria & Albert* steaming slowly up and down the lines of the assembled fleet. At between 2am and 3am the following morning Bournemouth was treated to the unusual sight of over 1,800 tired but happy passengers streaming ashore at the pier from the

were packed to capacity and demand remained high throughout the summer, with special trips being offered to witness every daylight arrival or departure. Excitement was increased by the fact that *Queen Mary* was in stiff, if unofficial, competition with the mammoth French liner *Normandie* for the Blue Riband of the Atlantic. Although *Queen Mary* did not manage to wrest the speed record from her rival until August 1938, there was always the possibility that the next trip might be the significant one and public interest remained high. The frequency of sailings to Southampton docks was increased whenever she was alongside and it was widely acknowledged that the new liner had added significantly to Cosens' profit for the season. On Whit Monday, 1 June, the BBC travelled on board *Premier* in order to broadcast a radio programme contrasting the veteran paddler, by now the oldest vessel on the British register to hold a passenger certificate, with the huge Cunarder which was, of course, the largest and newest.

At Weymouth, concern was caused by the decision of the G W R to introduce afternoon and evening cruises from the pier in one or other of their large steamers which had remained to view the evening illuminations.

Back at Weymouth it had been apparent for some time that the elderly, open-decked *Victoria* no longer provided an adequate degree of comfort or speed for long-distance excursions. On 19 April 1937 a special meeting was called to consider her replacement by the Southern Railway's paddle steamer *Duchess of Norfolk* which was lying for sale at Southampton. Having inspected her in drydock, Cosens submitted an offer of £4,000 which was quickly accepted and delivery was agreed for mid-June.

Duchess of Norfolk had been launched on 25 August 1911 at the yard of D. W. Henderson & Sons of Glasgow. The last ship to be built for the old London & South Western Railway / London, Brighton & South Coast Railway 'Joint Committee', she replaced *Alexandra* (which had also passed into the Cosens fleet) on the Portsmouth-Ryde ferry service. With a gross tonnage of 381 and dimensions of 190ft x 26ft, she was considerably larger and faster than *Victoria* and boasted a spacious deck saloon on the main deck aft, surmounted by a full width promenade deck.

Cosens applied to the Board of Trade to change her name to *Sovereign* but this together with several other suggestions was rejected until eventually the name *Embassy* was agreed upon. As soon as the ship was handed over she entered drydock at Southampton for survey and a temporary load line certificate was granted on the strict condition that Cosens undertook to complete all necessary repairs during the coming winter.

By the beginning of July 1937 *Embassy* had arrived at Weymouth for repainting and on Saturday 25 July she was thrown open to inspection by the great and good of the town. The ship was toasted in champagne and the mayor congratulated the company on the acquisition of such a fine ship, expressing the hope that they might be encouraged to resurrect the trips westwards from Weymouth to Torquay. On the following morning, Sunday 26 July, *Embassy* sailed on her first public excursion from Weymouth to the Isle of Wight with 300 passengers on board. On the bridge was Capt Bowering who had been promoted to his new command from *Victoria*. For the remaining six weeks of the of the season *Embassy* was based mostly at Weymouth undertaking long excursions to Swanage, Bournemouth, the Isle of Wight and, as the mayor had hoped, occasional trips direct to Torquay.

EMPEROR OF INDIA passes an anchored liner at the Spithead Review.
AUTHOR'S COLLECTION.

Her refit completed, EMBASSY backs out of Weymouth at the start of a long-distance excursion. It is interesting to note that although fine new carved name boards had been fitted, the ship carried her original railway crest in the centre of her paddle box decorations until her post war refit in 1946.
AUTHOR'S COLLECTION / SEWARD

A deck view taken on board PREMIER on 1 June 1937 emphasises the ship's vintage appearance and lack of covered accommodation. Note particularly how the curved boiler casing, with the funnel rising above, protrudes through the main deck.
G. E. LANGMUIR

In February 1937 the death was announced of Frederick Richards who had served the company all of his working life. He had been one of the crew which brought *Empress* from the builders yard in 1879, and had stayed on her until his retirement in 1931, serving the last thirty years as chief engineer. A remarkable record indeed.

On 14 July *Victoria* had a second brush with a torpedo. She was returning from Bournemouth to Weymouth with 200 passengers on board when an object was sighted floating off Anvil Point. Closer inspection revealed that the object was a torpedo, which was promptly taken in tow and brought back to Weymouth where it was returned to a grateful Navy. Apparently it had been lost from HMS *Inglefield* during firing trials in the Channel on the previous day. During September *Victoria* took over the Swanage service for nine days whilst *Bournemouth Queen* was being repaired.

At the end of the season both *Emperor of India* and *Embassy* required substantial repairs in order to obtain their load line certificates for the following season. Quotes were obtained from a variety of shipyards resulting in *Emperor of India* being dispatched to Willougby's of Plymouth and *Embassy* to White's at Itchen. It is interesting to note that the repairs to *Embassy* cost £1,232 on top of the purchase price of £4,000.

While she was in the hands of the shipyard, consideration was given to either building on a foc's'le head in the style of the *Monarch* or the Southampton Company's *Gracie Fields* of 1936, or of plating in the entire forward end of the ship to give a full-length promenade deck in the style of the *Bournemouth Queen*. Plans were submitted to the board showing the appearance of the ship in each guise, and White's quoted £860 and £1,275 respectively for the two schemes. The board decided that it preferred the full length promenade deck, but also resolved that the alterations should be carried out by the company's own workshops at Weymouth. By December, however, it had been decided that the scheme should remain in abeyance until *Embassy*'s speed had been tested following her major repairs. As no further references to the scheme appear in the minute books, it must be assumed that Cosens feared that the alterations would upset *Embassy*'s trim and speed, turning her into another slow *Emperor of India*. It is probably significant that even in her major post-war rebuild *Embassy* never was plated up to the bows, so we can only speculate how she would have performed had the 1937 proposals been carried through.

During the autumn Cosen's yard at Weymouth had been repairing a small motor yacht, the MY *Sheiling* which one of the excursion steamers had towed in with engine failure earlier in the season. By November all the work was complete but it proved impossible to obtain payment from the owners, so the Admiralty Marshal seized the vessel and put her up for sale. Cosens purchased her for £500 with the intention of selling her during 1938 but in the meanwhile her name was added to the company's fleet list.

Also during November it was discovered that Mr Alexander Taylor of Torquay was seeking to dispose of his paddler *Duke of Devonshire*. Cosens had been offered the ship by various brokers at prices ranging from £1,500 to £2,500, and had inspected her at Dartmouth. It was felt that she would be very useful on the Lulworth Cove service if she could be obtained sufficiently cheaply. An offer of £1,000 was made, and the ship passed into Cosens' ownership on 10 December 1937.

It was widely assumed that veteran *Premier* would be displaced by the resulting fleet reshuffle and disposed of immediately. In the event she was given a brief reprieve in November 1937 when Cosens secured a contract with the Air Ministry for the towage of bombing targets between Weymouth and the bombing range in West Bay, together with the repair of damaged targets. It was felt that *Premier* would make a suitable tug and that she should be retained for the time being.

The highly successful 1937 season, marked by the acquisition of the first replacement tonnage for many years, drew to a close with a significant financial development. Part of the company's capital was made up of £34,000 worth of debenture stock which was due for redemption on 1 January 1938. In view of the fact that the company was paying holders of the stock a guaranteed 5% per annum together with free season tickets, but could not find a satisfactory investment for its surplus cash at higher than 3%, it was decided redeem the stock at the earliest opportunity. This was done on 30 November 1937, leaving the company with no outstanding mortgages or debts. The company now had to draw on investments to provide working capital but this proved no problem, especially since the book value of their investments was considerably below their market price.

In February 1938, with *Embassy* and *Emperor of India* both back from their refits, the company chose the occasion of the AGM to confirm its plans for the coming season. As expected, *Empress* was to be replaced on the Lulworth run by the faster *Duke of Devonshire* and would in turn be transferred to the Portland service in place of the elderly *Premier*. *Premier*'s reprieve as a target tug had proved short-lived and the company regretfully announced that, after 79 years continuous service at Weymouth, the old ship was to be advertised for sale. In a statement to the press Mark Frowde emphasised that that the decision was:

> ...not on account of her seaworthiness. The vessel has gone through her BoT survey for the coming season, but in view of the company's purchase of the *Duke of Devonshire* and *Embassy* being put on last season it was decided not to apply for *Premier*'s certificate. The traffic at Weymouth would not warrant an extra boat on the station.

At 92 years old, *Premier* was truly a survivor from another age and her imminent demise stimulated a flurry of affectionate press interest. There was much talk of her early days on the Clyde when, in 1847, she was one of a flotilla of steamers which escorted the Royal Yacht during Queen Victoria's visit to Scotland. The Southern Times recalled the days when Victorian ladies in crinolines and young men in top hats had trodden her decks, and the summer evenings around the turn of the century 'when she used to run "eight-penny cuddle trips" with dancing on board to the music of the old town band'. It was estimated that during her long life the little ship had carried over two million passengers and that 'hundreds of couples had found romance between her decks, returned for a honeymoon cruise, and in later years taken their children for a trip on board.' Although considerably altered down the years, much of the ship's original fabric survived and there was hot competition between Cosens' employees to obtain souvenirs before she was despatched to the breaker's yard. Amongst the most sought-after objects were the

fine wood carvings of Aries the Ram which had adorned the foot of her main companionway ever since she was launched in 1846.

The ship was quickly sold for £290 to Thames shipbreakers T W Ward Ltd and on the cold, still morning of 29 April 1938, a large crowd gathered to watch her pass through Weymouth Town Bridge for the last time, in tow of Cosens' motorboat *Pearl*. *Premier* lay briefly at Custom House Quay to await the arrival of the steam tug *Brahman* which took her to Ward's scrapyard at Grays on the River Thames and into oblivion. With her passing, Weymouth lost a vessel which had been part of the harbourside scenery for, quite literally, longer than anyone could remember.

Bournemouth took this opportunity to press Cosens to build a new steamer for their station but the company, whilst acknowledging the desirability of such a vessel, replied that at the present time it would be impossible to obtain sufficient steel and, even if it was, that the cost would be excessive. In any case, the company was still congratulating itself on the

These pictures, taken on board PREMIER shortly before her departure for the breakers show:

Top the tiny engine house with its frosted glass windows which could be hinged up to the deckhead to provide additional ventilation. The large wheel with its associated steam steering engine was only used in emergencies, the ship normally being steered from the deck above. The ship's bell hangs from a beam forward of the wheel.

Bottom the port paddle box with the steps which provided the only means of access to the upper deck, a feature characteristic of the very earliest paddle steamers.

AUTHOR'S COLLECTION.

The old and the new: Shortly after her arrival at Weymouth, DUKE OF DEVONSHIRE is seen on 18 April 1938, moored alongside PREMIER in the Backwater. Preparations are being made to lower her mast. In the background are North Quay and Chapelhay before war damage and demolition took their toll. H. A. ALLEN COLLECTION

Towed by the launch PEARL, PREMIER passes through the Town Bridge for the last time on her way to the breaker's yard, 29 April, 1938. The photo is taken from the deck of EMPEROR OF INDIA. AUTHOR'S COLLECTION / SEWARD

P.S. CONSUL.

acquisition of *Embassy* and *Duke of Devonshire* and, in comparison to the veteran it had just sold, probably considered its new ships more than adequate.

On 1 April 1938 *Duke of Devonshire* arrived at Weymouth from Dartmouth and was officially renamed *Consul*, the BoT having rejected the company's first choice of *Marquis*. Work immediately began on refitting her for the season ahead. The chief alteration was the addition of a larger, elliptical funnel in place of her original, rather spindly affair. Her mast was also replaced and extensive internal renovations were undertaken to bring her up to the desired standard. All of the work was carried out in the company's own yard. Unlike *Empress*, which she was due to displace on the Lulworth service, *Consul*, in common with *Embassy* and *Victoria*, held a Class 3 passenger certificate which enabled her to trade outside Weymouth Bay to Swanage and beyond. This added considerably to the flexibility of the Weymouth-based fleet.

By early June the refit was complete and, under the command of Capt A. R. 'Pony' Moore, *Consul* sailed light for Bournemouth where she undertook her inaugural voyage on the Swanage run. She spent the early season at Bournemouth, but later returned to Weymouth from where she mostly operated on day trips to Swanage and Bournemouth, interspersed with local sailings to Lulworth and around the Bay.

The spring of 1938 was marked by three significant changes in company personnel. Firstly, in April, the retirement of Capt Leddy of the *Empress* was announced. Capt Leddy had been in the company's employ for many years and was well

known for his small stature. Indeed, he was so short that during his years as mate of *Premier* a small, rectangular window, immortalised as 'Leddy's peep-hole', was cut in the front of the wheel box to allow him to see better. Sadly, his health broke down during

With her refit completed, CONSUL *(ex-*DUKE OF DEVONSHIRE*) complete with her new elliptical funnel, steams across Weymouth Bay.* AUTHOR'S COLLECTION / KESTIN

CONSUL *embarking passengers at Weymouth on 22 July, 1938. Everyone in the photograph looks wonderfully relaxed: passengers read or admire the views, the master leans on the bridge rail, two deckhands attend the gangway and a member of the engine room crew takes a breath of fresh air by the starboard doorway.* AUTHOR'S COLLECTION.

Left to right: EMBASSY, EMPRESS and EMPEROR OF INDIA at Weymouth on 18 April 1938. In the background two of the GWR Channel Islands vessels – the cargo ship SAMBUR and either the ST JULIAN or ST HELIER - are laid up in The Cove, where Cosens undertook their annual mechanical overhauls. VICTOR GRAY COLLECTION

Capt Philip St Barbe-Rawle on the bridge of the MONARCH at Swanage pier, 1937.
VICTOR GRAY COLLECTION

1937 and after a winter spent at home on a retainer he was forced to give up his intended promotion to *Consul* and retire with the appreciation of the company and a pension of £1 per week.

In early May Mr Thomas Lynes, who had been a director since 1903 and Chairman of the Board since 1921, died after a short illness. Colonel G. P. Symes was appointed Chairman in his place, but never actually chaired a board meeting. He too was taken ill and died in June, leaving the vice-chairman, Mr J. Vincent, to succeed him as the company's third Chairman in six weeks.

The 1938 season was something of a disappointment. Poor weather and the popular Empire Exhibition in Glasgow conspired to reduce passenger earnings, although this was somewhat offset by a buoyant year in the engineering works. *Emperor of India*'s load line certificate was granted for only four instead of the usual five years due to her increasing age and the general deterioration of her shell plating. Comments began to appear in the minute books about the increasing costs of maintaining such an ageing fleet and protests were made against the rising price of bunker coal.

A small but potentially serious dispute broke out with the Board of Trade over landing rights at Lulworth Cove. It seems that the BoT had suddenly realised that Cosens were using a wheeled landing stage at Lulworth and wrote to ask on what authority they were doing so since the foreshore below high water was the property of the Crown. How this had escaped the Crown's notice for the last ninety years is a matter for conjecture but, now that the opportunity to gain income had been identified, it seemed determined to press the case. Correspondence passed

to and fro for many months but eventually, faced with the threat of losing their landing rights altogether, Cosens capitulated and agreed to pay a rent of £4 per annum for the use of the foreshore. Negotiations were also opened for the renewal of the lease on Castletown Pier which had lapsed in October 1937.

If things seemed a little dismal afloat, matters in the arena of international relations were far worse. In Europe, Hitler's expansionist policies had taken a sinister step with the occupation of Austria in March 1938 and throughout the summer tension mounted over Czechoslovakia and Hitler's demands that the Sudetenland be handed over to Germany. In Britain air raid shelters were prepared, anti-aircraft barrage balloons were deployed and gas masks issued.

On 28 September 1938 the British fleet was prepared for action and, under the terms of the dormant contracts that had been agreed shortly beforehand, the King's Harbour Master at Portland requisitioned most of the Cosens' fleet. All the ships except *Monarch* and *Empress* had already finished their seasons. *Monarch* was immediately withdrawn from Bournemouth and recalled to Weymouth, *Empress* was handed over to the Admiralty at Portland and *Victoria* was manned, coaled and provisioned. Only *Embassy*, which was already under repair, could not be handed over.

On the following day, 29 September, Chamberlain flew to Munich for the famous meeting at which it was agreed that Hitler should take the Sudetenland. In return he signed a document declaring his confidence in consultation as a means of avoiding war. Chamberlain flew home in triumph waving the piece of paper and declaring 'peace in our time'. Few people shared Churchill's view that both Chamberlain's policy of appeasement and the Munich Agreement were disasters of the first magnitude. The crisis appeared to be over, the mobilisation was cancelled, and Cosens' steamers were returned to slumber peacefully in winter lay up.

Another view by Mr. Bailey, the Bournemouth pierhead photographer, of passengers on board VICTORIA on 19 July 1934. Note the brass plaque commemorating the ship's war service, just below the timetable board
VICTOR GRAY COLLECTION.

CHAPTER EIGHT

TO WAR AGAIN

1939 TO 1945

An aerial view of Weymouth Harbour during the summer of 1939. CONSUL lies at the pleasure pier, while further up harbour EMBASSY and VICTORIA are moored at Custom House Quay and EMPRESS, together with a timber ship, at Trinity Quay. Two Channel Islands steamers lie in the GWR berths. On the left of the photo is Cosens' No1. slipway while in the top right hand corner the sheerlegs crane and the roof of the company workshops and cold stores stand out against the backwater.
WEYMOUTH LIBRARY

During the winter of 1938-9 Cosens were approached by Capt Shippick of the New Medway Steam Packet Company, offering to sell the steamer *Queen of Kent* for the sum of £10,000. This ship was the former Admiralty minesweeper HMS *Atherstone* which the Medway company had purchased and converted to passenger carrying after the Great War. Along with her sister ship *Queen of Thanet* (ex HMS *Melton*) she had operated on long excursions between Chatham, Southend, and Margate and across the Channel to Calais, Boulogne and Dunkirk. As such she might have seemed a suitable candidate to revive Cosens' cross channel traffic from Bournemouth, but the board clearly had no real desires in that direction and rejected her as 'too large for the company's requirements.' She reappears, however, later in this history.

Monarch was away from home for the first few months of 1939, undergoing repairs at Willoughby's shipyard in Plymouth. The agreed work was nearing completion when the BoT surveyor discovered that a further £1,000 worth of hull plates required renewal, and it was not until early April that the ship arrived back in Weymouth. At about the same time the death was announced of Mr Russell, chief engineer of the *Empress*, who had been employed by the company since 1900, and also of Capt Leddy who had retired during the spring of 1938.

Joint arrangements for the Bournemouth season were agreed at a meeting with the Southampton Company on 11 January. It was decided that only one steamer, to be provided by the Southampton Company, would operate between the start of the season on Good Friday 7 April and 13 May. During 1940 the same period would be operated by a Cosens' ship. From 14 May until 18 June one steamer from

EMPEROR OF INDIA steams through the Solent on a wet summer's day, 21 July 1939, H. A. ALLEN COLLECTION

each company would run and from then onwards, throughout the high season, two vessels would be provided by each company.

Bournemouth Town Council, who had been unsuccessfully asking for a meeting with the steamer companies to press for 'a greatly improved service', expressed relief that at least the former level of sailings was to be maintained but hoped that the summer of 1940 would see a significant expansion. It is interesting to note that, at the same time, they again refused permission for steamers to operate from the pier on Sunday mornings.

The peak season of 1939 saw the Southampton Company represented by *Bournemouth Queen* and *Princess Elizabeth*, and Cosens by *Monarch* and *Emperor of India*, together with frequent visits from Weymouth and Southampton by other units of the respective fleets.

On 17 June 1939, *Monarch* was disabled off Old Harry Rocks when a paddle arm in one of her wheels fractured and a float was badly damaged after striking some floating wreckage. She immediately dropped anchor and her passengers were taken off by *Bournemouth Queen*. As soon as temporary repairs had been effected *Monarch* limped first to Bournemouth Pier and thence to Poole where workshop staff from

MONARCH and CONSUL exchanging passengers at Swanage Pier. CONSUL has come from Weymouth and is transferring her passengers to MONARCH for the onward trip to Bournemouth. MONARCH has come from Bournemouth with passengers who will join CONSUL for an afternoon cruise to Lulworth Cove. In the evening, the procedure will be reversed. AUTHOR'S COLLECTION

Fleet Review. sailing bill
AUTHOR'S COLLECTION.

WEDNESDAY, 9th AUG.

NAVAL REVIEW
BY
HIS MAJESTY
KING GEORGE VI
IN
WEYMOUTH BAY
COSENS & CO'S. SALOON STEAMER
"EMPEROR OF INDIA"
will (weather and circumstances permitting) make a Special Cruise
From **BOURNEMOUTH** and **SWANAGE**
TO WITNESS THE
REVIEW OF THE FLEET
Of 160 Warships, comprising Battleships, Aircraft Carriers, Destroyers, etc.
Leaving **BOURNEMOUTH PIER** at **10.15 a.m.**   SWANAGE at **11.0 a.m.**
Note:—Passengers may join the Steamer at Poole at 8.0 a.m. on payment of 1/- extra.
FARE **8/6** (Children under 14 years **5/-**)   FROM SWANAGE **7/6** (Children under 14 years **4/6**)
THE "EMPEROR OF INDIA" WILL STEAM THROUGH THE
LINES OF WARSHIPS
AND AFTERWARDS TAKE UP A POSITION ALLOCATED TO HER TO WITNESS
THE REVIEW, RETURNING AFTERWARDS TO SWANAGE AND BOURNEMOUTH
A Special Luncheon will be served this day in the Spacious Dining Saloons at 3/6 per head
SPECIAL NOTICE:—In the event of the Review being postponed before the Steamer leaves Bournemouth all monies will be refunded in full. The "Emperor of India" will then make a cruise
THROUGH THE LINES OF WARSHIPS
Leaving Bournemouth at 10.30 a.m.   Swanage at 11.15 a.m.   Fares 6/6 & 5/6.
TICKETS NOW ON SALE:— Apply Cosen's & Co.'s Offices, The Corner House, 8, Bath Road, Bournemouth. Tel. 4180. Or the Steam Packet Office, Swanage. Tel. 2116.
For Conditions of Sailing see Weekly Programme
Early Booking Essential!

During the last days of peace passengers enjoy a tranquil cruise on board EMBASSY *from Weymouth along the Purbeck coast past Durlston Head to Bournemouth. Note how, in the course of a few years, hats have almost completely disappeared from men and women alike.*
H. A. ALLEN COLLECTION.

Weymouth were waiting to carry out a permanent repair. Letters of thanks were sent to the master of the *Bournemouth Queen* and also to Capt Rawle and Mr

Hardy, chief engineer of the *Monarch*, for the able and expeditious way in which they had dealt with the emergency.

A new competitor appeared at Bournemouth during July when a screw steamer called *Arpha*, owned by Guernsey Carriers Ltd, advertised excursions from the pier to the Channel Islands. About eighty passengers took advantage of her first trip on Saturday 1 July but, although *Arpha* continued to operate intermittently throughout the season, she appears to have had very little impact on the trade of the two main companies.

Although the immediate threat of war had receded following the Munich agreement it was clear that, behind the scenes, preparations were still being made. In May all British steamer companies were informed via the Coastwise Passenger Steamship Owners' Association that permission must be obtained from the BoT before any vessel could be sold to foreign buyers. Then it was announced that a major review of the Reserve Fleet would take place in Weymouth Bay on 9 August.

The review, of course, provided a major boost to Cosens' trade. For several days prior to the King's visit the warships of the Reserve Fleet arrived to take up their allocated positions, until over 130 of them stretched in precise lines across the bay. They included such famous vessels as the battleships *Revenge*, *Ramilles* and *Iron Duke*, the aircraft carrier

Courageous and Vice Admiral Sir Max Horton's flagship, *Effingham*. Of this impressive array of naval power, no fewer than 42 ships were to be lost during the impending conflict, the *Courageous* being torpedoed off Ireland less than six weeks later.

While the fleet was in, tens of thousands of sailors were given shore leave in Portland and Weymouth where they often proceeded to drink the pubs dry by lunchtime. All had to be ferried ashore by liberty boat and such was the pressure of numbers that, with shades of the pre-1914 Admiralty contract, several of Cosens' steamers were chartered to shuttle between the anchored warships and the pleasure pier. In addition the public flocked to Weymouth in droves to view the spectacle. On one day alone, 45,000 people arrived at Weymouth railway station and many of these went afloat in the steamers to view the fleet. The normal timetable was suspended and all of the Weymouth steamers were fully occupied in dealing with the crowds. The Bournemouth and Southampton ships were also frequent visitors but, to Cosens' relief, Weymouth Council refused requests from both Guernsey Carriers and Gondolier Motorboats of Poole to run from Weymouth during the review. Inconveniently, *Bournemouth Queen* was out of service with mechanical problems during this busy period leaving *Embassy* from Weymouth and *Lorna Doone* from Southampton to cover her services alongside their own commitments as best they could. The substantial revenue generated by the review went some way to offset the disappointing results of the early season.

The review itself took place on Wednesday 9 August 1939. The King arrived early in the morning and joined the Royal Yacht *Victoria & Albert* which was anchored in Portland Harbour, just off Bincleaves Pier. He spent the morning visiting the aircraft carrier *Courageous*, the cruisers *Effingham* and *Cardiff* and the destroyer *Exmouth* before setting off during the afternoon on the traditional stately progress up and down the long lines of warships. The King departed during the evening and the ships' companies prepared to sail their ships for their war stations. Weymouth Bay would never see such a large assemblage of warships again.

With the excitement over, the paddlers returned to their normal timetables, and the rest of the month passed relatively uneventfully in pleasant, settled weather. *Embassy* caused slight damage to *Emperor of India* whilst berthing at Bournemouth Pier, *Consul* went to the aid of a small boat becalmed between Swanage and Weymouth, and the motorboat *Diamond* towed a capsized sailing yacht in from Weymouth Bay. *Empress* suffered from a minor crime wave when first her compass and then her binnacle lamps were stolen by sailors on shore leave.

The tranquillity, however, was short-lived. On 25 August the worsening political situation in Europe triggered the Admiralty's plan to establish an examination and contraband control base at Weymouth. These two functions, although technically different, were in practice very closely connected and carried out by a pool of shared vessels.

The purpose of the examination service was to ascertain the identity and intentions of all vessels attempting to enter a British port, and to give warning of any attempted entry by unfriendly or suspicious ships. Contraband control, on the other hand, was intended to prevent any contraband of war from reaching the enemy by sea. Three British contraband bases were established simultaneously at Kirkwall, the Downs off Ramsgate and at Weymouth with the intention of preventing any ship entering the North Sea without first receiving the permission of

EMPRESS, in use as an examination steamer, stops a neutral ship off the east coast of Portland in the autumn of 1939. The Borstal buildings are prominent on the skyline while, on the cliffs to the right, the guns of East Wears Battery are ready to provide covering fire.
IMPERIAL WAR MUSEUM.

A contraband control party on board one of the chartered Lowestoft drifters, prepares to board the Dutch cargo vessel RHEA in the anchorage. IMPERIAL WAR MUSEUM.

The boarding officers examine the ship's papers. IMPERIAL WAR MUSEUM.

suspended, the remaining steamers returning to their home ports without any of the customary farewells. Since *Emperor of India* had already been withdrawn for repairs to her collision damage, it fell to *Consul* to operate Cosens' last pre-war passenger sailing. The following day, Sunday 3 September 1939, Britain declared war on Germany.

From their HQ in the Edward Hotel on Weymouth Quay, the examination and contraband control services swung into immediate action. The four paddlers were placed on an operational rota which involved each ship spending 24 hours on the outer patrol between Grove Point on the eastern side of Portland and St. Alban's Head, 24 hours on the inner patrol between Chequered Fort on Portland breakwater and White Nothe, and 48 hours in harbour. During their 48 hours alongside the crew were split into two sections and given 24 hours shore leave each. Those remaining on board for the first watch would immediately coal ship. For the first few months of the war coaling took place at Weymouth using the company's normal facilities, but thereafter each steamer would end its 48 hour patrol with a visit to the coaling jetty in Portland Dockyard before returning to Weymouth to lay over. This new arrangement was unpopular since coaling at Portland involved the whole crew and cut into the shore leave of those with the first 24 hours off. Those remaining on board ensured that a full head of steam was maintained and that the ship was ready to sail immediately in case of an emergency.

Whilst at sea the examination vessels would steam slowly to and fro along their designated patrol lines, awaiting the approach of any neutral ship from seaward. Often an incoming vessel had already been reported and her arrival signalled from Portland but, just as often, she might be unidentified and the paddler would approach with more caution. Since the lightly-built paddle steamers were armed only with a single machine gun and were not even fitted with protective screens around their open bridges, they would have stood little chance in the face of aggression. They depended for their protection on the heavy guns of East Wears Battery high on the side of Portland, Chequered Fort and the Nothe Fort, which were kept trained on each incoming ship until she had hoisted the correct signal indicating that she had been identified as friendly.

Once an incoming ship had been intercepted the examination steamer would range alongside and issue orders against the unauthorised use of wireless. If the weather was calm and the service not too busy, an examination officer and boarding party might be put on board at sea but, more frequently, the ship in question would be directed to the designated anchorage in Weymouth Bay.

Once at anchor the neutral ship would hoist a red and white blue-bordered flag indicating that she was awaiting examination. A boarding party of two officers and six men was then put on board from one of the drifters or a Cosens' motor boat and, having apologised to the master for the inconvenience

the Royal Navy. All ships entering the English Channel were advised to call voluntarily at Weymouth, since failure to do so would result in interception by a British warship and a compulsory diversion to the Downs.

On 26 August *Empress* and *Victoria* together with Messrs Basso's tug *Marina* were taken on charter by the Admiralty, followed two days later by *Monarch* and *Embassy*. All five were shared between the examination and contraband patrol services. In addition, the latter service had use of the Dundee, Perth & London Shipping Co's *London* as guardship, together with a yacht called *Mermaiden*, three Lowestoft drifters and up to six of Cosens' motorboats.

On 1 September Germany invaded Poland and on the following morning the skeleton service which had operated all week at Bournemouth was

The paddle minesweeper GLEN GOWER undergoes repairs outside Cosens' engineering works. Astern of her is GLEN USK, while the funnels of BRIGHTON BELLE and SNAEFELL (ex-WAVERLEY) are visible in the background.
C. COLLARD COLLECTION

caused, proceeded to seal the wireless cabin, inspect the ship's papers and cargo manifest and check that these corresponded to the cargo on board. Provided that all appeared to be in order the boarding party would go ashore with a summary of the manifest which would be sent by teleprinter to the Ministry of Economic Warfare. As soon as the ministry's consent to release the ship was received the boarding party would go out again to return the ship's papers together with a 'Navicert' or certificate of naval clearance, and the ship would proceed on her voyage.

If, on the other hand, the boarding party discovered suspicious cargo or an anomaly on the manifest, a full search party would be sent on board to make a complete examination of the cargo. By February 1940, 141,237 tons of cargo had been seized at Weymouth and the crowded anchorage had become an accepted part of the wartime scenery.

In November 1939, *Embassy* was replaced by *Consul* and withdrawn from the examination service. She was inspected by the Admiralty and, early in December, was delivered to Plymouth where she was converted into a minesweeper. Renamed HMS *Ambassador*, she was declared ready for naval duties on 12 March 1940. On 12 November 1939 *Emperor of India* was also requisitioned for minesweeping and, a couple of weeks later, was taken to Southampton for fitting out. Both ships took up their duties during early April and were not seen in Weymouth again until the war was over.

The period from September 1939 until May 1940 is often referred to as the 'Phoney War' and was an arduous but relatively uneventful period for the contraband patrol steamers. The weather throughout the winter months was appaling and imposed a severe strain upon the vessels and their crews but, fortunately, the enemy did not interfere with their activities.

During December and January the scene in

Weymouth Backwater was enlivened by the presence of four of P. & A. Campbell Ltd's large paddle steamers which, as HM paddle minesweepers *Glen Usk*, *Glen Gower*, *Brighton Belle* and *Snaefell* (peacetime *Waverley*), called for a major refit by Cosens' staff.

In February 1940, in an attempt to counter the threat posed by the recently developed German magnetic mine, a degaussing establishment was set up at Portland. Civilian labour, including the boys at the local Borstal, began manufacturing degaussing cables which, once installed in a ship's hull, neutralised the vessel's magnetic field and provided protection against magnetic mines. The coil factory was in production by 4 March and a naval staff of 8 officers, 12 non-commissioned officers and 100 ratings were engaged in installation. Four lighters were sent from Portsmouth to carry the coils out to ships and a tug named *Silver Dial* was provided to tow them. One of Cosens' coal barges was requisitioned and converted by the company into a wiping unit by fitting 48 submarine batteries. At the same time two of the company's motorboats were requisitioned for general ship-to-shore duties and to work with the wiping unit which required constant attendance. Cosens provided a crew for the *Silver Dial* and acted as managers for all the craft involved in the operation. Degaussing began on 6 March and by 15 March the time required to coil a ship had been reduced from two days to one. In the second half of the month 8 ships were fitted with coils and 32 used the degaussing range. Amongst these was HMS *Ambassador*, formerly the *Embassy*, which arrived on 16 March from Plymouth, used the range, and sailed later the same day for Dover. The operation appears to have continued until 4 July 1940 when both the *Silver Dial* and the wiping barge were sunk by enemy bombing. The barge was raised during August and placed on the slipway at Weymouth for survey.

Throughout this period the company was also

manufacturing 'skids' for the Admiralty. These were wooden rafts carrying heavy copper coils which, when towed along the surface, detonated any mines lurking below. The skids proved quite effective and, since they were generally destroyed in the resulting blast, provided a steady trade for Cosens.

In March 1940 the Yugoslavian steamer *Neti*, heavily laden with pyrites, dragged her anchors from the examination anchorage and went ashore on Weymouth sands. Two of Cosens' barges were hired to lighten her of her cargo, but one of these was overloaded and sank under tow in Weymouth Harbour, creating more work for the company in the subsequent salvage operations.

The relative lull of the phoney war came to an end during May with the German army's advance through the Low Countries. On 13 May the Dutch surrendered and on 26 May the retreat of the British Expeditionary Force to the Channel coast at Dunkirk triggered Operation Dynamo. During the 'nine day miracle' which followed, 338,226 men were evacuated from the harbour and beaches of Dunkirk by that extraordinary variety of ships and small craft which have become immortalised as the 'Little Ships of Dunkirk'. Cosens' part in the evacuation was small. The paddlers on contraband patrol could not be released from their duties and so the only large unit of the fleet present at the evacuation was *Emperor of India* which, together with the other units of the 10th Minesweeping Flotilla, crossed to Dunkirk on the evening of 27 May and returned to Dover the following morning, with 642 troops on board.

Dunkirk was not the only evacuation to take place during May and June. Between 18 May and 3 June several thousand refugees arrived at Weymouth from Zeebrugge, Ostende and Cherbourg in a variety of cross channel steamers, Belgian drifters and the Dutch liner *Volendam* to which the Cosens' steamers acted as tenders. These were followed between 31 May and 20 June by the arrival of 15814 British and Allied troops from Europe in thirty vessels and the re-embarkation of 9,156 French troops returning to their homeland. Finally, the period 20 to 28 June saw the evacuation of much of the civil population of the Channel Islands and the arrival of 55 ships which landed 25,484 refugees at Weymouth Quay.

The fall of the Low Countries and the subsequent surrender of France on 22 June enabled the Germans to base squadrons of fighters and bombers at airfields close to the Channel coast and by the beginning of July bombing of Weymouth and Portland had begun in earnest. On the morning of 4 July a formation of twenty dive bombers attacked Portland Harbour, severely damaging two anchored merchant ships and sinking the anti-aircraft ship HMS *Foylebank* at her moorings. The attack on HMS *Foylebank* only lasted eight minutes but in that time she was hit repeatedly and nearly half of her complement killed. Most of her main armament was put out of action immediately, but her surviving pompoms and machine guns continued firing until the ship was abandoned. One of her gunners, Leading Seaman Jack Mantle, was awarded a posthumous Victoria Cross for his heroism. Rescue ships came alongside to take off the survivors and as the morning passed HMS *Foylebank*, wracked by internal explosions, gradually sank. The *Consul* returning from patrol early in the afternoon to coal in the dockyard passed close by the burning wreck, her crew deeply shocked by what they saw. Her engineer at the time, Bob Wills, clearly recalled the vast column of black smoke which rose above her and the horrific sight of the bodies of her unlucky crew floating in the water which literally boiled around her sinking hull.

Three days later, on the afternoon of 7 July, at the same time as a short memorial service was being held alongside the wreck of HMS *Foylebank*, five paddle steamers of the 11th Minesweeping Flotilla were on passage from Portsmouth to Ardrossan when they reported being attacked by enemy aircraft south of St Albans Head. Of the five ships, HMS *Jeanie Deans*, HMS *Goatfell* (ex *Caledonia*), HMS *Scawfell* (ex *Jupiter*), HMS *Helvellyn* (ex *Juno*) and HMS *Mercury*, all of which were peacetime Clyde pleasure steamers, the last two received the most damage. HMS *Mercury* was hit by a bomb abreast the gun on her foredeck and suffered nine casualties. Both she and HMS *Helvellyn* put into Portland where they remained for a week while repairs were carried out by Cosens' staff.

The aircraft which had attacked the minesweepers then turned westwards towards Portland Harbour where they dropped a further twenty bombs before heading back across the Channel. *Victoria*, which was also off St Alban's Head at the eastern extreme of her patrol area, reported being fired on by a Messerschmitt but fortunately escaped without casualties. An interesting postscript to the incident was the story, widely maintained by Cosens' staff, that a fire-watching platform subsequently erected on the roof of the Southern National bus depot at Radipole Spa was constructed from plates removed from HMS *Mercury* during repairs.

During July and August 1940 the threat of invasion increased substantially and precautions were taken all along the south coast. Bournemouth Pier was breached on 5 July to prevent its use by the enemy. Playlands, Cosens' former coal store at Swanage, was taken over by the ARP and air raid shelters were built at the company's slipways and works at Weymouth. On 7 July an elderly cargo ship named *Kenfig Pool* arrived at Weymouth for use as a blockship. In the event of invasion it was intended that she would be swung across the harbour entrance and scuttled, a manoeuvre which was practiced several times during July and August. During September when invasion seemed imminent she was actually swung into position each night. Although it is yet to be confirmed from official sources, Bob Wills who was chief engineer of the *Consul* at the time, staunchly maintained that all of the paddlers on contraband patrol were also fitted with scuttling charges around their seacocks. The intention was that, if the *Kenfig Pool* had to be used in anger, the

nearest paddlers to the scene would steam into position and sink themselves in any gaps left between the blockship and the piers.

On 27 July Weymouth suffered its first air raid, and from then on raids over the town and Portland increased in frequency and severity until they became almost a daily occurrence. In order to deprive enemy aircraft of directional guidance the light on the Shambles Lightship off Portland was extinguished on 1 August and the vessel herself towed into Portland five days later. After coming to Weymouth for repairs by Cosens she spent the remainder of the war at Portland. On 11 August a particularly severe raid took place with 57 bombs falling on Weymouth, where the harbour area was clearly the chief target, and a further 32 on Portland. The Weymouth to Portland railway was damaged; 40 houses destroyed and another 463 damaged; Admiralty oil storage tanks on Chesil Beach were pierced and set alight and several ships damaged. On 13 August a large formation of bombers passed overhead without attacking but on the following day, 14 August, the dockyard suffered heavy damage. A number of bombs fell on the Coaling Pier where *Consul* had a very narrow escape. Her moorings were quickly cast off and the ship went full astern from her berth where one of the bombs fell a few seconds later.

In addition to the heavy raids, bombing and machine gun attacks by single aircraft were common and large numbers of mines were laid by aircraft.

These presented a particular hazard to the contraband patrol steamers, and Bob Wills recalled a number of incidents during his time in the *Consul*. He first joined the ship in November 1939 as second engineer under Mr Goss, during which time the ship was commanded by Capt Bowering with Mr Bartlett as mate and Bernie Ridout as cook/steward. On 1 July 1940 he was rated chief engineer and was joined by his close friend and fellow apprentice Reg Willshire as second engineer. Working in six hour watches the two of them managed the engine room assisted by a single greaser who split his time equally between them. During the autumn of 1940 the crews of the examination vessels were required to transfer from Cosens to Royal Naval Patrol Service pay and conditions, and negotiations were held with all concerned. Most agreed, but Capt Bowering of the *Consul* refused to do so unless the Admiralty guaranteed not to move him from Weymouth. As a result he was given seven days notice and replaced by Capt Carter assisted by mate Alf Pavey, and this combination of officers stayed in the ship for the remainder of her time on the contraband patrol.

On one occasion Bob recalled being out on patrol when a lone bomber made a diving attack on *Consul*. He had noted that bombs were normally dropped in sticks of five but, on this occasion, only four descended and disaster was narrowly averted. On another occasion a minesweeper exploded a mine a short distance ahead of *Consul* with such force that the

CONSUL , looking extremely dilapidated in her rust-streaked wartime grey paint, moored above Weymouth Town Bridge. The boat moored alongside her bow is Weymouth's original rowing lifeboat, the AGNES HARRIET, which subsequently spent many years as Cosens' diving boat before being sold to a local fisherman.
AUTHOR'S COLLECION

paddler's hot well tank was perforated. With her vital boiler water draining uselessly into the bilges, the ship was forced to return quickly to Weymouth for repairs.

One still night *Consul* was quietly anchored just to seaward of the contraband anchorage when she received an Aldis light signal informing her that she was lying almost on top of a mine and that she was to move immediately. Not surprisingly, this piece of news induced considerable tension amongst the crew. The anchor was raised very, very gingerly with every attempt being made to limit the clatter caused by the steam windlass and the cable coming on board. The ship then got under way and paddled slowly away from the scene, leaving two minesweepers to detonate the mine which exploded, as Bob recalled, 'like a huge white mushroom, right where we had been laying'. Having escaped destruction once again, *Consul* became the butt of affectionate jokes to the effect that she was so rusty that there was not enough metal left in her even to explode a magnetic mine.

Apart from being painted grey and having some of their saloons temporarily subdivided to provide increased sleeping accommodation for the crew, the paddlers on contraband patrol were very little altered from their peace-time state. Their only armament was a single machine gun operated by a marine gunner, occasionally supplemented by the rifles carried by the examination officer or other crew members. These were of little practical use against heavily-armed

aircraft, but served to keep crew morale up and sometimes to provide light relief.

Both Bob Wills and Reg Willshire recalled the occasion on 17 November 1940 when they had watched a single enemy raider circling over Weymouth and dropping the parachute mine which devastated the Chaplehay area of Weymouth, killing 12 people, destroying 77 houses and damaging 879 others. Even in this dreadful event was a glimmer of humour: the marine gunner had bravely let fly at the raider with the *Consul*'s machine gun but the tracer, looking for all the world like bent pins, curved harmlessly into the sky and fell well short of its target. The enemy aircraft, having dropped its mine, loosed a single burst of fire at the impertinent little paddler below, at which point the gallant marine gunner fled immediately for the lower saloon and was not seen again until the ship docked.

On another occasion the *Consul*'s RNVR examination officer, a local draper called Mr Dennis, almost killed a member of the crew. He was inordinately proud of his rifle and, to everyone's alarm, always insisted in keeping an additional round 'up the spout'. One day he tripped, the rifle discharged and the bullet missed a stoker by a hair's breadth, embedding itself in the woodwork of the main companionway. As Bob Wills remarked, it was only the ability to see the funny side of situations which kept the crews sane during the dark days of 1940-1.

During September 1940 it was unofficially discovered that the Admiralty planned to reduce the number of ships on the contraband patrol at Weymouth and in November official notification was received that *Victoria* and *Empress* were to be withdrawn and replaced by the Southern Railway paddle steamer *Freshwater*. This pretty little steamer had been built in 1927 for the railway's passenger ferry service from Lymington to Yarmouth, Isle of Wight. She was requisitioned on 11 November on the understanding that she could be recalled to her home route should an evacuation of the island become necessary in the face of invasion. She arrived at Weymouth on 18 November to be fitted out for her new role at Cosens' yard. *Victoria* moved up through the bridge to lay up on 29 November and was officially relieved from her duties on 6 December. *Freshwater*'s refit was completed on 14 December when she left the Backwater for sea trials before relieving *Empress* on 16 December. *Empress* immediately passed up through the bridge to join *Victoria* in lay up. Eleven days later, on 27 December 1940, *Consul* too was withdrawn from the contraband patrol and joined her consorts in reserve.

For all three ships the war was effectively over. Although their names were submitted to the Small Boats Pool and the Ministry of Shipping promised to keep them in mind for further employment, nothing arose. In September 1941 they were considered for use as local minesweepers, but rejected. In August 1942 all three were slipped for bottom cleaning and maintenance and it was agreed to allow the local Sea Cadet Corps to use one of them for static training purposes. A further inspection in May 1943 also failed to bring any employment and it was not until the flurry of activity preceding D Day that the steamers were finally, if briefly, reactivated in April 1944.

Monarch, by now renamed HMS *Exway*, and *Freshwater* remained under requisition and maintained a reduced contraband patrol service until 1944. After the fall of the Low Countries the need for the contraband and examination services declined dramatically and the two ships, working alternate 24 hour patrols, were more than adequate to deal with the demand. Throughout the war HMS *Exway* was commanded by Capt Philip St Barbe Rawle, whose father had commanded the ship before him. In a 1943 newspaper interview Rawle recalled 'The first time I came on board the ship was when I was three years old. I still remember getting into trouble with my mother for getting my white sailor suit dirty playing with the seamen and for copying their language'. The chief engineer was Lieut C. C. Hardy who had been in charge of the engine-room since 1933, but the ship's oldest inhabitant was former engineman E. A. Le Seur, now rated Sub Lieut RNVR, who had been on the ship since 1920 and admitted that he knew 'every cog and piston by its Christian name'. The great affection in which the old ship was held is illustrated by a statement made by Cosens general manager, Mr C. Kaile, in February 1943:

We were sorry to have to change her name, of course, but it doesn't matter what her name is or if her gay black and gold paintwork and her two well-known funnels have gone battleship grey again. It is as *Monarch* that she is known and loved right along the coast. We have received many anxious enquiries about her welfare from former holiday-makers who hope they will meet her again after the war.

If the end of 1940 saw a reduction in the company's activities afloat, the exact reverse was true of the workshops and slipways that, since the outbreak of war, had been busy with ship repairing and marine engineering on behalf of the Admiralty.

By the beginning of September 1940 the Admiralty floating dry dock at Portland had been sunk by enemy bombing, creating a sudden increase in demand for slipway facilities. The Admiralty pressed Cosens to extend their No 1 slip by 50ft to enable larger vessels to be handled but, rather cheekily, enquired how much the company would be prepared to contribute towards the building costs. Cosens responded that the present slip suited them very nicely and in view of the fact that the extended slip would still not be large enough to accommodate their biggest steamers, nor were they permitted to charge the Admiralty to use it, they felt unable to make any contribution.

Negotiations flowed to and fro and eventually the Admiralty agreed to bear the full cost of £2640. Weymouth Corporation was concerned that the extended slipway might prove an obstruction to the harbour and in particular that it would protrude into the area used by the GWR Channel Island steamers to swing inside the harbour. Permission to start construction was only granted on the strict condition that Cosens would agree to remove the extension at one month's notice.

The enlarged slipway also benefitted from a wider cradle. By the beginning of March it was declared ready for use but a trial, in which one of Cosens' motorboats was hauled up, revealed faults in the levels of some of the rails which carried the cradle. These faults caused considerable delays until they were finally rectified in March 1942, at which time an application was also made to construct a plate rolling shop and workshop along the northern side of the slip.

No sooner had the problems been solved than it was suggested that a further extension should be constructed. In September 1942 both No 1 and No 2 slipways were reconcreted and in May 1943 No 1 slip was taken out of use while further construction work took place. Cosens must have regretted ever agreeing to the scheme, as the Admiralty contractors worked painfully slowly and deprived the company of one of its key assets at a critical point in the war. During June Cosens themselves were busy constructing a new cradle for the slipway but, by December, the slipway was still not finished. Frustrated by the delays and alarmed by the errors made by the contractor during the previous extension, Cosens appointed their own civil engineers to keep an eye on the project. It was as well they did so for more unacceptable variations in gauge and gradient were discovered, and much of the work had to be done all over again.

The slipway was finally completed in January 1944. The stationary steam engine, which had hitherto provided the power for hauling up the cradle, was dismantled and put into store at the Backwater works and its boiler sold to the Admiralty for £40. In its place a new 20 ton winch was installed on the side of No 2 slipway with its hauling cables passing in tunnels under the public footpath which separated it from No 1 slipway. New toilets and air raid shelters were also provided on No 2 slip. The new winch was powered by a V8 petrol engine which proved something of an art form to drive. Skilled throttle and clutch control were required and the new engine defeated so many operators that, over the years, it became the personal province of Reg Willshire who 'had the knack' and was regularly called out when a ship needed to be slipped or relaunched. To add to the complexity, two large sections of fence also had to be removed on each occasion in order to give the winch driver a clear view across the footpath and down the slip. The whole performance provided a fascinating spectacle for passing members of the public. Repairs and extensions aside, both slipways were used to full capacity throughout the war, and the same was true of all the company's other shore facilities.

The blast from the landmine which the crew of the *Consul* had watched falling onto Chaplehay on 17 November 1940 was so powerful that the slipways, ice factory, main office and engineering works all suffered damage. Worse was to come, however, on Saturday 3 May 1941 when incendiary bombs fell on the engineering works and the stores were completely gutted. Company staff were praised for their fire fighting efforts which prevented the fire from spreading. Temporary repairs were immediately put into effect, but the matter of long term renovations was complicated by the fact that the lease on the property, which was owned by Weymouth Corporation, was due to expire during 1943. Cosens were understandably reluctant to invest in a major rebuilding project unless and until the lease was renewed on satisfactory terms. An agreement was reached in January 1942 with the Corporation agreeing to extend the lease for two years after the end of the war on the basis of temporary repairs only.

In July 1941 the company purchased a property known as New Court on West Street just behind the works but, during the autumn, was required by the Council to demolish it together with several adjoining properties which they already owned, and to clear the site. This was completed by November 1941 and in March 1942 a further small parcel of land on Ferry's Corner was purchased from a Mr James.

On Thursday 2 April 1942 bombs fell in St Nicholas Street causing extensive damage to the Cold Stores and engineering works and killing a Mr T. L. Pavey who had worked for the company since 1895. Once again, as soon as permits for the necessary materials were obtained, repairs were put in hand. At the same time a decision was made to replace some of the antiquated equipment in the fitting and boiler shops with more modern, labour-saving machinery. Under wartime conditions this was not easy to locate but over the following few months a mixture of new and second hand lathes, milling, punching and shearing machines and a portable air compressor were obtained, and quickly proved their worth.

In September 1942 capacity was further increased by the arrival, on loan from the Ministry of War Production, of a barge fitted out as a floating workshop, complete with welding plant. The ministry also paid for the construction of a gridiron on North Quay opposite the fire station at the foot of Boot Hill. The new facilities were chiefly used in connection with the conversion of Thames lighters into invasion barges. Rudders and stern tubes were fitted on the gridiron and the rest of the work carried out afloat. In September alone, 38 barges were converted in this way. In November a 50 year lease was obtained on a portion of Quay adjoining the No 1 Slipway on Nothe Parade, and the 10 ton wooden crane, for so long a landmark outside the Backwater engineering works, was found to have serious rot which necessitated the jib being shortened at both ends.

1943 saw further, steady improvements in plant. By the spring the company was running desperately short of storage space for coal and materials needed to fulfil their many Admiralty contracts and, in August, an area of land measuring 310ft x 110ft in front of the Backwater works on Commercial Road was requisitioned for their use. More than 70 ships were repaired at Weymouth during the year, together with others, such as the Isle of Man Steam Packet Co Ltd's *Victoria* and *Lady of Mann* at Portland.

One interesting job was the reconversion of the Weymouth blockship *Kenfig Pool* to commercial use. With the threat of invasion greatly reduced it was decided that blockships were no longer required and Cosens spent much of August 1943 making her ready for sea again. When she finally sailed for dry-docking at Southampton on 16 October and thence to the Clyde. Cosens provided the engine-room crew. The chief engineer was Mr Derriman, formerly of the *Victoria*, who was on his last trip to sea before retirement. Bob Wills went as second engineer and Reg Willshire as third.

By the end of 1943 plans for D-Day, the allied invasion of mainland Europe, were beginning to take shape, and in November Cosens were approached by the Director of Naval Contracts regarding the creation of a landing craft repair base at Weymouth. If 1943 had been a record breaking year for the company's ship repairing staff, 1944 looked set to be even busier.

By March 1944 all the details had been finalised and arrangements were being made to cope with the domestic needs of the large number of extra workmen who had been directed to the company's employ 'in connection with the coming operations'. So great was the demand that the British Restaurant at the Sidney Hall, on the opposite side of the Backwater to the engineering works, was unable to cope with the victualling so a special hut had to be erected at Cosens' expense in which the expanded workforce could be provided with four square meals a day.

At the beginning of April the first landing craft began to arrive for docking and attention to underwater fittings. On 1 May Weymouth and Portland were officially commissioned as a U.S. Navy Advanced Amphibious Base and Weymouth harbour became a major embarkation point for infantry landing craft. During May no less than 55 landing craft of all types were slipped and the workforce laboured around the clock to keep pace with demand. As May turned into June activity became intense with troops and vehicles pouring into the area to embark on the growing armada of invasion ships which filled the harbours until the night of 5-6 June when they sailed for France and D-Day.

Immediately following the invasion there was no reduction in the shipyard work. Indeed, it became even more intense with the regular dockings and maintenance jobs supplemented by a steady stream of landing craft and other vessels returning from France for damage repairs. Amongst the long list of vessels handled appeared the paddle steamers *Queen Empress* in June and *Scawfell* and *Golden Eagle* in October 1944, the latter being one of the largest vessels ever to pass through the Town Bridge into the Backwater. After July the number of vessels handled per month began to decline and by August most of the imported workforce had left.

Between the outbreak of war in 1939 and VE day, over 1,200 vessels passed through Cosens' hands. With the colossal expansion of the engineering department and the fact that the cold storage facilities were working to capacity, it was hardly surprising that the company recorded its biggest ever turnover during 1944 and, for the second year running, was able to declare a 15% dividend. It is ironic that with no steamer service running at all the company was able to invest more retained profit than at any time since the previous conflict in 1914-18.

The run up to D-Day also saw the reactivation of *Consul*, *Victoria* and *Empress* from their lay-up in the Backwater. During March 1944 Capt Shippick, this time representing the Ministry of War Transport, visited to Weymouth to inspect the three ships together with HMS *Exway* and *Freshwater* 'with a view to their being used locally.' Their role was to act as 'Invasion Steamers', carrying troops out to transports anchored in the Bay and landing casualties brought back from the invasion beaches. All were required to be ready for sea trials before 20 April, and were ordered to be slipped and refitted at the earliest opportunity.

HMS *Exway* and *Freshwater* were still under the white ensign, but *Consul* was formally requisitioned on 7 April, followed by *Victoria* and *Empress* five days later. *Embassy*, which was lying in the River Tyne, was also inspected and sent south to join the Plymouth

Special Services Command on similar duties.

Consul, *Empress* and *Victoria* were all supposed to be manned by civilian crews but great difficulties were experienced obtaining suitable men. All of Cosens' own hands were either at sea already or engaged in essential shipyard work. In the end a number of men were recruited from the Hull area but caused nothing but difficulties. A surviving letter from Capt Carter of the *Consul* dated 15 July 1944, gives some idea of the problems encountered.

Between 1 April and 14 July, no less than fourteen hands left the ship under unusual circumstances. Six left due to accidents or illness, four deserted, one was discovered to be an army deserter and was arrested, and the rest were dismissed for a combination of insolence, insubordination, incompetence, drunkenness and failing to keep watches. Capt Carter added somewhat desperately:

> I consider that no investigation as to character, conduct or ability was carried out. In some cases they have been in trouble with the local police and have caused a lot of trouble to the masters and officers of the ships, also in many cases have been sent here without any previous experience whatever of vessels or boats. In spite of assistance and help they have been of no use to this class of vessel and the conditions of service they are engaged upon.

The deserters were all taken to court where the prosecution argued successfully that, since the steamers were required to sail without prior warning and at short notice, the absence of crew members might cause serious delays in loading transports or unnecessary hardship to wounded troops waiting to be landed. In his defence one of the deserters, a fireman aged 17 from Grimsby, unwittingly confirmed the suspicion that the steamers were not heavily employed during this period. When he had been sent to join the ship, he claimed, he had been told that he was going to sea. However, since then 'most of the time they were lying in harbour and had never gone more than three miles out'. With impeccable logic he argued that had he actually been at sea he 'would never have left the ship'!

Consul, *Empress*, *Victoria* and *Monarch* were indeed only lightly used during the D-Day period and were all released from Government service in November 1944. But if these four ships had spent their war close to home, the same could not be said for *Embassy* and *Emperor of India*.

Embassy, it will be recalled, was initially employed on the Weymouth Examination Patrol until relieved by *Consul* in November 1939. After conversion into a minesweeper at Plymouth she was commissioned as HMS *Ambassador* on 12 March 1940 and sailed to take up her duties at Dover. From then until June 1940 she was a member of the 10th Minesweeping Flotilla of the Dover Command, together with the other paddle steamers *Sandown*, *Duchess of Rothesay*, *Emperor of India*, *Gracie Fields*, *Kylemore*, *Medway Queen* and *Princess Elizabeth*. In April *Kylemore* was replaced by the P. & A. Campbell paddler *Brighton Belle*, and the flotilla was kept busy sweeping the narrow, dangerous

EMBASSY formerly HMS AMBASSADOR, photographed after her return to Weymouth in 1945.
AUTHOR'S COLLECTION / SEWARD

EMBASSY formerly HMS AMBASSADOR, photographed after her return to Weymouth in 1945.
AUTHOR'S COLLECTION / SEWARD

waters of the Dover Strait and Thames Estuary.

At the beginning of June 1940 the flotilla sailed to Portsmouth to reorganise and HMS *Ambassador*, herself replaced by the railway paddler *Ryde*, was sent first to Southampton and then to Sheerness where she arrived on 23 June. There it was announced that she was to become the Attached Paddle Minesweeper to the 60th Minesweeping Group based at Port Edgar on the River Forth.

The 60th was a minesweeping training flotilla and HMS *Ambassador*'s role was to work in cooperation with smaller vessels in training both seamen and stokers.

Extracts from a surviving logbook from 1941 give an interesting insight into the ship's important but monotonous routine on the Forth.

Sept 13.	Sailed 0745 from Leith to degaussing range, Burntisland, thence, after 6 runs, proceeded to Port Edgar. Alongside 1147.
15	0945 proceeded on H. P. trials between Forth Bridge and Oxears Gate. Made fast again 1121. Loaded ammunition.
16	1420 Speed trials on range. 1600 secured in Port Edgar.

17	0810 Sailed for Rosyth to coal. 0835-1035 anchored in fog. 1125 alongside.
	1530 sailed for Port Edgar then off to anchor.
18	Speed trials
19	Sweeping past Oxears Gate
22	Exercising
23-28	Sweeping
29	Sailed for Rosyth Basin

This was a day typical of the ship's routine:

0830	Sail
0905	Oxears Gate
0940	West Ears Gate
1045	Out sweeps to starboard
1107	In sweeps to starboard
1125	Out sweeps to port
1207	In sweeps to port
1350	Out sweeps to starboard
1435	In sweeps to starboard
1505	East Inch Gate
1515	West Inch Gate
1615	Oxears Gate
1730	Alongside. Trainees landed by tug earlier.

HMS Ambassador remained on the Forth until early in 1944 when she moved to the Tyne. During April, she was inspected and sent south to Plymouth for use in connection with the D-Day landings. As part of the Plymouth Special Service Command she spent the next eight months on transport, tendering and other local duties before being sent to Dartmouth to de-store.

On 5 December 1944 Cosens received a letter officially releasing the ship from naval duties and informing them that she would be laid up at Salcombe. Mr Ward and a B.o.T. surveyor met at Salcombe on 18 January 1945 to carry out a survey as a result of which it was estimated that essential repairs would cost between £10,000 and £15,000. The government asked Cosens to take on the reconditioning themselves on low priority and, following the usual negotiations, an agreement was reached. A passage crew was sent to Salcombe to collect the ship which, battered and worn but with her peacetime name restored, arrived back in Weymouth harbour on Sunday 9 September1945.

Emperor of India's war began in a very similar manner to *Embassy*'s. She was formally requisitioned as a minesweeper on the evening of 12 November 1939 but, owing to a delay in sending a crew, did not 'enter into pay' until 22 November. She sailed from Weymouth a few days later for conversion at Thornycroft's yard, Southampton. Her peacetime fittings and panelling were stripped out and put into store, only to be destroyed in a bombing raid later in the war.

Her refit was completed by 25 February when, sporting the pennant number J106, she joined *Embassy* as a unit of the 10th Minesweeping Flotilla at

Her decks crowded with rescued troops, EMPEROR OF INDIA arrives at Dover from Dunkirk , 28 May 1940.

The gun crew on EMPEROR OF INDIA's paddle box take shelter as a mine is exploded by gunfire.
B JACKSON COLLECTION /
T. PIKE

Dover. The flotilla's routine was dramatically interrupted on 27 May when it was ordered to Dunkirk as part of the evacuation fleet for the British Expeditionary Force. *HMS Ambassador* (*Embassy*) and *Duchess of Rothesay* were at Southampton at the time so took no part, but the rest of the flotilla sailed in company on the evening of 27 May. They loaded from the beaches during the hours of darkness before setting off on their return trip early on the morning of 28 May. *Brighton Belle* was sunk on passage.

The remaining ships set off again the same evening for another crossing, this time to Dunkirk Harbour, but it is not clear whether *Emperor of India* was with them. Her officially recorded total of 642 troops carried suggests that she made only one return trip, in which case we must conclude that she suffered some serious mechanical defect or other major problem. The emergency was so acute that no high-capacity, shallow draft paddle steamer would have been allowed to lie idle in port without a very good reason indeed.

Whatever the case, it is clear the *Emperor of India* remained in the Dover area throughout the evacuation, during which another of her consorts, the Southampton Company's *Gracie Fields*, was lost and the rest of the flotilla made numerous independent crossings. When the emergency was over the flotilla moved to Portsmouth to re-organise. Casualties amongst paddle minesweepers from all flotillas had been so severe that a major reshuffle was required and at the same time it was announced that *Emperor of India* was to be converted into an anti-aircraft bofors gunship. She sailed for Sheerness at the end of June and spent the next two months fitting out for her new role.

On 1 September 1940 she arrived at Harwich to join the Nore Command of the Thames Local Defence Flotilla. Fitted with 2 pounder Bofors guns fore and aft, 20mm Oerlikons on each sponson, eight machine guns and four rocket projectors, her role was to put up a hail of anti-aircraft fire against enemy attacks on shipping in the Thames Estuary.

The coming of the New Year saw enemy bombing raids intensify, with London and the Thames as the chief targets. As the London Blitz was reaching its height mines were also being sown from the air in the estuary, shipping was being bombed and Harwich and the Medway towns were receiving regular raids. More paddle steamers were converted into anti-aircraft 'Eagle Ships' and hastily joined the defences. The large local paddlers *Royal Eagle*, *Golden Eagle* and *Crested Eagle* were joined in May 1941 by *HMS Aristocrat*, formerly the Clyde paddler *Talisman*, and a further group, consisting of the Clyde steamers *Jeanie Deans*, *Jupiter*, *Juno* and *Caledonia* were converted in London Docks. *Juno* was bombed and sunk in her fitting out berth, but the remaining ships joined the Thames Flotilla shortly afterwards.

Although none of *Emperor of India*'s own logs or records for the period have yet been located, enough contemporary accounts exist to piece together a clear impression of what life on board must have been like. The Thames Estuary is a maze of tide-swept sandbanks and narrow shipping channels where navigation is a precise art even in daylight. During wartime with the navigation buoys blacked out *Emperor of India* frequently operated during the hours of darkness and in dreadful weather conditions escorting convoys in and out of harbour. In addition to the daily air raids there were also unseen enemy mines to avoid, and one can only wonder at the skill and stamina which the ship's navigating officers displayed. Even when alongside at Harwich or operating close to base, there was no respite. Harwich was frequently bombed and day in–day out *Emperor of India* had a key role in helping to put up an effective anti-aircraft barrage. The defences were not always successful and, in April 1941 during a particularly severe raid, the paddle minesweeper *Marmion* of the 12th Flotilla was sunk at Harwich.

Emperor of India continued with her duties at Harwich throughout 1942 and most of 1943 but, as the air raids gradually decreased and D-Day approached, the requirement for anti-aircraft cover was replaced by an urgent need for accommodation ships. Accordingly, in July 1943, she was stripped of her armament and sent up river to Ipswich as an accommodation ship. Contemporary records are frustratingly contradictory regarding her movements at this period but, although we cannot be absolutely certain of the date of her conversion or renaming, we do know that she was in use at Ipswich in May 1944 under the new name of *HMS Bunting*.

She continued in this mundane role until the end of the war and at some stage was moved to Wivenhoe where she was finally released from Government service during 1946. In June it was reported that she was being made ready for sea, and a month later she was once again moored in Weymouth Harbour. She had arrived under tow as her starboard paddle wheel was almost completely missing. Whether the wheel was damaged by a mine or floating wreckage during her time as an Eagle Steamer and hastened her

HMS EMPEROR OF INDIA, bristling with guns, during her period as an anti-aircraft ship on the Thames. It is claimed that the sheer weight of her armament made her sit so low in the water that she was only capable of a speed of 6 knots.
IMPERIAL WAR MUSEUM

EMPEROR OF INDIA lies between her peace-time rivals, LORNA DOONE and BALMORAL at Harwich. Of the three ships only EMPEROR OF INDIA returned to passenger service, the others being so worn out that they were scrapped after the war.
IMPERIAL WAR MUSEUM

demotion to accommodation vessel, or whether it happened during her time at Ipswich has yet to be established.

The return of the battered *Emperor of India* marked the end of the war for Cosens' fleet. Five steamers had served with distinction and all had survived. *Empress* and *Victoria* claimed to be the oldest paddle steamers requisitioned during the conflict, whilst *Monarch* as HMS *Exway* was undoubtedly the oldest to fly the white ensign. The motorboats too had played their part, which is described more fully in Chapter 3.

The demands of the conflict had masked one important event ashore earlier in the war. On 1 March 1942 Mr Mark Frowde, the company's managing director, resigned due to ill health. He had first joined the company in a junior position in 1890, and had become joint manager in 1911. He had been largely responsible for steering the company through the major financial restructuring of 1915-6 and for maintaining its finances in such a sound state through the difficult years between the wars. He remained on the board but was granted a pension of £600 p.a. in recognition of his long and invaluable service.

In his place Mr C. H. J. 'Charlie' Kaile was appointed as General Manager and Company Secretary. Mr. Kaile had been associated with the company for 40 years and, with Mr J. M. 'Sharky' Ward as Works Manager and Marine Superintendent and Mr G. Pearce as Assistant Secretary, the company was blessed with an experienced team to see it through the war years.

Now, with the fleet safely home, this same management team concentrated its collective thoughts on the full restoration of peacetime passenger services.

Safely back in Weymouth in the summer of 1946, the battered EMPEROR OF INDIA awaits her post war refit. AUTHOR'S COLLECTION / SEWARD

CHAPTER NINE
PLANNING FOR PEACE

It should come as no real surprise that, as soon as D-Day was over and the allied foothold in Europe firmly established, British industry began to plan for peace. Cosens were no exception although, having enjoyed record turnover in their engineering and ship repairing departments throughout 1943 and 1944, they were perhaps a little more complacent than was wise.

In August 1944 Mr Kaile presented a report to the board on the possible post-war activities of the company, as a result of which he was instructed to look into the 'prospects of building new pleasure steamers'. He immediately approached the Scottish shipbuilding yards of A. & J. Inglis and Ailsa but, due to the volume of orders on hand, neither felt able to give the matter their immediate attention, nor promise delivery for some years after the war. Mr Kaile then approached the Admiralty to enquire whether any amphibious craft suitable for conversion into pleasure steamers might be available at the end of the war, but was told that no information was yet available.

These enquiries reveal the basic dilemma which had faced the company ever since the loss of *Majestic* during the Great War. Should they take the risk of a major capital investment in a large, fast, new ship capable of reviving the cross-channel and long-distance trips from Bournemouth; or should they content themselves with their current, elderly fleet possibly supplemented by further cheap, second-hand tonnage? There can be little doubt that their ability to carry out all of their own repairs and maintenance in their own yard, combined with the fact that the existing ships had already reached bottom book value and could depreciate no further, must have swayed the company heavily in favour of the latter course. However, enquiries continued in both directions.

The idea of converting redundant landing craft was not unique to Cosens, and history reveals that several other companies were thinking along similar lines. On the River Medway in 1947 the New Medway Steam Packet Company acquired a former landing craft and converted her into the 147ft motor vessel *Rochester Queen*, whilst at Poole, J. Bolson & Sons Ltd converted three similar craft and ran them from Bournemouth during the 1946 season.

It is clear that Bolsons were far more proactive than Cosens at this period. In 1914 Jake Bolson had been begun operating his first 'Skylark' motorboat from Bournemouth beach and since 1922 had been the leesee of the Skylark Shipyard at Hamworthy where he built and maintained his own boats together with a wide variety of yachts, launches and commercial craft. Between the wars his business had flourished and by January 1931 had been incorporated as a limited company under the name of J. Bolson & Sons Ltd. By the outbreak of war the company's fleet consisted of two small motor vessels, four motor launches, three speedboats and numerous rowing boats.

The war years saw a massive expansion of the company's shipbuilding activities. Initial Admiralty orders for wooden launches and motor minesweepers led to the acquisition of further shipyard sites in Poole and the construction of assault landing craft. As D-Day approached production soared to one landing craft per day, a new slipway capable of handling 190ft tank landing craft was installed, the workforce rose to over 800 and steel shipbuilding and repairing was introduced. Just like Cosens, Bolson's turnover and facilities benefitted greatly from the war, and the approach of peace found them in a stronger financial position than ever before.

Anxious to consolidate this position, Bolsons contacted Cosens in August 1944, explaining that they were considering post-war expansion and offering to buy out their Bournemouth steamers and goodwill. Cosens replied by asking precisely which steamers Bolson's had in mind and whether they would be prepared to purchase the whole company.

Bolsons made it clear that they were really only interested in the Bournemouth station and would not wish to purchase the Weymouth steamers unless Cosens absolutely insisted. They offered to absorb established employees, to negotiate over the figure for goodwill, and requested a valuation of all relevant steamers. Cosens, apparently flustered by Bolson's enthusiasm, prevaricated and responded that 'in view of the problematical date when the war will be ended combined with the current uncertainty regarding the industrial situation, no useful purpose would be served by further discussing the matter.'

Bolsons were not to be put off by this response but insisted that they were genuinely interested and kept up the pressure. They did their best to persuade Cosens to avoid any delay in establishing the post-war services by planning ahead and negotiating immediately, but all to no avail. In the end, despite offering to buy the whole of the company's operation, Bolsons had to content themselves with asking Cosens to let them know as soon as they were willing to negotiate and writing at six monthly intervals to repeat their offer.

Cosens' prevarication was not, however, entirely due to indecisiveness. Unbeknown to Bolsons, other

CONSUL (left) and EMBASSY at Weymouth after the war. CONSUL's poor condition put her future very much in the balance and it was not until November 1946 that a decision was reached to rebuild her. Astern of EMBASSY is the coaster COLDWITH FORCE while in the Cove is the French railway steamer BORDEAUX. This ship had been seized by the Germans after the fall of France but was reclaimed at the end of the war and sent to Weymouth where Cosens carried out her refit during 1945.
AUTHOR'S COLLECTION / SEWARD

irons were in the fire. During the autumn of 1944 Mr Kaile had been in contact with various ship brokers, enquiring about the availability of new and second hand tonnage, and this fact had clearly reached the ears of other shipowners. In November a meeting was held with one of these brokers, Messrs T. W. Tamplin & Co, at which it was revealed that The General Steam Navigation Company of London 'might be inclined to take an interest' in Cosens.

Cosens' board found the proposition interesting and an initial meeting between the two companies took place in London in January 1945. The General Steam Navigation Company was one of Britain's best known and longest-established shipping companies which, in addition to its extensive coastal and continental cargo fleet, had for many years run a large fleet of excursion steamers on the Thames estuary. Most of these had been paddle steamers but, shortly before the war three large twin screw motor vessels had entered the fleet.

The development and operation of these three fine ships had given the General Steam Navigation Company more experience than any other British company of the practicalities of operating modern screw vessels on long, cross-channel day excursions. When they heard that Cosens were seeking quotes from A & J Inglis and Denny of Dumbarton for a twin

screw diesel vessel in the 235 to 250ft range it was quite natural that they should take an interest. Exactly what they had in mind is still unclear, but in September 1945 they were proposing a large increase in Cosens' share capital. It would appear that General Steam Navigation Company intended to purchase all of the new shares, thereby funding the building of a new cross channel steamer for Bournemouth and acquiring a large or controlling interest in Cosens.

Whether or not the Cosens fleet would have been allowed to retain its own identity is a matter for pure conjecture. In either case, had a large, modern, cross channel motor vessel been based at Bournemouth after the war, the rest of this history might have been very different. Although it was estimated that such a vessel should be capable of earning 10% of her capital cost per annum, the Government's subsequent refusal to allow landing day excursions to France until 1954 suggests that it was as well that the plan did not go ahead.

As it was, by October 1945 discussions with the General Steam Navigation Company were reported to be in abeyance and nothing more was heard of the matter. Instead of an agreement to built a new cross-channel steamer the last communication was an offer to sell their elderly paddle steamer *Laguna Belle* of 1896. Having completed her war service, the old ship was considered unfit for further use on the Thames and was lying at Southampton awaiting a buyer when Cosens were offered first refusal. Whether the General Steam Navigation Company, having noted Cosens' apparent preference for cheap, elderly, second hand ships, was making a serious offer or having a gentle joke at the Weymouth company's expense is for the reader to decide. Cosens politely declined the offer and shortly afterwards the worn out, 49 year old *Laguna Belle* was towed away to a Belgian breaker's yard.

Thus, between November 1944 and November 1945 both Bolsons and the General Steam Navigation Company were negotiating to gain control of Cosens' Bournemouth operations. In view of this interest it was decided that a full valuation of the company's physical assets should be commissioned. The results which were received from C. W. Kellock & Co Ltd, Cosens usual brokers, in July 1945 placed the following values on the company's vessels:

Consul	£5,250
Emperor of India	£12,000
Embassy	£10,000
Empress	£2,500
Monarch	£6,750
Victoria	£3,750
Pearl (MV)	£650
Ruby (MV)	£700
Miss Dorset	£500
Miss Weymouth	£500
MY *Catherine*	£500
Two Crane Barges	£700
Dumb Hopper Barge	£50
Five Dinghies	£150
Five Flats	£100
Five Rafts	£250
TOTAL	£44,350

In addition, a separate survey valued the company's slipways, workshops, cold stores, properties, plant and machinery at £49,360, giving a total of £93,710. The valuations, however, were at 1939 prices. Within a very short while another surveyor was to point out that if the earning potential and replacement costs of the ships were taken into account the actual worth of the vessels to the company should be significantly increased. *Victoria*, for example, would take 18 months and £100,000 to replace.Her market value was therefore estimated at £15,000. This argument was to have a significant effect on subsequent negotiations.

In the same week that these valuations were delivered to the company, yet another take-over offer was received. This time Messrs. Cook, Painter, Spofforth & Co of Bristol, acting on behalf of an unknown client, sought to secure an option on the whole of the company's shares. At a meeting in Bristol during November an increase in the company's capital was proposed and an offer made for the whole of the 12,520 ordinary shares. By January 1946 Cosens had declined this option but offered a

gentleman's agreement not to negotiate with any other parties for a period of two months provided a firm offer of £16 per share was forthcoming. Correspondence flowed to and fro. The deadline was extended and by April Cosens were insisting that the name of the purchaser be revealed and a firm offer made. Faced with this ultimatum the potential purchasers identified themselves during May as the Charterhouse Finance Corporation of London (presumably acting on behalf of another, unknown client), and offered £15 per share. This was conditional upon a full valuation and report, their offer being acceptable to 90% of the ordinary shareholders; and upon a continuity of effective management being guaranteed. This final condition together with the contents of the financial reports reveal that it was Charterhouse's clear intention to continue and expand Cosens' traditional excursion steamer and ship repairing businesses.

The first report, by marine architects and engineers James Dewar & Son, provides us with a wonderful analysis of the condition of the fleet and ship repairing facilities at the end of the war and is worth quoting selectively.

Commenting on the six paddle steamers the report began:

As you are aware, these craft are all old, the youngest being 35 years and the oldest 67 years; but it is to be born in mind that:

These vessels only operate during daylight and in the summer season.

For six months in every year they are laid up in charge of a care and maintenance squad which has the company's repair facilities at its disposal.

Major items required for the annual refit and renewal of passenger certificates are dealt with on the company's premises, in consequence of which all work required by the Board of Trade, or recommended by the crews, can be carried out efficiently and at a lower cost than would be the case if the owners had to contract out. One would normally expect to find extensive wastage of material in a vessel 67 years old; but there is remarkably little evidence of this due to the steelwork having been thoroughly chipped and painted every year, with the result that the main structure has been, very largely, kept free from rust and although the craft, by their outline and general appearance, can be seen to be of some antiquity, there is no reason to suppose that they cannot continue to operate for several years to come. Indeed , with such care and attention as they receive, the question of their replacement is likely to be governed more by economics than by any consideration of the vessels' condition. They must necessarily be uneconomical in operation by modern standards; but since they are not running in competition with more modern craft, this point has never been considered.

The report then explained that in the cases of *Monarch*, *Embassy* and *Emperor of India* the terms of the wartime charter party allowed Cosens to carry out full post war refits and obtain load line and passenger certificates entirely at the expense of the Ministry of Transport. The remaining ships had been returned from war service with a cash settlement. In the cases of *Empress* and *Victoria* the cash sum had comfortably covered the refit costs but *Consul* was a different matter. Cosens had received a cash settlement of £3,000 but a survey had revealed considerable wastage of the hull plating above the waterline and the costs of repairs were estimated at between £15,000 and £20,000. No decision had yet been made as to her future.

The motorboats, harbour craft, slipways and repair facilities were all found to be in good condition and capable of producing good post war income. The surveyor reiterated the fact that Cosens' own book values for their ships were based on 1939 figures and, taking into account earning potential and replacement costs, were far below their actual worth to any potential purchaser. The possibility of a new long distance ship was mentioned. Cosens had recently received a quotation of £175000 from Denny of Dumbarton for a 235ft twin screw diesel vessel and another of £128,000 for a 245ft ship from A. & J. Inglis but in view of the cost and the attitude of the existing board who 'were not so much concerned with the replacement of their existing craft as with extending their activities' this option was regarded as unlikely. Instead it was suggested that Charterhouse might consider the purchase and conversion of an ex-Admiralty vessel at half the cost of a new vessel.

The report concluded:

Our investigation leads us to the following conclusions:

The passenger side of the business can be profitably carried on for several years with the existing craft because, although the cost of operation, maintenance and annual refit of these vessels must necessarily be greater than would be the case for new vessels, the company is in a position to carry out its own repairs and is not in competition on the earning side.

This can be implemented by the provision of new small craft operating from the beaches. Such craft could be built in time for the 1947 season.

A new vessel for the 1948 season or a converted Admiralty vessel for the 1947 season, carrying the necessary certificates for cross channel service could reasonably be expected to earn good dividends, and could be used for coastal runs of greater length than the existing craft are suitable for, on days when she was not required to cross the channel.

The repair side of the business could be profitably developed independently or alongside the shipowning side , as there is no competition nearer than Poole, Southampton or Dartmouth.

We have been unable to find any contingent liability on technical grounds or any reason to suppose why this company should not operate as satisfactorily in the future as it has in the past.

The second report, by chartered accountants Thompson McLintock, concentrated on the company's financial records. The authorised capital of the company was 14560 ordinary shares at £2 each, of which 12,520 or £25,040 had been issued. There were approximately 300 shareholdings which were mostly quite small and held by residents in the Weymouth and Bournemouth areas.

For the company's three main departments of marine activities, ship repairing and refrigeration, the following fascinating gross profit figures were produced:

YEAR	MARINE	REPAIR WORK	REFRIGERATION	TOTAL
1935	£6,215	£ 369	£1,349	£7,933
1936	6,769	968	1,375	9,112
1937	6,189	1,360	1,360	8,909
1938	2,810	2,631	1,167	6,608
1939	5,690	827	782	7,299
1940	4,174	1,474	1,173	6,821
194	5,366	3,070	loss 698	1,141
1942	2,871	5,294	684	8,849
1943	3,179	9,496	1,689	14,364
1944	4,105	9,127	1,946	15,178
1945	2,050	10,840	1,178	14,068

The receipts of the marine department were further analysed, as follows:

YEAR	1935	1936	1937	1938	1939
Passenger fares	£23,603	£23,166	£27,970	£25,632	£22,630
Charters	424	107	1,158	134	3,004
Weymouth motor boats	1,669	1,391	1,484	1,423	1,854
Stewarding (net profit)	1,296	1,345	1,595	1,150	720
Barge earnings	150	150	150	150	150
Sundry marine receipts	51	38	33	32	16
Salvage and winter trading	20	398	65	25	-
Speed boats	705	864	762	639	605
TOTAL	£27,918	£27,456	£33,217	£29,185	£28,979

To these gross trading profits were added the income from the company's extensive investments in gilt-edged government securities, building society accounts and local trades. These totalled £141,526 and had not been drawn upon for many years. After deduction of directors' fees this yielded the following Net Profit figures:

1935	£11,713
1936	£12,908
1937	£12,754
1938	£ 9,491
1939	£10,023
1940	£ 9,527
1941	£ 7,417
1942	£ 9,393
1943	£15,490
1944	£15,739
1945	£15,449

Thus, on the basis of book values, the company was shown to be in a position of considerable financial

strength. The only problems related to the valuation of the fixed assets - in particular the ageing paddle steamers - and to the associated issue of depreciation. As already discussed, the most recent valuation of the ships was at 1939 prices and therefore bore little relationship to the actual revenue-generating value of the vessels. Thompson McLintock were of the opinion that the value of the fixed assets was actually nearer to £90000 and suggested the following revaluation:

	BOOK VALUE	NEW VALUATION
FIXED ASSETS		
Floating craft	£2,894	£44,350
Properties and plant	£2,264	£49,360
INVESTMENTS	£139,355	£141,526
Total	£144,513	£235,236
LIQUID ASSETS AND CURRENT LIABILITIES		
Surplus		£3,488
Deficit	£ 512	
NET SURPLUS ASSETS		
On book value	£144,001	
Per new valuation		£238,724

Clearly, the price placed upon the fixed assets would have considerable bearing on any offer which Charterhouse were prepared to make for Cosens. The issue of depreciation was also a difficult one, for the amount allowable by the Inland Revenue for wear and tear on the steamers had long since been exhausted. Future depreciation was estimated at between £400 and £500 per annum and this amount would have to be taken from future net profits after taxation - potentially a considerable drain.

Thompson McLintock concluded that, these complications aside, Cosens' books revealed a long period of successful trading in a business which was 'well established and singularly free from competition'. Although post war conditions might differ considerably from those before 1939 and the pre-war trading figures therefore needed be used as predictors with considerable caution, Cosens were regarded as a financially sound and very experienced company which should have little difficulty in re-establishing and developing their pre-war pattern of trade.

Informed by these reports Charterhouse decided to proceed and a special meeting was called in Weymouth on 1 July at which the directors considered a draft agreement. A number of amendments were recommended, an agreement reached on 29 July and the offer circulated to shareholders for ratification. Bolsons of Poole continued to show an interest in purchasing the Bournemouth steamers but their approaches were regularly rejected.

Arrangements for the take-over seemed to be going smoothly when, during August 1946, another contender in the form of the Southampton, Isle of Wight & South of England Royal Mail Steam Packet Company Ltd, entered the fray by issuing an increased offer of £20 per share to all shareholders.

One of the Southampton Company's directors,

A fascinating aerial view of Weymouth, taken late in 1945. VICTORIA and EMPRESS, their refits virtually complete, lie outside Cosens' engineering works in the Backwater. Below the Town Bridge the dilapidated CONSUL can just be made out awaiting her fate at Custom House quay, while EMBASSY at Trinity Quay has already received her new full-width saloon. Extensive bomb damage is evident in the foreground.
BILL MACEY COLLECTION

Mr E. C. Redman, had for some time held a block of Cosens shares and was therefore in a position to keep his own board closely informed about developments. There can be little doubt that the Southampton Company must have been deeply apprehensive about the possibility of Cosens being taken over by Charterhouse. At the very least it might lead to the end of the comfortable, long established, joint-running arrangements at Bournemouth. At worst, an injection of new capital leading to the building of a fast new long distance excursion ship would certainly mean competition at Bournemouth and might even eat into the Southampton Company's own traditional excursion trade from the Solent and Isle of Wight piers.

Alongside these defensive motives for a take over there were the undoubted attractions of acquiring a healthy business with good trading profits, extensive investments and a ship repairing facility which might well save the Southampton Company money on refitting its own vessels. Then of course there would be the effective end to all competition at Bournemouth and the potential to plan the future development of the excursion fleets in a more integrated and rational manner.

Cosens, however, were bound by their July agreement with Charterhouse and were therefore unable to recommend the higher offer to their shareholders. The impasse eased at a special meeting on 19 September when it was disclosed that Charterhouse had been in direct contact with the Southampton Company. They had enquired whether,

in the event of them deciding not to proceed with their option, the Southampton Company would be willing to offer £20 a share to all those company shareholders who had already ratified with Charterhouse at the lower price.

On 23 September a letter was received from the solicitors of the Charterhouse Finance Corporation stating that since the number of ratifications of their offer did not come up to the minimum percentage stipulated, they did not intend to proceed any further. Charterhouse had withdrawn. At the same time the Southampton Company notified Cosens that it had decided to purchase all of the directors' shares at £20 each, without compensation. It has been reported that the Southampton Company finally paid the sum of £170,000 to obtain some 70% of Cosens' shares.

As soon as the share transfers had been registered a meeting was called at Cosens' head office on Custom House Quay on 4 November 1946. The five existing directors, Messrs. Dunn, Simpson, Horton, Frowde and Vincent, tendered their resignations and were immediately replaced by Mr E. C. Redman, Mr F. C. Thatcher and Capt. W. V. J. Clarke of the Southampton Company. Mr Redman was elected to the chair and Mr C. H. J. Kaile, Cosens' existing general manager and company secretary, was invited to join the board. Mr Redman paid tribute to the retiring directors and Mr Vincent, the outgoing chairman, wished the new board every success. Control had formally passed to the Southampton Company and an era had come to an end.

The joint meeting of the old and new board of Directors, 4 November,1946. Back row, left to right: C. H. J. Kaile, W. V. J. Clarke, R. L. Horton, J. B. Simpson, A. H. M. Dunn. Front row, left.to right.: F. S. Thatcher, E. C. Redman, M. C. Frowde, J. Vincent.
AUTHOR'S COLLECTION.

CHAPTER TEN
THE FLEET REBUILT
& SERVICES RESTORED
1945 TO 1949

While negotiations about the ownership of the company were going on behind the closed doors of the boardroom, Cosens' workshop staff were fully occupied with preparing the steamers for a return to passenger service.

As already recorded, the terms of the wartime charter agreement allowed Cosens to recover the entire cost of restoring *Monarch*, *Embassy* and *Emperor of India* from the government whilst, in the case of *Empress* and *Victoria*, the lump sums received would comfortably cover the refit costs. *Consul* was a different matter. Her survey revealed extensive wasting of her hull plates and the lump sum received would only pay for a fraction of the work which was needed. Her future was therefore very much in doubt and she was placed firmly at the bottom of the refit priority list.

Empress and *Victoria* had spent much of the war laid up in Weymouth Backwater and had therefore received far less punishment than the rest of the fleet. Their simple passenger accommodation had been left more or less untouched, no major renewals were required and the Ministry of War Transport estimated that each of them could be refitted within 28 days at a cost of £925 and £1,100 respectively.

Work therefore went ahead immediately and both ships were completed during the summer and autumn of 1945.

Work was still underway on *Empress* when she was chartered by Independent Film Producers Ltd to take part in a new film version of Charles Dickens' 'Great Expectations'. The film, starring John Mills, was being made at Denham Studios and the company was hunting for a steamer which could easily be converted into a cross channel packet of the William IV period for use in location shots on the River Medway. *Empress* suited them ideally and, once the licences were obtained for the scarce materials needed, Cosens' shipwrights under the leadership of chief shipwright W. Banbury set about transforming the ship.

Their task was not assisted by the fact that the company's carpenters' shop at 9 Commercial Road had been gutted by fire on the evening of 24 January with the loss of much stock and equipment. Plans had been drawn up to rebuild the shop to an improved design but meanwhile all the work on *Empress* and the other ships had to be carried out in a temporary workshop leased from Messrs Theo. Conway Ltd.

Notwithstanding the problems and shortages, the shipwrights completed their unusual task within a

EMPRESS in full disguise during the filming of 'Great Expectations'.
AUTHOR'S COLLECTION.

month. Enormous, 13ft paddleboxes decorated with symbols of the rose, shamrock and thistle were constructed over *Empress*'s own dainty ones. A 20ft, bell-mouthed extension was added to her funnel, her foremast was lengthened to 70ft, an 85ft mainmast was added, and both were fully rigged with sails and spars. A false clipper bow was fitted and adorned by a magnificent pine figurehead depicting the famous contemporary ballet dancer Moira Shearer, carved in Cosens' yard by a local man, Mr Fred Calder.

As soon as the work was completed most of it was dismantled and stowed on deck for the passage to the River Medway. With Capt 'Pony' Moore in command, Bob Wills in the engine room and a crew of seven, *Empress* left Weymouth on 26 September for what turned out to be quite an eventful voyage. Mr A. R. Holmes, designer of *Empress*'s film disguise, was on board for the trip and recalled:

Leaving Weymouth just after daybreak, the *Empress* arrived at Southampton about 2 p.m. Here R.N. control took charge of her for coaling and other attentions. Next morning we swung off Netley for compass adjustments and set sail for the Medway at 12.30 p.m. Off Hayling Island we had quite a thrilling quarter of an hour. We were passing a shore practice range where firing was in progress with pom poms or bofors guns. Suddenly we found that shells were pitching in the sea all round us, either "riccos" or "overs". Anyway, whatever they were, one flew over the bridge with a vicious crack and burst only a few yards from the starboard sponson. It called forth a certain amount of "interesting" comment from our skipper.

Empress survived her encounter and steamed onwards, passing Beachy Head at midnight and arriving off Dover just before dawn. Since navigating the Downs in darkness was prohibited, she had to slow down and dawdle until daybreak when she once again pressed on at an average of 10 knots, arriving at Gillingham some 24 hours ahead of schedule on the afternoon of the 28 September. Here she was met by a team of Cosens' shipwrights who transformed her once again for her starring role.

Filming took place further downstream in the low-lying, marshy landscape around Darnet Ness Island and Colemouth Creek. One scene, which involved a fight between the two convicts Magwitch and Compeyson, was shot at low tide on the mud flats of Darnet Ness. As soon as filming was completed the two shivering actors were rushed by launch to *Empress* which was lying just off shore, to thaw out in the steam-heated bath tubs which had been specially installed in the paddler's main cabin.

The most complex of *Empress*'s scenes, however, was the one in which a police boat, in hot pursuit of the escaping Magwitch, is drawn into the paddle wheels of the speeding steamer and destroyed. The scene, which employed stunt men, was a dangerous one and had to be rehearsed several times. During the filming the entire crew on deck, together with the thirty extras employed as passengers, were required to wear full period dress and Bob Wills always maintained with some mirth that Capt Moore looked so much the part 'that he was the only one who didn't need make up.' Much amusement was also caused by the fact that the film company employed a man whose sole task it was to conceal himself behind the bulwarks aft with a barrel of fish scraps which were tossed overboard to ensure that a good flock of seagulls were following the ship whenever the cameras were rolling. Filming continued throughout October and early November after which the ship's disguise was removed and placed into store. *Empress* left the Medway on Sunday 11 November

Filming continued throughout October and early November after which the ship's disguise was removed and placed into store. *Empress* left the Medway on Sunday 11 November in company with a small Royal Marine landing craft which had been attached during filming and whose crew slept and messed on board the paddler. *Empress* was supposed to escort the landing craft as far as Ramsgate but immediately ran into strong north east winds which forced both craft to seek shelter off Southend. *Empress* had not been provisioned for a long period at sea and very soon both food and water were running short. Southend Pier was still under military control and *Empress* was refused permission to go alongside, so all available buckets and containers, including the water tanks from the lifeboats, were sent ashore in the landing craft. The Royal Marines faired no better with the water but, after considerable argument, were allowed to land one man to buy bread. Unable to obtain fresh water at Southend *Empress* could not wait for the weather to moderate, but was forced to sail for Dover on Tuesday 13 and experienced several hours of very heavy weather off the North Foreland. Capt Moore reported that both food and water had been severely rationed and, since none of the crew had

In a still from the film Capt. Moore, in full period costume, sounds the ship's whistle. The picture has been signed by John Mills who has also inscribed the message 'I wish I looked like this , Skipper'
AUTHOR'S COLLECTION.

washed for several days, they arrived in Dover looking like scarecrows. With her food and water topped up *Empress* proceeded to Newhaven where she berthed for the night of 15 November. The next day, in rapidly deteriorating weather conditions, she set off again and experienced a fast but extremely rough ten hour passage back to Weymouth where she arrived shortly before a severe south easterly gale set in. After the austerity of the war years the ship's film role attracted considerable local interest and her crew became temporary celebrities. *Empress* returned briefly to the Medway in the spring of 1946 to complete the filming and some months later the whole crew were given a tour of the studios, met an number of contemporary film stars and were entertained at a private preview of the film.

By October 1945, with *Empress* away filming and *Victoria*'s refit effectively completed, *Embassy* had moved to the top of the priority list. Much had already been achieved but now the bulk of the company's resources were directed her way and some major structural alterations undertaken. Her main deck saloon aft, which had previously been narrow with open walkways along either side, was now extended to the sides of the ship and plated in. Associated with this was a major remodelling of the passenger accommodation. On deck a new bridge structure with enclosed wheelhouse was fitted and a large wooden deckhouse was erected abaft the funnel to cover the main companionway.

A new ventilating system was installed to replace the one removed during her naval service, and it was also decided to accept a quote from the Sturtevant Engineering Company of Sutton, Surrey, to improve the ship's steaming qualities by converting her from natural draught to induced draught for the sum of £460.

Too big to fit onto the Weymouth slipway, she was sent to Castletown at Portland during February for attention to her hull. Major wastage of the shell plating in the area beneath the main paddle shafts was discovered, which required some inventive engineering to solve.

Also during February, a plan to convert *Embassy*, *Monarch* and *Emperor of India* from coal to oil burning was announced. Quotes were sought from a number of manufacturers and one accepted from Todd Oil Burners Ltd for £995 per vessel. Conversion to oil firing was a fairly major undertaking, involving complete replacement of the furnace fronts, installation of oil fuel burners, pumps and associated pipework, and the replacement of the ships' coal bunkers with oil fuel tanks. In the event it was discovered that *Monarch*'s low pressure boiler was unsuitable for conversion so, along with *Victoria* and *Empress*, she remained coal fired until the end of her career. *Embassy*, *Emperor of India* and *Consul* were all successfully converted.

Some delays were evidently encountered with *Embassy*'s oil firing equipment and since the company was anxious to have her back in service by the beginning of September 1946 it was decided to

VICTORIA passing outwards through Weymouth Town Bridge on 31 October, 1945. Although she is looking smart in her post-war livery, her refit is not quite complete and she has still to be fitted with her lifeboats and davits. AUTHOR'S COLLECTION.

postpone her conversion until the winter. Thus, she ran sea trials in August and completed her brief 1946 season still sporting her tall, thin pre-war coal burner's funnel, but otherwise in post war guise. During the winter of 1946-7 the oilfiring gear was fitted and in February 1947 a new, shorter, fatter, elliptical funnel completed the transformation.

As soon as Embassy had moved to Castletown, Monarch became the focus of the Weymouth workshop's attention. In February she was placed on the slip to have her hull drill tested, and a great deal of essential work was identified. The wartime extension made it just possible for the slipway to accommodate Monarch and Cosens saved thousands of pounds by completing all the work on their own premises.

The ship was stripped to deck level and spent most of the spring on the slipway for extensive replating to be undertaken before returning to the backwater on 3 June to complete her fitting out. When the engine-room steam piping came to be reassembled it was discovered that several pipes no longer fitted precisely, revealing that the unconventional slipping method had caused a slight but significant hogging of the hull. She finally ran trials and was declared ready for passenger service at the end of August.

Cosens' first post war passenger sailings took place on 1 June 1946 when Empress and Victoria began running local trips from Weymouth. The pre-war arrangements at Lulworth were quickly reinstated and Mr Miller, the local fisherman who had sole rights to the beach in the cove, agreed to act as the company's agent there. At Portland an agreement was reached for one of the larger units of the Home Fleet to be opened to visitors between 2 pm and 6 pm each Saturday and Sunday, and special landing platforms were erected on board the two steamers to ease the transfer of passengers.

At Bournemouth and Swanage matters were not

so simple. Both piers had been breached as an anti-invasion precaution and urgent plans were being prepared to restore them sufficiently for at least a limited steamer service to be re-introduced during August. On 12 July representatives of both Cosens and the Southampton Company went to Swanage to view the 3ft wide bridge which had been thrown across the 40ft gap in the pier, whilst at Bournemouth a temporary metal walkway was constructed to reunite the pierhead with the beach

Cosens had hoped to open the steamer service on 1 August but, in the event, the honour of carrying out the first post war call at Bournemouth fell to the Southampton Company's Princess Elizabeth on Monday 19 August. Having arrived on a day excursion from Southampton, the ship was treated to a civic welcome before crossing to Swanage where she was also the first steamer to call.

Embassy and Monarch completed sea trials during August and opened their season at Bournemouth on Monday 2 September. By working in close co-operation with Princess Elizabeth it was possible to maintain a regular Bournemouth to Swanage ferry service, together with a variety of longer day trips to the Isle of Wight, most of which were taken by Embassy. Monarch frequently began and ended her day at Weymouth, offering a full day excursion to Swanage and Bournemouth and using the time while her passengers were ashore to slot into the Swanage ferry schedule.

The 1946 season lasted barely a month and was bedevilled with wet and windy weather which led to many cancellations. At Bournemouth, where the season closed on 2 October, only 29,646 passengers were carried, compared with 127,658 in the full length season of 1938. Things cannot have been helped by the competition from the three ex-landing craft which Bolsons had hastily converted to carry 271 passengers each and put into service from Bournemouth pier. Named Bournemouth Skylark Nos.

4 - 6, they came into service in May and offered an hourly service to Swanage; two hour cruises around Studland Bay, Shell Bay and Poole Harbour; a variety of non-landing Sunday morning cruises; and single evening trips to Poole. It is not surprising that both Cosens and the Southampton Company complained bitterly to Bournemouth council about 'unrestricted competition by vessels which do not conform in any serious respect with the standards expected from our companies'. The council ruled that as soon as the pier became available to the paddle steamers, Bolsons would be restricted to operating the motorboat trips which had existed before the war. The steamers reclaimed the Swanage service on 2 September and, too large to operate from Bolson's own jetty, the 'Bournemouth Skylarks' were put up for sale in August at £20,000 each. All three were sold abroad during 1947.

At Weymouth, in stark contrast, things were remarkably optimistic with the 1939 figures exceeded on all routes. 32,477 passengers sailed to Lulworth, 50,033 visited warships and 49,850 took other excursions, compared with 17,865, 6,819 and 45,287

respectively during 1939. The travelling public at Weymouth was clearly making the most of the benefits of peace.

While all this was happening the board was wondering what to do about *Consul*. With the exception of her engine and boiler she was in extremely bad condition and the £15,000 estimate for reconditioning did not compare favourably with the £3,000 lump sum received from the government. What should be done? It was decided to look into having a new hull built in which the old engines and boilers could be re-used. Charles Hill's ship yard in Bristol, which at the time was building the large new paddle steamer *Bristol Queen* for P. & A. Campbell Ltd, was approached and representatives came to Weymouth to measure the existing ship and discuss requirements. Their subsequent quote of £43,000 was regarded as too expensive, the concept of a new hull was abandoned and the ship's future once again hung in the balance. Mr Ward was asked to draw up costings for an in-house rebuild but, after several changes of heart, it was not until November 1946 that the new, Southampton-controlled board finally gave

MONARCH stern-first on Cosens' slipway with her funnels removed. Behind her buckled bow can be seen the steam yacht FLORINDA, whose panelling was used in EMPEROR OF INDIA's refit. AUTHOR'S COLLECTION / SEWARD

With Weymouth seafront in the background, EMPRESS diplays the white-painted bulwarks which significantly altered the appearance of the steamers in post war years. Behind her funnel, Cosens' motorboat landing stage can be seen running out from the beach.
AUTHOR'S COLLECTION / KESTIN.

their go ahead. The old ship had cheated the ship breaker once again.

As well as working on the refit of their own ships the company's shore staff were busy in other directions as well. At the end of 1945 they had obtained a contract to refit a large cargo ship, the *Bordeaux*, which was lying in The Cove at Weymouth. Then, in September 1946 Cosens obtained an Air Ministry contract which gave them the management of three ministry vessels and the maintenance of all targets, rafts and moorings in connection with the bombing range in West Bay. This required additional storage for moorings, vehicles, etc. and a lease was taken on part of Messrs Betts & Co's timber stores.

A rare picture of EMPRESS's simple but homely lower deck saloon. Note the potted plants on the tables and the gimballed oil lamp on the wooden panelling
AUTHOR'S COLLECTION / MISS M. MORRIS

The contract brought useful income to the company but sadly, when it came up for renewal in September 1947, Cosens were defeated by a lower tender. On top of all this there were hard negotiations with Weymouth Council regarding the renewal of the lease for the main engineering works on Commercial Road, and the terms under which rebuilding, repairs and improvements to these and the fire-damaged carpenters shop were to be completed.

Instead of beginning at Easter as in previous years, the start of the 1947 season was delayed until May when *Monarch* and *Embassy*, the latter complete with oil firing and large new funnel which had been fitted in February, opened the sailings alongside the Southampton Company's *Princess Elizabeth* and *Upton*.

On Sunday 11 May the battleship HMS *Vanguard* arrived at Portsmouth carrying home the King, Queen and the young princesses from their Royal Tour of South Africa. Three of the Bournemouth steamers were completely filled for the trip to see the arrival and *Victoria* had to be sent from Weymouth to take the overflow.

On 12 July, *Monarch* suffered an embarrassing accident whilst approaching Bournemouth pier. The incident began when a bather decided to swim round the pier head just as the *Princess Elizabeth* was about to make her departure at 2.40 pm The man ignored shouted warnings and was about to be drawn into the

steamer's paddle wheels when a rope was thrown and he was hauled to safety on the pier. *Monarch*, meanwhile, had been making her approach and had put her stern line ashore. In the confusion, however, she had drifted off the pier to such a strange angle that it was obvious that she could not come alongside normally. The master ordered the stern rope to be released and went astern intending to make a fresh approach, but the floating rope became entangled in the paddle wheel. Completely disabled, the ship began to drift towards Boscombe where it was feared she might go aground.

The situation was saved by Jake Bolson who rushed out with two of his motor launches, *Skylark 5* and *Skylark 7*, towed *Monarch* out to a safe anchorage in the bay and took off about 50 passengers. The rope was cut away but one of the paddle box brackets was found to be broken, so *Embassy* towed *Monarch* as far as Brownsea Island where the tug *Wendy Ann* took over and berthed her safely at Poole Quay. Replacement parts were sent from Weymouth and, by working all night, her engineers had *Monarch* in service again the following morning. Cosens were subsequently forced to settle a substantial and unwelcome salvage claim from Bolson.

The season was blessed by almost unbroken good weather which lasted right through until the autumn. Passenger figures soared to unprecedented levels at Bournemouth with 193,757 coming up the gangways,

whilst at Weymouth figures remained about steady except for a steep increase in the numbers using the motor boats and speedboats from the beach. *Monarch* returned to Weymouth at the end of September as usual but such was the demand at Bournemouth, that *Embassy*'s season was extended until 16 October and, retained by public demand, it was not until 23 October that *Bournemouth Queen* made the last departure of the season.

The end of the season saw the retirement of Mr James Halford, Cosens' agent at Bournemouth and a familiar figure on the pier. He had joined the company in 1900 as purser on the *Albert Victor* and had subsequently served in most of the fleet until 1925 when he came ashore to replace Rex Sydenham

VICTORIA arrives at Lulworth Cove.
AUTHOR'S COLLECTION.

Passengers enjoy a cup of tea in VICTORIA's very similar saloon.
AUTHOR'S COLLECTION / MISS M. MORRIS

MONARCH at Bournemouth Pier during September 1946, showing the temporary walkway which was constructed to connect the bare pier head to the shore while reconstruction of the breached pier neck took place.
B. JACKSON COLLECTION

The ship that never was: A plan from Cosens' drawing office shows a conjectural design for a steamlined, 190ft. paddle steamer named VICEROY. It seems probable that this was a draughtsman's idea of what might have resulted had the plan to build a new hull around CONSUL's engines and boilers gone ahead.
AUTHOR'S COLLECTION

as the Bournemouth agent. He retired on a small pension to concentrate on the garden at his home in Swanage and his successor was Captain Howard Baker working in conjunction with Mr Martin Harvey who was responsible for advertising.

Emperor of India, meanwhile, had finally returned from war service in July 1946. One paddle wheel was missing and she was in an advanced state of dereliction. To make matters worse, all of her internal panelling and fittings had been destroyed in an air raid whilst in store in Southampton, and replacement materials were almost impossible to obtain. Indeed, timber was in such short supply that for many months none could be found to re-deck either her or *Consul*. Cosens' workshop staff were faced with their biggest challenge yet and for the next year or so worked between the two ships, completing jobs as and when suitable new or second hand materials could be liberated from a range of imaginative sources.

In the spring of 1947 *Emperor of India* went onto the Castletown slip for a lengthy period of major hull repairs. While she was there it was discovered that

her high pressure cylinder had cracked and been welded sometime during the war. Close inspection revealed other fractures and the cylinder was condemned. It was removed through a hole cut in the side of the ship and sent to Cowes where J. Samuel White & Co copied it and made a replacement casting. By September 1947 the new cylinder had been hoisted back into place, hull repairs were complete and *Emperor of India* had returned to Weymouth backwater where reconditioning continued.

It was then that the ingenuity and craftsmanship of the workshop staff led by Mr Ward came into full play. Plans of the original 1906 accommodation layout were obtained from her builders and the workforce set to work to create an interior which, when finished, would equal that of any ship built for service on the south coast.

Pitch-pine stairways were made from the timbers of derelict quarry cranes, and other timber was obtained from a variety of wrecks. Large quantities of the finest teak were recovered from the former steam

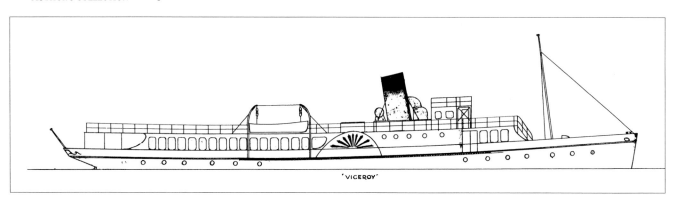

'VICEROY'

The workers who rebuilt EMPEROR OF INDIA, gathered beside the ship on Castletown Slipway, Portland during 1947.
AUTHOR'S COLLECTION / M. PROWSE

yacht *Florinda* which had originally been owned by Lilly Langtry (made famous as one of King Edward VII's mistresses) and had spent the war years as an accommodation ship at Poole and Portland. Cosens bought her and stripped her of all useful materials before selling her remains on to a local man who broke her up on the mud outside Weymouth fire station.

The new interior was truly impressive. The ceiling of the main dining saloon aft had no fewer than 448 beautifully cut and polished panels, whilst the side panelling was of oak and mahogany, with 60 teak window frames. The saloon included a large pantry and horseshoe shaped bar, and the tables throughout the ship were constructed of polished oak and mahogany with ornamented ash legs. A stairway led down to the lower aft saloon which had two bars, comfortable seating and was panelled in walnut veneered weyrock and oak.

Forward on the maindeck was another saloon fitted out in similar splendour and, below this, comfortable crew's quarters together with six officer's cabins, each with wash basins and modern fittings. Other accommodation included galleys for passengers and crew, refrigerator rooms, baths and store rooms.

On the upper deck was a large modern deckhouse complete with confectionery bar and an ice cream parlour, purser's and wireless cabins, and a splendid new bow-fronted bridge structure with enclosed wheelhouse and a captain's cabin below. The decks were completely relaid with over 30,000 ft of planking. The ship was converted to oil firing and fitted with a large elliptical funnel.

Almost unrecognisable as her pre-war self, *Emperor of India* made her inaugural, two hour cruise in Weymouth Bay on Monday 12 July 1948 under the command of Capt St Barbe Rawle, Commodore of Cosens' fleet. Fifty guests were entertained to lunch during the trip, and amid the toast and speeches repeated congratulations were heaped upon the workshop staff who, it was asserted, had transformed a virtual wreck into 'the most up-to-date and palatial passenger vessel on the south coast'. The following day, 13 July, she sailed for Bournemouth where she took up her duties as Cosens' principal long-distance steamer.

Early season returns on the Swanage ferry had been disappointing in 1947 so it was decided that only one steamer would operate at Easter 1948. Thus *Embassy* opened the season on 29 March but only managed to complete two trips due to poor weather.

Bottom left: *With her refit nearing completion but still unpainted, EMPEROR OF INDIA has her mast and funnel fitted in Weymouth Harbour. The dockside crane is in the process of stepping the foremast while the new outer funnel lies on the quay behind the ship's deckhouse.*
AUTHOR'S COLLECTION

Bottom right: *EMPEROR OF INDIA's new funnel and the boilermakers who built it, on the quay outside the Backwater engineering works.*
AUTHOR'S COLLECTION / M. PROWSE.

The completed EMPEROR OF INDIA, seen here in Southampton Water on 7 September 1949, was a magnificent ship although some argued that her new paint scheme made her look unnecessarily top-heavy.
BRITISH RAILWAYS

Victoria and *Empress* began at Weymouth on 3 and 10 May respectively, whilst *Monarch* opened a modified Swanage ferry service on 10 May which took into account that this season the Southampton Company was represented by just one steamer, *Bournemouth Queen*. On 13 July the much-heralded return of *Emperor of India* took place, returning Bournemouth to its usual strength of four steamers.

Unfortunately, *Emperor of India* did not prove to be an unqualified success. Even before the war she had tended to sit low in the water and had never been able to attain the speeds of which she should have been capable. The post war refit had simply exacerbated the problem. The tremendous weight of material which had gone into her caused her to squat even lower in the water, and her increased 'top hamper' further increased her tendency to take on a list. When this happened, or if there was any sea running, her paddle boxes became choked with water and her speed dropped dramatically. Her chief engineer, 'Benbow' Allen, attempted to improve matters by having her solid sponsons aft of the paddles replaced by slats through which the wash would surge and foam in an alarming manner, but with little success. The strain on her paddle wheels caused frequent mechanical failures and she quickly developed a reputation for unreliability. Thus, although undoubtedly the most luxurious ship on the station she was also the slowest and was frequently as much as one and a half hours late in returning from the Isle of Wight.

A typical weekday morning in 1948 would see the steamers leaving their overnight berths at Poole Quay for Bournemouth. The long distance ships were already well laden with passengers who preferred to embark at Poole rather than face the long queues at Bournemouth where the pier was still being rebuilt. Either *Bournemouth Queen* or *Emperor of India* would depart at 10 am for Yarmouth, continuing either to Southampton or Ryde and Portsmouth Harbour. The other would set off at 10.15 am around the Isle of Wight. On Fridays these trips were combined to give alternate ships a day off. The first departures for Swanage were at 10.30 am and 11.00 am, taken by *Embassy* and *Monarch* alternately and continued for the rest of the day. A small 'German' or 'Steamer Band' was often provided for the entertainment of passengers, and on busy days during 1948 the 'Neptune Melody Makers' were frequently to be seen perched on top of *Monarch*'s tiny midships deck house. At the beginning of the season the new agent, Capt Baker, experimented with concentrating three ships on the Isle of Wight run with only one on the Swanage ferry, but this proved unworkable and the status quo was soon restored. *Princess Elizabeth* would often arrive around the middle of the day on an excursion from Southampton, whilst Cosens' *Victoria* was a regular visitor from Weymouth. She would normally lay at the pier while her passengers were ashore, but occasionally put in a relief run to Swanage and, on at least one occasion, ran an advertised half-day excursion to land at Lulworth Cove.

Another 1948 innovation was the introduction of Thursday night 'Showboat Cruises' by *Emperor of India*, departing from Bournemouth at 8.30 pm and returning at midnight to Poole Quay where a fleet of coaches would be waiting to transport her passengers home to Bournemouth. A range of cabaret and music artistes were engaged to provide the entertainment and, with her extensive and comfortable accommodation, *Emperor of India* proved popular in the role. Between 1949 and 1952 she alternated week and week about with the Southampton Company's *Lorna Doone*, and the 'Showboat Cruises' quickly became an established part of the programme.

The indifferent weather during the peak season of 1948, combined with the reduced spending power of the public (many had spent their war gratuities and savings during 1947) led to a £20,000 fall in profits. 102 trips had been cancelled at Weymouth, 22 at Bournemouth and the beach motorboats had been unable to work on 20 days. Despite all this, passenger

Capt. 'Pony' Moore and members of the EMBASSY's crew seated beside the ship's enormous new deck house. The lack of white tops to the officers' caps suggests that the date is Easter 1948. On the right is 'Ma' Waddington, a greatly respected and long-serving stewardess, who tended to the needs of female passengers in the 'Ladies Cabin' on many of Cosens' Bournemouth steamers. Unusually, she is not wearing her customary white uniform.
KEN MOORE

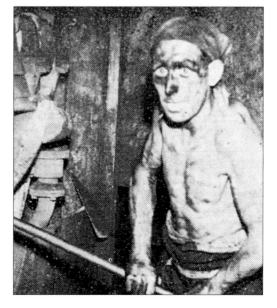

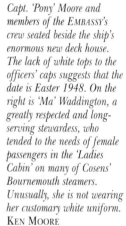

On 20 August 1947 the Bournemouth Echo published this photograph with the comment: 'How many holiday makers sweltering at 93° in the shade on the decks of the S.S. Monarch as she left Bournemouth Pier last Saturday gave a thought for the stokers down below? Here stoker George Williamson is seen poking up the ship's fire with the thermometer at 140°.'
VICTOR GRAY COLLECTION

EMPEROR OF INDIA and MONARCH at Bournemouth Pier in August 1948. All ships had to use the eastern side of the pier until 1951 when the rebuilding of the western landing stage was completed.
AUTHOR'S COLLECTION

EMBASSY in Weymouth Bay, showing the larger funnel which was fitted when she was converted to oil firing during the winter of 1946.
AUTHOR'S COLLECTION / KESTIN

figures had been above pre-war levels and, on sunny days, the steamers at Weymouth and Bournemouth as well as at Southampton were all stretched beyond their capacity. The Southampton Company sought to ensure that adequate capacity would be available during 1949 by ordering a new, multi-purpose motor vessel named *Balmoral*, and purchasing two large, second hand paddle steamers from the New Medway Steam Packet Company. These ships, the *Queen of Kent* and *Queen of Thanet* were originally Admiralty minesweepers and had been offered to both Cosens and the Southampton Company. A joint deputation travelled to Rochester to view them when it was decided that they would be more appropriate for the Southampton fleet, and were duly renamed *Lorna Doone* and *Solent Queen*.

It was intended that *Solent Queen* should become the principal Southampton excursion steamer,

releasing *Princess Elizabeth* to spend more time on the Southampton-Cowes ferry run which was suffering from a shortage of suitable tonnage. *Lorna Doone* was to be sent to Bournemouth to partner *Emperor of India* on the long excursions, freeing *Bournemouth Queen* to relieve *Embassy* from the Swanage ferry. *Embassy* was to become Weymouth's long-distance steamer and would be joined later in the season by the refurbished *Consul*.

With *Emperor of India* back in service the workshop staff had been able to use the remainder of 1948 and the spring of 1949 to concentrate on *Consul*. She was finally completed in May 1949 having undergone an equally thorough if slightly less luxurious rebuild. Having been stripped to a bare hull and extensively replated, she emerged with similar modifications to *Embassy*: saloon lengthened and extended to the hull sides and accommodation remodelled; a new bridge structure with enclosed wheelhouse; a large deckhouse over the maindeck stairway; oil firing and a well-proportioned, elliptical funnel.

As each ship had returned to service she had been given a modified post-war paint scheme in which the bulwarks were painted white down to main deck level. Whilst this undoubtedly made them look brighter and more modern, it suited some better than others. In the case of *Emperor of India* it simply made her look even more top heavy and low in the water. All three oil burning ships had curious curved casings fitted to their funnels. *Consul*'s was relatively discreet and fitted to the back of the funnel, whilst *Embassy* and *Emperor of India* had much larger affairs attached to the front edge. These casings contained the fan engines which were intended to blow air up the funnels, increasing the draught through the boilers and thereby improve their steaming qualities. This

CONSUL on the slipway at Weymouth, showing the full extent of her post-war dereliction.
AUTHOR'S COLLECTION / SEWARD

system was designed by Cosens in preference to the sealed, pressurised stokehold system favoured by some other companies and was often referred to as 'induced draught'. The other fitting at the base of the funnel was a large, cylindrical tank containing foam which could be sprayed directly into the boiler room in case of fire.

An interesting twist occurred in September 1948 when Cosens were invited to purchase the Paignton Pier Company together with the South Western Steam Navigation Company for the sum of £100,000. The latter company was the owner of the 1897 paddle steamer *Pride of Devon* which they had bought from the New Medway Steam Packet Company in 1946. The ship had operated cruises from Torquay during the 1947 and 1948 seasons but now her owners were in financial difficulties. Cosens declined the offer on the grounds that 'in view of the national situation the

Back in service at last, the reconstructed CONSUL lands passengers at Lulworth Cove during the summer of 1949.
B. JACKSON COLLECTION

While passengers embark for her 2.30p.m. sailing to Swanage, MONARCH rests at Bournemouth Pier on 15 August, 1949.
H. A. ALLEN COLLECTION

present time was not opportune to widen the scope of the company's interests.' The company probably still had unhappy memories of *Alexandra*'s experiment at Torquay in the 1920s. *Pride of Devon* was laid up at Southampton until sold to the breaker in 1951.

1949 was another year of prolonged good weather. It was the Southampton Company's turn to provide the Easter steamer, and *Bournemouth Queen* operated alone from Good Friday in temperatures that were more akin to mid summer. During April she suffered a serious breakdown and was replaced for ten days by *Princess Elizabeth*. When the new *Lorna Doone* arrived on 5 May to take over the long distance sailings, *Bournemouth Queen* transferred to the Swanage ferry where she was joined four days later by Cosens' *Monarch*. *Embassy* partnered *Lorna Doone* from Whitsun until 24 June when she was relieved by *Emperor of India* and returned to Weymouth. A non-landing cruise to Cowes Roads was reintroduced as a Sunday destination, with arrivals carefully timed to avoid disruption to the Southampton Company's established calls.

Embassy should have arrived at Bournemouth on 9 May but was delayed by a serious mishap on the Castletown slipway. While she was being launched, a downhaul wire broke and the ship, which was already partially afloat, damaged 20 bottom plates before she could be hauled ashore again. £2,750 worth of damage was caused and the ship was over a week late entering service.

Weymouth enjoyed an exceptionally good service during 1949. Not only did it benefit from the presence of *Embassy* as the principal long distance steamer but *Consul* finally returned to service during May. After a press preview she was moored just below Weymouth Town Bridge and thrown open for public inspection on 9 and 10 May, before making her first passenger sailing on Monday 12 May. Weymouth now had four steamers in place of the usual two and local people were able to benefit from a 250% increase in passenger capacity, greatly improved accommodation and a far better selection of sailings. *Embassy* or *Consul* went to Swanage and Bournemouth on most weekdays and while there *Embassy* would usually offer an onward afternoon tea cruise towards the Isle of Wight whilst *Consul* came from Bournemouth to Lulworth Cove via Swanage at least once a week. The prewar practice of Lulworth passengers from Bournemouth going outward by the Swanage service steamer and changing at Swanage was not resumed until 1950.

Some unwelcome competition arose at

Weymouth when the Channel Islands railway steamers introduced day trips to Guernsey and Thursday afternoon cruises along the coast. 885 passengers embarked on the first trip to Guernsey. Cosens were concerned about the potential loss of trade, and also about the lack of outside work coming into the slipway and engineering departments. In an attempt to open new avenues they revived their moribund diving department; engaged a specialist shipping clerk to develop their role as a local shipping agent; and tendered to carry out conversion on two ships belonging to the Redcliffe Channel Islands Steam Ship Company. This company, owned by a Mr Metcalf, had announced its intention of operating a service between Weymouth, Alderney and Sark, beginning at Whitsun 1949. Work was completed on the first ship, the ss *Radford*, and her consort, the ss *Radbourne*, arrived in the Backwater on 14 May 1949. However, Mr Metcalf never paid his bills, Cosens issued a writ and by December the company was in receivership. The *Radbourne* passed to Cosens in lieu of debts and became something of a fixture in Weymouth Backwater. She was finally sold for £9,000 and left Weymouth during October 1952. A more successful tender was for the refit of the Air Ministry vessel *Buoymoor* which was completed during March 1949.

During April there was a new arrival at Poole in the form of the 200 ft oil barge *Brownsea* which had been purchased by the Southampton Company and moored in the Wareham Channel. Fitted with flood lights for working at night she had a capacity of 450 tons of oil and was used for bunkering by the oil fired steamers of both fleets. An equivalent vessel was needed at Weymouth and in December Cosens were able to purchase the *Shell Mex No 6* for £450. Built in Rotterdam in 1925 she was 91 ft in length with a gross tonnage of 86.15. Her engines and crew

accommodation were removed and, after conversion into a dumb barge, she was renamed *Melway* in February 1950. For the next eleven years she became a familiar part of the Weymouth scene, being towed by one of Cosens' motorboats from her berth in the backwater to refuel either *Consul* or *Embassy* in the lower harbour.

The pattern of sailing from Bournemouth was much as in previous years. The advent of the speedy and reliable *Lorna Doone* threw *Emperor of India*'s shortcomings into an even more vivid light and it is significant that she retired to Weymouth on 27 September to be replaced by *Embassy* which closed Cosens' extended season on 14 October. With hindsight it is clear that 1949 with its excellent weather, greatly improved fleet and general sense of optimism marked the peak of post war steamer services along the Dorset and Hampshire coasts.

Shell Mex 6 on the slipway for conversion into Cosens' Weymouth oil fuel barge MELWAY.
B. JACKSON COLLECTION

Capt. Cooke brings a rather rust-stained MONARCH *into Poole Quay towards the end of the 1948 or 1949 season. He is using the flooding tide to swing the ship round to moor bows-out, making her next departure far easier.*
B. JACKSON COLLECTION.

CHAPTER ELEVEN

STEADY DECLINE
1950 TO 1960

1950 opened on a gloomy note. Analysis of the 1949 passenger figures showed that, despite the favourable weather, passenger income had dropped by over £6,000 and the expanded fleet had not been justified. This disappointment was blamed on the fact that wages and pubic spending power were down, wartime gratuities had all been spent and that competition from buses and trains had increased significantly. The situation was not helped by the dramatic rise in the price of fuel oil which made the newly-converted steamers far less economical than had been anticipated.

Things were little better in the works department which had now completed all the post war refits and was finding outside work harder to obtain. Income had dropped by £51,000 in comparison with the previous year and it was clear that economies would have to be made.

The first casualty was the veteran *Monarch* which had been due for her load line survey during the spring. Discussions with the Board of Trade, whose survey requirements had recently become far more stringent, revealed that between £3,000 and £4,000 would be required to obtain another three year passenger certificate. Such expenditure could not be justified so the old ship was sold for £900 to the British Iron & Steel Corporation for breaking up. Cosens' board admitted that the decision was 'a terrific wrench' and sent a message of sympathy to the ship's many supporters on the loss of 'a grand old friend'.

After 62 years in the company's service, *Monarch* had become as much a part of the south coast scene as the piers and harbours themselves. Despite her dated appearance and fine, almost delicate lines, she had remained a favourite amongst passengers and crew alike and was always said to be one of the very best seaboats in the fleet. It is not surprising that when, on 22 February 1950, she left her berth outside the Backwater works for the last time, the entire workforce and a large crowd of Weymouthians turned out to bid her an emotional farewell.

As a result of *Monarch*'s withdrawal, *Embassy* was transferred to Bournemouth for the whole of the 1950 season, taking the veteran's place on the Swanage ferry. This reduced Weymouth to three steamers once again, with *Empress* and *Victoria* operating the local sailings whilst *Consul* went to Swanage and Bournemouth on four days a week. The pattern of sailings was broadly the same as previously, with the exception that *Consul*'s Bournemouth to Lulworth sailings now began at Swanage, with Bournemouth passengers using the Swanage ferry steamer to make the connection. Oddly, the return leg of the sailing went direct to Bournemouth with Swanage passengers remaining on board until the ship called there on her way back to Weymouth. Afternoon cruises to the Isle of Wight that had previously been taken by *Consul* were now operated by *Embassy* and *Bournemouth Queen* whilst the Weymouth vessel substituted on the ferry.

Some additional competition appeared at

MONARCH and her tug at Weymouth Pleasure Pier awaiting departure for the breaker's yard, 22 February 1950. Note the 'dustbin lid' caps which were fitted to the funnels of all the steamers during winter lay-up to prevent rainwater entering the boilers.
AUTHOR'S COLLECTION / SEWARD

Bournemouth in the form of three converted Fairmile motor launches belonging to the Poole & Solent Navigation company. These three vessels, named *Matapan*, *Dunkirk* and *Anzio*, had been offered to Cosens in February but were declined, and now operated in opposition to both Cosens and Bolsons from the pier. The company lasted for only one season after which *Matapan* and *Dunkirk* were taken over by Bolsons and *Anzio* sold away.

Consideration was given to basing a steamer at Torquay once again during 1950. A group of ships' masters visited Torquay, Lyme Regis and Exmouth to inspect the landing facilities but the debate was settled prematurely by the departure of *Monarch* which left the company without a spare ship. Cosens also declined an invitation to run from Bognor Regis pier, but the Southampton Company agreed to operate at least one trial trip during the season. Strenuous efforts were made to encourage coach operators to bring tours to both Weymouth and Bournemouth to connect with steamer excursions, an aspect of the company's business that was to become increasingly important in the decade ahead.

Three factors conspired to make 1950 one of the worst years in the company's history. The first of these was the poor weather throughout the season and the second was the outbreak of the Korean War in June. At the time nobody could predict how far the situation might escalate and a general atmosphere of anxiety and retrenchment prevailed. The final and most serious factor was the epidemic of polio which originated and had its centre on the Isle of Wight. Fear of infection caused passenger figures to the Island to fall away dramatically and, even in the height of the season, it was common for round the Isle of Wight sailings to be cancelled for lack of demand, with *Emperor of India* or *Lorna Doone* returning to Poole to lay up for the day.

By the end of August it was decided to withdraw

one ship from each company. *Emperor of India* retired to Weymouth and *Bournemouth Queen* was transferred to Southampton, leaving *Embassy* and *Lorna Doone* to alternate between the Swanage and Isle of Wight services. The disastrous season closed early at the end of September, with Cosens' passenger receipts a further £23,500 down on 1949.

During 1950 a meeting was held between the two steamer companies and Mr G. A. Preece to discuss the decline in the number of his customers patronising the Yarmouth to Southampton excursions. This led to a development which was to have a profound effect on the Bournemouth steamers from 1951 onwards.

In addition to Preece's Holiday Camps Ltd which operated several camps on the island, he had a major interest in a coach company and, most significantly, was chairman of the Totland Bay Hotel and Pier Company. The pier had been declared unsafe in 1931 and no steamers had called since then. Preece wished to see it restored and neatly turned the discussion about the Yarmouth traffic into a suggestion that the steamer companies might find it to their benefit to invest in rebuilding the pier.

A summer morning in Weymouth Harbour. EMPRESS is still at her overnight berth on Trinity Quay, while VICTORIA is going astern down the harbour to collect her first passengers of the day from the Pleasure Pier.
AUTHOR'S COLLECTION

An official company postcard sold on board the new MONARCH, the last vessel in the fleet to retain a narrow main deck salloon aft. The open alleyway around the saloon can be clearly seen.
AUTHOR'S COLLECTION

The board thought long and hard about the scheme and in September 1950, on learning that Brickwoods the brewers had also taken a large financial interest, agreed to invest £6,000 in the scheme on the condition that only Cosens' and Southampton Company's steamers be allowed to operate from the pier. Refurbishment of the pier went ahead during the spring of 1951 while the two steamer companies considered how to make the best use of their new destination.

It was decided that Cosens would operate a direct Bournemouth to Totland service several times each day, while the long distance excursion steamers would call as appropriate. More significantly, the Southampton Company would introduce a new route from Southampton and Southsea through the Solent

Stewardess with the ship's dog, on board EMPRESS at Weymouth pier.

Right
Chief Steward George Morris serves passengers on the foredeck of EMPRESS in Lulworth Cove.
AUTHOR'S COLLECTION /
MISS M. MORRIS

to Totland. *Bournemouth Queen* was withdrawn from Bournemouth to cover the new service and left the resort short of a steamer.

The solution to this shortfall lay in the purchase of the British Railways Portsmouth to Ryde ferry steamer *Shanklin* which was lying for sale at Southampton. Built in 1924, the 412 g.r.t paddler was a close sister to *Embassy* in her pre-war guise and was still coal-fired. She was inspected at Southampton in November 1950 and bargaining continued until May 1951 when a purchase price of £7,000 was finally agreed. Curiously, though, she was not purchased by the Southampton Company but by Cosens. She was drydocked at Southampton where Thornycrofts hurriedly completed essential work before, resplendent in Cosens colours and renamed *Monarch*, she sailed direct to Bournemouth to begin service on 9 July 1951, a day of high winds and rain.

It fell to *Lorna Doone* to make the first call at Totland on 17 June 1951, and thereafter the previously non-landing afternoon cruises to Totland became landing trips and the Yarmouth steamer called at both piers. When *Emperor of India* joined *Lorna Doone*, *Embassy* and *Consul* at Bournemouth on 25 June the high season programme commenced, but with adjustments to include Totland.

The Swanage service was reduced from two ships to one, initially *Consul* except when she was rostered

Monkey business on board EMPEROR OF INDIA. For a period during the early 1950s passengers were offered the opportunity to have souvenir photographs taken with a pair of chimpanzees who travelled on board. Here, Commander Brown, Bournemouth Piermaster; Alf Pover, Chief Engineer; the Chimps' keeper and Eric Playter, Mate are seen with the chimps in the ship's wheelhouse.
DORCHESTER LIBRARY

EMBASSY at Totland Bay Pier.
AUTHOR'S COLLECTION

to go to Lulworth in which case *Embassy* would substitute. *Consul* alone was not really suited to the Swanage service at peak times, as she was smaller and slower than *Embassy* and could only use two gangways as compared with the latter's four. The two ships therefore swapped services from 4 July, with *Consul* offering three return trips each day to Totland.

Consul was due to return to Weymouth as soon as *Monarch* arrived at Bournemouth but was prevented from doing so by a disaster which occurred at Southampton on 22 June. *Solent Queen*, the Southampton Company's key Solent excursion steamer, was gutted by fire whilst on the slipway preparing for the season ahead. She was declared a constructive total loss and consequently, as soon as *Monarch* was ready, *Lorna Doone* was recalled from Bournemouth to take her place. Thus it was, in July 1951, that the Southampton Company came to withdraw from Bournemouth leaving the Cosens steamers with the bay to themselves for the first time in almost 100 years.

Consul remained at Bournemouth to partner *Monarch* on the two ship Swanage service, whilst *Emperor of India* and *Embassy* shared the Isle of Wight sailings. By early July it had become apparent that the new arrangements were not generating any additional traffic to the island, but that the same

number of passengers were merely spreading themselves between more ships, so the number of Totland sailings was reduced. Weymouth had to make do with the two veterans *Empress* and *Victoria*, the latter, remarkably, still offering regular day trips to Swanage and Bournemouth, with an onward afternoon cruise to Totland.

An already difficult season was made worse by poor weather which caused sailings to be cancelled on no less than 30 days from Bournemouth and 26 from Weymouth. The Festival of Britain events in London deflected many visitors from coming to the seaside whilst increased competition from coach and rail tours and significant pay rises for staff cut further into the profits. On the bright side, Cosens managed to negotiate a reduction of the charge to use Bournemouth pier to £500 p.a., to include the provision of a small ticket office at the pier entrance and in June the main Bournemouth steamer office moved to a new location on the West Cliff close to the pier approach.

At Weymouth the main No 1 slipway which had been extended during the war was shortened again to clear the swinging berth used by the Channel Island steamers. The work was carried out at the Admiralty's expense and was completed by mid November, just in time for Cosens to begin converting a wooden motor minesweeper, *MMS 1035*, into a floating laboratory for the Admiralty Underwater Weapons Establishment (AUWE) at Portland. This was a major job and, together with one or two other refits, kept the reduced workshop staff fully employed for the next year.

With the bad experience of 1951 still very much in mind, Cosens decided to abandon the Easter sailings in 1952 and open the Bournemouth season with *Consul* in mid-May. Local pressure, however, caused a change of heart and the parent company sent *Princess Elizabeth* to operate for five days between Easter Sunday and the following Thursday. The decision was well justified, for the weather was kind and on her first afternoon trip to the Island she was filled to capacity.

Consul entered service as planned during May to be joined in turn by *Embassy*, *Monarch* and *Emperor of India*, leaving Weymouth to be served once again by the elderly *Empress* and *Victoria*. When *Monarch* had gone to Southampton for docking and load line survey during May it had been discovered that her shell plating was severely corroded. The necessary replating, together with the cost of her 1951 refit now added up to considerably more than her initial purchase price and Cosens must have been wondering how much of a bargain they had actually obtained.

Consul and *Monarch* shared the Swanage service as before, but the Isle of Wight sailings were completely reorganised. One steamer - usually *Emperor of India* - sailed at 10am for Totland or Yarmouth returning to Bournemouth at midday before repeating the trip during the afternoon. In this way passengers could enjoy either a half day cruise, a full day with time

A close up view of MONARCH's bow rudder. Both she and EMBASSY were fitted with bow rudders which greatly improved their manoeuvrability when going astern from piers. Controlled by a seaman from a manual wheel in the bows the rudder had to be pinned securely in a midships position before the ship went ahead again.
AUTHOR'S COLLECTION.

MONARCH and EMBASSY in drydock together at Southampton on 9 May, 1952. AUTHOR'S COLLECTION / DOCKS & INLAND WATERWAYS EXECUTIVE.

The Mersey ferry J. FARLEY at Custom House Quay in September 1952. AUTHOR'S COLLECTION

Her conversion to a floating laboratory completed, J. FARLEY is manoeuvred by Cosens' launch PEARL down Weymouth Harbour and past the laid up MONARCH.
AUTHOR'S COLLECION / M. PROWSE

Able seaman Desmond Palmer on board EMBASSY in 1952
MRS. P. HART

ashore or the option of a connecting coach tour of the Isle of Wight with the West Wight Motor Co. An increasing emphasis was placed on coach tours and much of the Bournemouth manager's winter activity was devoted to canvassing coach companies as far away as the Midlands, in the hope of obtaining regular advanced group bookings. Indeed, as the season progressed it was found desirable to alter the return time of the afternoon steamer to the Island from 2.15pm to 3.45 pm, allowing passengers from Totland more time ashore at Bournemouth. This had the effect of generating through coach traffic from the East Wight resorts of Shanklin and Sandown and

provided additional coach capacity at Totland for the combined tour, demand for which often outstripped the seats available. *Embassy*, whose reliability and timekeeping were better, was generally employed on the full day trips to Southampton Docks or Round the Island.

A high spot of the 1952 season was the arrival at Southampton of the new Blue Riband holder, the giant American liner *United States*. On the occasion of her first arrival *Embassy*, *Emperor of India* and *Monarch* braved wet and windy weather to take capacity loads from Bournemouth to Southampton. On a number of subsequent occasions demand was so great that a relief steamer had to be provided and it was on one of these days that *Consul* made her only known sailing from Bournemouth to Southampton.

As the season was drawing to a close in September a strange vessel arrived in Weymouth to berth briefly outside the head office, before moving up through the town bridge to the Backwater works. She was *J Farley*, a Mersey ferry built in 1922 for Wallasey Corporation. Rumours began to fly as the uninformed surmised that she must be a replacement for one of the older units of the Cosens fleet. The explanation was, in fact, far more prosaic. The old steamer had been purchased for conversion into another floating laboratory for the AUWE, and Cosens had won the valuable contract for the work. Whilst lying in the Backwater she was stripped of her accommodation and machinery with several of her auxillaries later finding their way onboard the Cosens paddlers as replacements. In February she was placed on the No 1 slip where her massive beam required alterations to the cradle and her weight caused damage to the rails and problems for years to come. The *J Farley* contract represented a very useful income for Cosens which, together with other work for the Admiralty and Prison Service, encouraged the company to re-equip the machine shop in the hope of attracting precision work resulting from the national re-armament programme.

During December there was an addition to the fleet when the Southampton Company's Poole oil barge *Brownsea*, together with a depot ashore, was officially transferred into Cosens' ownership for the sum of £1000. Sadly this was followed a month later by a far more significant disposal.

The old *Victoria* of 1879 was due for her load line survey and a preliminary report showed that the poor condition of her hull combined with the general antiquity of the vessel would make her uneconomic to repair. She was quickly sold to the British Iron & Steel Corporation for £1850 and was allocated to Pollock Brown's scrapyard at Southampton. At 8am on the morning of 22 January 1953 she slipped almost unnoticed out of Weymouth harbour and turned her bows eastwards for the last time. On the bridge for the final voyage was Capt 'Pony' Moore who commented:

> It was like parting with an old friend. At least she never suffered the indignity of being towed there, but went under her own power. Everyone felt it a bit as we dipped our ensign to the Anvil Point

VICTORIA entering Lulworth Cove towards the end of her long career.
AUTHOR'S COLLECTION

lighthouse keeper who saluted us when we went by, and when the Southampton steam packets sounded their sirens in the Itchen.

The shipbreakers worked quickly and within a matter of weeks *Victoria* with her quaint oscillating engines and beautiful, sea-kindly hull was no more than a memory.

At the beginning of 1953 a small but extremely significant piece of financial restructuring took place. It will be recalled that, prior to the take over by the Southampton Company in 1946, Cosens had considerable investments and reserves which allowed them to declare a healthy dividend even in years when the trading profit was minimal. This situation still existed and was causing distortion to the parent company's consolidated accounts and problems with taxation. In order to avoid further overpayment of tax, to comply with the new Companies Act and to reflect more accurately Cosens' actual trading position, a major redistribution of funds took place. £95000 was transferred from the general and investment reserves and £36,118 from the profit and loss account, into the capital reserve account. The resulting debit balance of £18,181 in the profit and loss account represented the net results of Cosens' trading activities for the period 1946-52. The parent company now had access to greater capital reserves and was able to offset Cosens' trading loss against

their own tax bill. Unfortunately for Cosens' shareholders, however, no dividend could be declared for 1952.

The departure of *Victoria* meant that *Consul* was retained at Weymouth for the 1953 season, leaving *Monarch* to maintain the Swanage service alone. 1953 was also the first season in which no Easter sailings were provided at Bournemouth as it would have been too costly to commission *Consul* for a few days and then lay her up again. *Consul* still went to Bournemouth on two days a week and would put in a couple of crossings to Swanage while her passengers were ashore. On Fridays she sailed back from Swanage to Lulworth, Bournemouth passengers having been brought across in *Embassy* which then took *Consul*'s through passengers onwards to Totland Bay. This arrangement was extremely popular with Swanage residents as it represented their only direct sailing to the Island, all others being via Bournemouth and often involving a change of steamer.

On her Weymouth days *Consul* frequently operated the popular short trips to Portland harbour to land passengers on board which ever major warship was open to the public. Not infrequently this would be an aircraft carrier and, to assist berthing alongside, *Consul* often sailed in daylight hours without her mast.

CONSUL dressed overall and with a full load of passengers hurries towards the Spithead on a special cruise to witness the arrival home of the Queen and the Duke of Edinburgh from their Commonwealth tour, 14 May 1954. Note the light gantry fitted to her funnel during the previous winter. FOTOFLITE

The high spot of the 1953 season came in June when the Coronation Review was held at Spithead. The review itself took place on Monday 15 June, but on the previous Thursday *Embassy*, *Monarch* and *Consul* sailed for Southampton where, for the next five days, they effectively became units of the parent company's fleet, operating on a mixture of public and charter sailings.

Consul spent most of Friday, Saturday and Sunday operating short public cruises round the fleet from Southsea, in partnership with *Bournemouth Queen*. She returned to Southampton each evening and on at least one occasion was pressed into service on the parent company's regular Southampton to Ryde run. *Embassy* and *Monarch* spent the same period based at Southampton, running a mixture of official and charter cruises in company with *Balmoral*, *Vecta* and *Princess Elizabeth*.

Emperor of India, meanwhile, remained at Bournemouth. On 11 and 12 June she ran long day trips via Totland to view the fleet, and on Saturday 13 June sailed at 9am for Southsea. While her passengers were enjoying an afternoon ashore she undertook a charter to the Portsmouth & Langstone Conservative Association before returning to Bournemouth in the evening. These were *Emperor of India*'s only post-war visits to South Parade Pier and she experienced great difficulty in getting away on her return sailing. She did not respond well to her rudder when running astern and at one stage seemed to be in danger of going ashore on Southsea beach. Only when Capt Rawle ordered all passengers to her starboard side did she respond to her helm and disaster was averted!

On the following day, Sunday 14 June, *Emperor of India* ran a similar long day trip from Bournemouth and Swanage before sailing light during the evening to join the rest of the fleet at Southampton. The Swanage service had already been suspended for four days and now Bournemouth was without any steamer to offer direct sailing to the review - a stark contrast to pre-war practice.

On the day of the review itself the steamers, heavily laden with passengers, converged on Spithead to take up their allotted anchorages and watch the royal progress through the fleet. What a sight it must have been. *Emperor of India* and *Consul* sailed from Southampton in company with *Balmoral*, *Vecta*, the Thames steamers *Medway Queen*, *Royal Sovereign* and *Royal Daffodil* and the Bristol Channel paddlers *Bristol Queen* and *Cardiff Queen*. *Embassy*, *Monarch* and *Bournemouth Queen* came from Southsea where they had already run some short morning cruises. When the review itself was over some of the steamers remained at anchor to view the fireworks and illuminations whilst others, including *Monarch* and *Embassy*, landed their passengers and ran separate evening cruises.

On the next day the fleet dispersed. *Consul* steamed home to Weymouth, *Emperor of India* and *Embassy* went direct to Bournemouth, *Monarch* went to Poole to coal and life returned to normal.

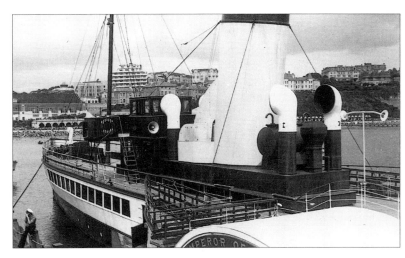

EMPEROR OF INDIA at Bournemouth Pier on 19 August 1954, showing fascinating detail of her deck layout.
DORCHESTER LIBRARY

The review proved to be a tremendous financial success for Cosens with over £14,000 clear profit made in less than a week. This, together with workshop income generated from the conversion of the *J Farley*, refits to the RAF mooring vessel *Rafmoor* and the War Department's *Tigris*, plus a contract to construct high speed marker buoys for the AUWE, helped to offset the effects of mediocre weather and rising costs allowing a 10% dividend to be declared once again.

1953 also saw the revival of several calling points on the Isle of Wight. Ventnor pier reopened to shipping on 25 May and *Embassy* made a number of calls during the season. The rebuilding of Sandown pier landing stage was still not quite complete but an inspection was made and Cosens were invited to call again from 1954. *Embassy* also made occasional calls at Ryde, which had not been visited since 1951, and revived regular sailing to Southsea for the first time since the war. *Emperor of India* finished her season on 11 September, followed one by one by the rest of fleet until *Embassy* brought the curtain down at Bournemouth on 1 October and retreated to lay up at Weymouth.

During the 1953 season *Emperor of India* fractured several arms in her paddle wheels. Although Cosens tried to persuade their insurance company that this was due to heavy weather damage, the reality was that ship sat too low in the water causing the wheels to be too deeply immersed and the paddle boxes to choke with water. This had thrown a great strain on the wheels and it was clear that extensive rebuilding was required. The work, which was carried out at Weymouth, took most of the winter and spring and involved the complete removal of the outer faces of the paddleboxes. At the same time some major repairs were carried out to the boiler. It was the last major job to be planned by Mr J. M. 'Sharky' Ward who retired at the end of 1953 and was replaced as Works Manager and Marine Superintendent by his assistant, Mr Donald Brookes.

Christmas Day 1953 very nearly saw the end of the *Embassy*. For many years it had been the tradition in Weymouth for large crowds to gather on the

harbourside at around midday to watch the traditional cross-harbour swim. On this particular occasion *Embassy* was moored on Custom House Quay and many of the onlookers boarded the unattended ship to use her as a grandstand. Once the swim was over the crowds dispersed to their Christmas dinners and no more was thought of the matter until a passer by, walking along the quay late that evening, noticed that the ship was unusually low in the water. With great presence of mind he called the fire brigade who quickly rushed two pumps on board. It was discovered that with the engine and boiler rooms flooded and over seven feet of water in the saloons, the ship was in imminent danger of sinking. It was not until 4am the following morning that the critical point had been passed, and pumping continued throughout most of Boxing Day. At the time of the accident *Embassy*'s condenser doors had been opened up for maintenance and an open outlet valve, normally above the waterline, had been submerged when the ship listed under the weight of the crowd watching the swim. Water had begun to flow into the ship and after the crowd had deserted her a syphon effect had continued the flooding. The accident caused over £1,000 worth of damage and led to the introduction of a rota of Captains and Chief Engineers to patrol the laid up ships during the winter months.

A Royal occasion opened the 1954 season when *Embassy*'s first sailing on 14 May took her from Bournemouth to Southsea and then to anchor in Spithead to witness the arrival home of the Queen and the Duke of Edinburgh from their long Commonwealth tour on board the new Royal Yacht *Britannia. Consul* and *Monarch* were also there having emerged early from their refits and sailed light to the Solent where they collected their passengers. They then retired to lay up and emerged for the main

season in the usual order with the repaired *Emperor of India* bringing up the rear on 22 June. Regular passengers would have noted that during the winter each of the ships had been fitted with a curious, tall metal bracket extending upwards from the forward end of the funnel. This was a result of a change in regulations which now required the steamers to display two white steaming lights at night, the aftermost being significantly higher than the forward one. Cosens solved the problem by using the funnel brackets as a characteristically economical substitute for costly mainmasts.

On 29 June 1954 *Emperor of India* was in trouble when she threw a paddle float near the Christchurch Ledge buoy at 4.30pm whilst on passage from Bournemouth to Totland and was forced to anchor. *Embassy* was lying at Totland ready to leave at 5.00pm for Bournemouth and Swanage whilst *Emperor of India* had been due to sail for Bournemouth direct at 5.15pm. *Embassy* embarked both groups of passengers and with 600 on board set off to her consort's aid. She moored alongside *Emperor of India*, embarked an additional 250 passengers, and sailed for Bournemouth. Bearing in mind that her certificate was for 622, she looked a remarkable sight as she berthed at the pier at 7pm with over 850 passengers crowding her decks. Her task was not yet over, for the passengers rescued from the *Emperor of India* had been on their way to Totland, so *Embassy* had to retrace her steps to the Island where she arrived at 8.20pm. From there she returned light to Poole. Meanwhile, passengers for Swanage had been transferred to *Monarch* at Bournemouth and *Emperor of India* had limped home to Poole where her damage was repaired overnight.

The pattern of sailings was much as in the previous year, but the season was dogged by exceptionally bad weather. There were 13 blank days and 49 cancelled trips at Bournemouth, 13 blank days at Weymouth and 71 occasions when the steamer could not call at Lulworth. The bad weather slowed the lumbering *Emperor of India* down even further and led to a number of complaints from the inclusive coach tour operators who were very concerned about her habitual failure to arrive back in Bournemouth at the agreed time of 6.30pm The situation threatened to lose vital business for the company and it began to be suggested that she and *Embassy* should exchange rosters. During July it was decided to reduce the weekend fares on the Swanage service to 3s 6d in an attempt to attract custom away from the overcrowded buses which operated between Bournemouth and Swanage. Advertisements were placed in the local press but the experiment was declared a failure and fares returned to 4s 6d before the end of the season.

The only additions to the 1954 programme were the newly revived calls at Cowes, where *Embassy* had to be used because the restricted waters demanded a ship with a bow rudder. No sailings to Cowes had been operated since before the war due to the demolition of the Victoria Pier, but a decision was made towards the end of the 1954 season to experiment with using Fountain Pier. The new service attracted considerable support and negotiations were opened with local coach companies for onward connections to Osborne House during the 1955 season. Towards the end of the season *Embassy* experienced some problems with her bow rudder and switched places with the *Monarch* which even, on one occasion, did a sailing around the Island. The fact that the coal-fired steamer performed so creditably on these occasions said much for the quality of her hard-worked firemen. While berthing at Totland in high winds at 11.30am on 17 September, *Monarch* fouled the pier, broke a stanchion and buckled two gangways. A decision was made to return passengers to Bournemouth by means of the Yarmouth ferry and a special train from Lymington while *Monarch*, her afternoon sailings cancelled, battled her way homeward without passengers.

Overall the season was a dismal one. The steamers often ran practically empty and revenue was over £20,000 down on the previous year. The shipyard at Weymouth completed refits on the *Rafmoor* and Trinity House *Light Vessel No.78*, but was otherwise quiet. An £8,206 deficit for the year on the

EMPRESS's compact oscillating engine. The piston rods connected directly to the cranks on the paddle shaft, the necessary movement being created by the cylinders themselves rocking to and fro. The engineer, invisible to the passengers above, controlled the engine from the large wheel in the centre of the photo, orders from the bridge coming by way of the voice pipe and engineroom telegraph above.
AUTHOR'S COLLECTION / HERBERT

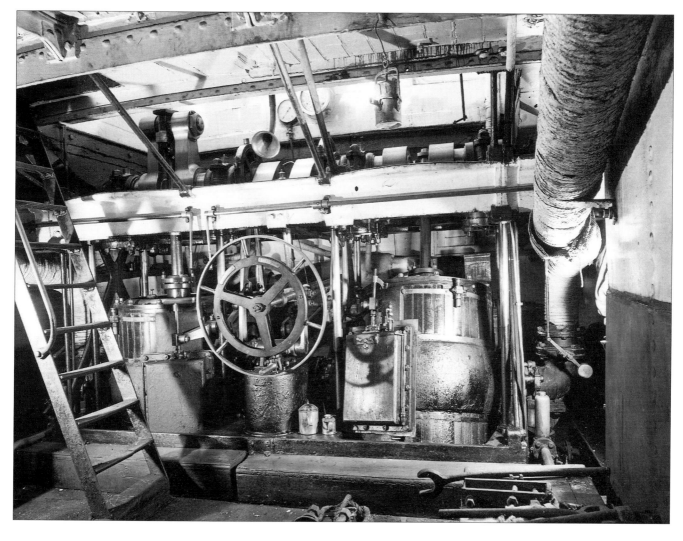

Capt Francis Merryweather,
last master of EMPRESS.
AUTHOR'S COLLECTION /
M. PROWSE

profit and loss account was carried forward and no dividend was declared for 1954.

Thankfully the weather during 1955 proved much kinder and the steamers were once again well-patronised. *Embassy* opened the season at Bournemouth on 23 May and the steamers were deployed as in 1954. The planned coach connection from Cowes to Osborne House did not materialise as the Southern Vectis Bus Company were unable to return passengers to the steamer before 4.30pm, which would have made her unacceptably late arriving back at Bournemouth. Instead, after initial objections from Southern Vectis had been withdrawn, arrangements were made for the Osborne House excursion to be offered by Pink's Coaches in connection with the Totland steamer. Calls at Shanklin were also reintroduced.

Some unease was caused by the fact that Messrs Bolson's motor launches were operating from the pier while their own beach jetty was under construction. It was feared that their presence might lure passengers away from the steamers and suspicions were increased when Bolson's introduced an early season service between Bournemouth and Swanage. Bolson's assured Cosens that they would withdraw the service as soon as the paddlers arrived on station and were true to their word. Passenger figures were monitored very carefully but it was finally decided that, as the smaller motor vessels did not start running until after the morning steamers had departed, there was little to fear.

Just after Whitsun, a strike by railway workers brought the movement of coal to a virtual standstill and led to a shortage of bunkers for the coal-burning *Monarch*. The Swanage service had to be severely curtailed and it was not until 18 June that a full service resumed.

When *Emperor of India* came into service on 21 June, she was put on the longer sailings around the Island, to Southampton Docks and elsewhere in place of *Embassy* except for the weekly trip to Cowes where the latter's bow rudder made her far more suitable. Although transferring *Emperor of India* to the long-distance sailings made sense in terms of her superior facilities and accommodation, it did nothing to reduce her time keeping problems and complaints continued to roll in. On 14 July she missed a day's sailings after her circulating pump broke down. Then, on 19 July she encountered a strong north east wind and an ebb tide in the Solent and fell so far behind schedule that Capt Rawle decided that rather than continue to Southampton Docks he would turn off Fawley and endeavour to arrive back at Bournemouth at the advertised time. His decision infuriated passengers and there were many demands for fares to be refunded. The incident brought discussions about her future to a head and that same evening the Bournemouth manager, Capt Baker, decided to transfer her to the Swanage ferry service from 25 July. *Embassy* reverted to the long distance trips and *Monarch* took her place on the shorter Isle of Wight connections.

Emperor of India with her beautifully appointed saloons was, of course, extremely popular on the Swanage service but the ludicrous situation of the company's largest and most expensive ship maintaining its shortest service was all too apparent. The Board was told that she simply floated too low in the water that a little weight might be saved if she refuelled each day and carried the minimum possible amount of oil in her bunkers. At the same time it was quietly suggested that the company should cut its losses by scrapping her immediately and transferring *Consul* to Bournemouth.

This solution, however, was a step too far for the Board who privately knew that its implementation would result in the complete closure of the Weymouth station. Although no public announcement was made until August, they had already decided that 1955 was to be the veteran *Empress*'s last season and had put her in the hands of a broker. By August an offer of £1,660 had been accepted from the British Iron & Steel Corporation for scrap.

On 2 September, a few days before the end of her season, *Empress* went to the rescue of a small boat which was seen drifting about three miles off Osmington. The boat's engine had broken down, one of her oars had snapped and she was in danger of being swamped when her five occupants managed to attract attention by waving their shirts on the end of the remaining oar. *Empress*, on her way home from Lulworth, took off the frightened family and towed their boat safely back to harbour.

Seven days later on the afternoon of 9 September 1955 *Empress*, under the command of Capt Francis Merryweather, cast off on her last trip to Lulworth, a voyage she had been making with remarkable regularity for the past 76 years. The afternoon was distinctly blustery but the sun broke through the clouds as she made her final departure under the watchful eye of a small group of local well-wishers, numerous journalists and a BBC outside broadcast crew. Upon her return she slipped alongside with a minimum of fuss, disembarked her 71 passengers and paddled quietly up harbour to her customary berth at Trinity Quay to destore and await final orders.

These came a few days later when the old ship slipped quietly out of Weymouth under her own steam, bound for Pollock Brown's scrapyard at Northam, Southampton, where she berthed beside her erstwhile rival, the Southampton Company's *Bournemouth Queen*. Happily, several members of the public suggested that *Empress*'s fascinating oscillating engines - the last of their type afloat in a British ship - should be preserved and the enlightened shipbreaker agreed to donate them to the Southampton Museum Service. When the city's new maritime museum opened in the Old Wool House some years later, the engines took pride of place and may be seen there to this day.

Capt Merryweather was less fortunate. With only nine years service in *Empress* he was a relative newcomer to the company and, having no replacement ship to go to, was forced to leave Cosens' employment immediately after her last passenger sailing, leaving Capt Rawle to deliver her to the breakers.

Another employee to leave at the end of the season was the Bournemouth manager, Commander Baker, who departed amidst rumours that he had become involved with a company who intended to run a rival ship, the motor vessel *Rochester Queen*, at

Bournemouth during 1956. He was replaced by Lt Commander T. Johnson, DSC, RN (retired) who took up his post on 1 January 1956.

Emperor of India finished her season on 1 September and retired to Weymouth to await developments. These were not long in coming. During October a Mr Barnaby, Thornycroft's chief naval architect and a board member of the parent company, was called in and by early December a large model of the ship had been constructed and tank tests carried out at Thornycrofts in Southampton. These confirmed Chief Engineer Alf Pover's long-held belief that some structural alterations to the sponson and paddle box supports would result in a significant increase in speed. Thornycrofts quoted for the work which was carried out, together with strengthening of the boiler, when the ship went to Southampton for her dry docking and load line survey during April 1956. The heavy box beams supporting the sponsons aft of the paddle wheels were cut away and replaced by lighter struts known as palm stays together with internal bracing inside the sponson houses above the sponsons. This was intended to improve the flow of water past the wheels and prevent choking of the paddle boxes. When *Emperor of India* returned to Weymouth at the beginning of May she made the passage in a very satisfactory $4\frac{1}{2}$ hours and everyone concerned expressed their optimism that the alterations had proved a complete success.

The winter of 1955-6 was a very good one for the works department which was operating at full capacity from October onwards. Most significantly, Cosens signed a five year contract with British Rail for

A company postcard of EMPEROR OF INDIA *in 1956 showing how low she sat in the water. The light bracket on the funnel was fitted and the landing platforms on her paddle boxes removed during the winter of 1953-4.*
AUTHOR'S COLLECTION

the refits of their four Weymouth-Channel Islands vessels, the cargo ships *Roebuck* and *Sambur* and the passenger steamers *St Helier* and *St Julien*. *Roebuck* was completed on a trial basis during the autumn before the contract was confirmed, but in subsequent years a clear pattern developed with one passenger and one cargo ship completed before Christmas and the other pair in the new year.

The ships under refit were always laid up in The Cove at Weymouth where they towered impressively above the quayside cottages. The whole workforce, including the engineers from the paddlers and extra hands taken on for the purpose, turned out to complete the task and specialisms soon developed. Work on the steam turbines of the passenger steamers was regarded as particularly delicate and was always carried out by the same small teams of staff.

The BR contract provided the stability and regular income which the works department had lacked for some years and was supplemented by a variety of other work. During the winter of 1955 refits of an inshore minesweeper, the RAF vessel *Rafmoor* and *MFV 1528* were carried out, which contributed towards an overall trading surplus for the year of £4,844. Although insufficient to eliminate the large accumulated deficit it did give some slight feeling of optimism and a 5% dividend was declared.

With *Empress* scrapped, 1956 found *Consul* alone at Weymouth, while the other three ships reverted to their pre-1955 arrangements at Bournemouth. Various economies and improvements were attempted, the most significant being the decision to

abandon the use of the oil barge *Brownsea* in Poole Harbour and bunker from road tankers instead. The contract was let to British American Petroleum of Southampton and, after every last drop of oil had been removed from her tanks, *Brownsea* was sold in July 1956 for £3,250.

The new Bournemouth manager, Commander Johnson, introduced experimental weekly tickets between Swanage, Bournemouth and the Isle of Wight and cut the mid season afternoon and showboat fares. A man was engaged to tout at the pier entrance and every effort was made to obtain more bookings from coach companies. On board the ships the crews were once again issued with uniform BUFF FUNNEL STEAMERS jerseys and the new catering manager, Mr Milton, attempted to improve the tone by insisting that all his staff wore white stewards' jackets and did not smoke on duty. It was also decided to stop running the motorboats from Weymouth beach at the end of the season.

The company Chairman, Mr Redman, stepped down in May having been appointed as chairman of the parent company. He was replaced by his vice Chairman, Mr Thatcher, one of whose first tasks was to host a reception on board *Emperor of India* during her inaugural afternoon trip to the Island on Tuesday 19 June. The full board was present, together with the Mayor of Bournemouth and invited members of the corporation. Mr Brookes and the consultant, Mr Barnaby, went along to monitor the ship's performance, and everyone present declared themselves delighted with her increased speed. Indeed,

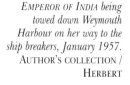

EMPEROR OF INDIA being towed down Weymouth Harbour on her way to the ship breakers, January 1957. AUTHOR'S COLLECTION / HERBERT

she was now so much more powerful ahead than astern that Capt Rawle nearly caused himself severe embarrassment when coming alongside Bournemouth Pier at the end of the trip. He rang down 'full astern' at his long-accustomed moment, but the ship carried her way past the landing stage and very nearly grounded on the beach. At long last it appeared that the old ship might be able to keep to her schedules.

Sadly, however, other circumstances conspired to ensure that the 1956 season was a disaster. The whole summer was plagued by bad weather and from mid season onwards the shadow of the developing Suez crisis led to a sharp decline in passenger numbers and a steady increase in fuel prices.

On 28 August *Monarch*, commanded by Capt Harry Defrates, went to the assistance of a small sailing dinghy which was in difficulties off Old Harry rocks. The two occupants were rescued and the dinghy was lifted on board *Monarch* to be landed at Poole Quay later that evening.

Although *Emperor of India*'s alterations had certainly improved her speed, her troubles were far from over. Through the peak season she suffered a series of breakdowns, mostly associated with her boiler that many claimed had been 'strained' by so many years of over-exertion. One night during August she was caught at anchor in Poole Harbour by a violent gale which gave her a severe buffeting and caused her to drag. One of Harry Roses's tugs had to be called to her assistance and an unwelcome salvage claim followed. Whether it was due to damage sustained during this incident or due to a weakness introduced by the new sponson supports is unclear, but shortly afterwards she suffered another breakdown due to sponson beam defects.

Circumstances were so adverse that the season was brought to an premature close with *Emperor of India* making her last sailing on 7 September 1956, followed by *Monarch* and *Consul* on 21 September and *Embassy* seven days later. An immediate decision was made to operate only two steamers from Bournemouth during 1957, and Mr Brookes was asked for his opinion on which should be disposed of. He prepared careful estimates of scrap values, depreciation, running costs and book values for each vessel, all of which pointed to the *Emperor of India*. She was by far the most expensive to operate, ran for the shortest season, and her lack of a bow rudder meant that she incurred an additional charge for a tug each time she departed from Poole Quay. She still sat too low in the water and her boiler was constantly giving trouble. It was estimated that £1,500 worth of repairs would have to be carried out before the boiler could pass its next Board of Trade survey. The old steamer's fate was sealed, and she was placed in the hands of a broker during December.

When the draft revenue accounts were circulated to the directors in January 1957 the true extent of the crisis became apparent. Although both the works and cold store departments had turned a reasonable profit, the marine department had made a loss of

Capt A. R. 'Pony' Moore (1894-1960) on the bridge of CONSUL shortly before his retirement. Born at Rochester, he went to sea in sail at the age of 14 and served deep sea before returning home in 1926 to take command of the Medway Steam Packet. Co's paddle steamer AUDREY. He moved to Weymouth in 1930, married Cosens stewardess Rose Brookes, and subsequently commanded PREMIER, CONSUL, EMPRESS and EMBASSY, finishing his career in CONSUL from 1952 to 1956.
KEN MOORE

£17,220, resulting in an overall net loss for the company of £3,899. This could not be allowed to continue and on 29 January the Board met to discuss whether to maintain the steamer services at Weymouth and Bournemouth or to cut their losses and close the marine department immediately.

A lively discussion ensued. Mr Payne expressed the view that the company, having already met with Bournemouth Corporation, was morally committed to offering a service during 1957 and felt that, given reasonable weather, there was a good chance of making a profit with two ships. Messrs Thatcher and Redman, acutely aware of their responsibilities to the shareholders of the parent company, argued that it would be unacceptable to keep trading unless detailed analysis suggested that a profit could be made. Mr Kaile felt that the time had come to sell the steamers.

In the end the decision was deferred to a special board meeting on 18 February. In the meanwhile Mr Kaile was asked to prepare a detailed breakdown of daily steamer earnings, passenger figures and weather conditions for July and August 1955 and 1956 and Mr Brookes was instructed to delay any expenditure on refits.

While all this was happening P & A Campbell Ltd, who had finally withdrawn their south coast steamer operations from Brighton at the end of the 1956 season, offered their steamer *Glen Usk* on charter to Cosens. A more inappropriate piece of timing is hard to imagine, and the offer was politely declined.

During the same week Capt 'Pony' Moore, a long-serving employee of the company, retired. Faced with a shrinking fleet and dwindling chances of employment it was a good moment to go. He was

THE PIER, SWANAGE

K 9344

The Swanage Service: A large crowd awaits MONARCH as she sweeps into Swanage Pier.
AUTHOR'S COLLECTION

given a lump sum of £28 - £1 for each year of service - and was sold the motorboat *Sapphire* at a reduced price of £100. With Cosens no longer operating from the beach he saw a gap in the market and began operating *Sapphire* from Weymouth Pleasure Pier.

The board met, as arranged, on 18 February. Having considered all the available evidence it was unanimously decided to continue to run excursion sailings during 1957, but on a greatly reduced basis. The season would be significantly shorter with *Monarch* beginning at Bournemouth and *Consul* at Weymouth on 9 June, followed by *Embassy* at Bournemouth on 1 July. All the services were

First officer Arthur Drage and a seaman on watch in MONARCH's wheelhouse
AUTHOR'S COLLECTION

scheduled to finish at the end of the first week in September. Fares were increased on all but the Swanage service to take account of rising fuel prices and Bournemouth Corporation co-operated by reducing the pier tolls and providing a ticket booth, rent free, at the pier entrance. It was earnestly hoped that, by concentrating the available passengers on two instead of three ships, a profit could be made in 1957.

Two other factors influenced Cosens' decision to carry on. The first was the quick sale of *Emperor of India* in early January to Belgian shipbreakers at the remarkably high price of £15,750. Only two months earlier her scrap value had been estimated at £4,000, but the Suez Crisis had led to a severe shortage of scrap tonnage and caused a meteoric rise in prices. This timely windfall was boosted further by the second factor in the form of the company auditor's agreement to write off a further £14,257 as exceptional depreciation. Added to ordinary depreciation these two sums enabled the debit the on profit and loss account to be wiped off and put the company - on paper at least - in a far healthier position. The parent company, however, made it clear that there would be no stay of execution at the end of the season if further losses were made on the steamer services. 1957 could easily have been the end of the story.

A large crowd turned out to watch *Emperor of India* pass stern first through Weymouth Town Bridge for the last time on a cold and gloomy January day. After turning in the harbour she was moored at the Pleasure Pier from where she departed on 24 January

Down below, the engine room was always an attraction. MONARCH's engine can be distinguished from EMBASSY's by the fact that MONARCH's inclinometer was fixed to the engine entablature, whilst EMBASSY's was on the bulkhead beneath the maker's plate.
B. JACKSON COLLECTION

in tow of the tug *Bulldog* bound for Van Heyghen Freres' breakers yard at Ghent. Subsequently rumours began to circulate that her hull had survived the breaker's hammer and had been seen in use as a dumb barge on the European waterways. Despite numerous enquiries, however, this story has never been confirmed and it seems probable that *Emperor of India*, the ship that never was quite right, was reduced to scrap in the spring of 1957.

During the winter, both *Embassy* and *Consul* had their large, post-war deckhouses removed. The reason for this appears to be a combination of two factors. Firstly, especially in *Embassy*, there was little room between the lifeboats and the corner of the deckhouse, which caused severe congestion when crowds of passengers were attempting to disembark at piers. Secondly, the deckhouses significantly increased windage and may have made the handling of the shallow-drafted paddlers even more difficult at piers. Whatever the reason, the deckhouses were lifted off the ships and dumped on the quayside outside the engineering works on Commercial Road where, until they eventually disintegrated, they were used as rather distinguished garages.

With only two steamers at Bournemouth the 1957 timetables were, of necessity, very different to the past. During the early season *Monarch* alternated between Isle of Wight and Swanage sailings but as soon as *Embassy* joined her on 1 July reverted full time to the Swanage service. *Embassy* offered a mixture of her own and *Emperor of India*'s old rosters, and a fair variety of sailings was still on offer. In addition to the regular service to the Island there was generally one sailing to Southampton Docks each week calling at Totland Bay and, on alternate weeks, at Cowes as well. There was also a Round the Island sailing each

week calling at Totland in both directions and touching at Shanklin on alternate weeks.

At Weymouth, *Consul* maintained her usual cruises to Lulworth Cove, the Shambles Lightship, or Portland Bill and Harbour, and went to Swanage and Bournemouth twice a week. While she was there she would either put in a crossing or two on the Swanage ferry, or offer an afternoon cruise from Swanage to Lulworth Cove.

The weather in June was excellent but deteriorated steadily through the peak season.

MONARCH's lounge bar
PSPS ARCHIVE

Back at Swanage once again, MONARCH *makes her approach to the pier.* AUTHOR'S COLLECTION

Taken from the top of Weymouth's gasometer in about 1957, this view reveals detail of Cosens' engineering works. Moored at the quay are the RAF vessel SALMOOR, under repair by Cosens with the launches PEARL and RUBY moored alongside and EMBASSY with LAUREL LEAF and another launch alongside. On the quayside between the two ships are the deckhouses removed from the EMBASSY and CONSUL during the winter of 1956-7. Above SALMOOR the buildings are, from left to right: part of the carpenters' shop, the boilermakers' shop and the black-painted main office with its brick chimney stack. Behind the office is the roof of the cold store. The building with the sign writing is the fitting shop with the lean-to former blacksmiths' shop, later used as a machine shop, built into the angle with the office.
CAMERA CORNER

Notwithstanding this disappointment the steamers carried reasonable loads and every effort was made to exploit new markets. *Embassy* took over the evening Showboat Cruises in August, with timings changed to leave Bournemouth at 8.00pm and return at 10.30pm but, with her more limited accommodation, she was never as well-suited to the role as *Emperor of India*. Interchangability of tickets was agreed with the Hants & Dorset Bus Co to and from Swanage, and the new pier booking- kiosk proved a definite benefit.

There were of course one or two setbacks. *Embassy*'s fan engine failed and *Monarch* fractured a paddle float during August. Concern was felt about British Railway's introduction of combined rail and ferry excursions from Bournemouth to the Island and Bolson's motor launches once again appeared on the Swanage service, skimming off a percentage of Cosens' customers in the process.

Monarch finished on 12 September 1957 with *Embassy* and *Consul* due to follow a week later. In the event *Embassy* did not complete her last week due to the poor weather and *Consul* was withdrawn two days earlier than planned, on 17 September, due to naval manoeuvres in Weymouth Bay. When the accounts were finalised it was confirmed that, despite the poor weather, the steamers had managed to make a small profit and that the service would therefore be continued into 1958. Everyone concerned breathed a collective sigh of relief.

During the winter it was announced that the parent company intended to withdraw *Princess Elizabeth* from service at the end of the 1958 season. She was in excellent condition and Cosens discussed the possibility of buying her to replace the older and more expensive, coal-fired *Monarch* at Bournemouth.

It will remain a mystery why they did not do so. It is probable that the Board of Trade regulations applying to an elderly vessel on change of ownership would have resulted in expensive repairs and alterations being demanded, but these could have been avoided by transferring the ship from one company to the other on long-term charter. Equally,

Capt. Harry Defrates on the bridge of Monarch in June1960. He joined the company after the war, initially serving as mate in the first MONARCH. In 1951 he took command of VICTORIA before moving to CONSUL (1952), MONARCH (1954-6), CONSUL (1957-9) and MONARCH (1960).
J. MEGORAN COLLECTION

30p

Paddle Steamer "Embassy"

COSENS & CO., LTD.,   Tel: Bournemouth 24021

COMMENCING SUNDAY AUGUST 12th, 1962

JAZZ and TWIST BOAT

EVERY SUNDAY 7.30 - 12.0
Bournemouth Pier   Sailing 8.15 p.m.

with

THE PINE CITY STOMPERS

the fabulous

SANDS BEAT COMBO

the accordians of

CHRIS AND CHARLIE

GUEST STARS

A Starlight cruise for young and old along the spectacular
Dorset coastline with continuous Bar and Buffet

TICKETS 10/-   STEAMER OFFICE, PIER APPROACH
                                BOURNEMOUTH 24021

Late transport arranged by Hants & Dorset

WAVERLEY PRESS (BOURNEMOUTH) LTD., Lincoln Avenue, Bournemouth

Showboat sailing bill
AUTHOR'S COLLECTION

the alleged loss of her Class 3 passenger certificate in 1952 may have mitigated against her use outside the Solent. Whatever the reason, the suggestion must have been financially unattractive to one or other company and no more was heard of it. At the same time Bolsons expressed an interest in selling their passenger business at Bournemouth but Cosens declined the offer.

The arrangements for the start of the 1958 season were almost unaltered from 1957. *Embassy* began on Whit Sunday 25 May, was joined by *Monarch* on 1 July and the two ships settled into their familiar routine. New developments included the introduction of a 'Dorset Tour' in co-operation with the Southern National Bus Company. Bournemouth passengers travelled by steamer to Swanage where they joined their coach for the tour, and the arrangement proved extremely popular. The number of late evening cruises was increased and Commander Johnson negotiated with the railway to allow passengers the option of travelling outwards by steamer via Totland to Yarmouth before returning by ferry to Lymington

and thence to Bournemouth by train. A special cheap non-landing afternoon cruise to Swanage was also introduced, sailing from Bournemouth at 4.15pm and returning from Swanage at 5.00pm

By August, however, financial analysis had revealed that the greatest profits were being made on the shorter runs and *Embassy*'s long distance trips were abandoned in favour of a basic shuttle service between Bournemouth, Totland and Yarmouth. On most Wednesdays *Embassy*'s morning trip to the island was fully booked and it was therefore decided to put on an extra trip departing from Bournemouth at 2.30pm and returning at 7.30pm As a result two ships were needed in the evening to bring back the afternoon passengers together with those who had travelled outwards in the morning and spent the whole day on the island. *Monarch*, after completing four double crossings to Swanage, therefore had to cross to Totland each Wednesday evening to bring home the overflow - no mean task for an elderly, coal-fired steamer. *Embassy* meanwhile would return to Bournemouth in the evening, put in a return sailing to Swanage and then set off on her evening Showboat cruise.

The steamers were kept very busy and performed creditably throughout the season despite another summer of wet and windy weather. The only recorded problem was with *Embassy*'s smoke emissions which frequently reached mammoth proportions. A trail of black smoke marked her passage to and from the island and there were complaints about her unsociable behaviour at both Bournemouth and Poole. Representatives from Todd Oil Burners, the makers of the installation, were called in to advise but only small improvements were achieved. Consideration was given to fitting a Thornycroft patent funnel which, had the plan gone ahead, would have considerably altered her appearance.

The poor weather resulted in a smaller profit being made by the steamers during 1958, but they were still in the black and the service continued more or less unaltered into 1959 which, thankfully, was blessed by exceptionally fine weather. At the beginning of June *Embassy* was still in drydock at Southampton undergoing her load line survey, so it fell to *Monarch* to open the Bournemouth season, followed a few days later by *Consul* at Weymouth. *Embassy* followed on 29 June. For the first time in many years a company guidebook entitled 'The Buff Funnel Book' was produced and sold around the decks of the ships, together with official postcards, by a crew member. *Monarch* was kept exceptionally busy carrying large loads on the Swanage service, and the only significant alteration to the timetable was the replacement of *Consul*'s 2.15pm afternoon cruise from Bournemouth towards the Needles with a shorter trip to Hengistbury Head, returning at 3.45pm.

The weather remained so good into September that *Monarch*'s season was extended by a week and *Embassy*, the last ship to lay up, carried on until 24 September. The season's earnings were up by about

19% which, although superficially pleasing, still disappointed the board. They reasoned that the exceptional weather should have resulted in a massive increase in passenger numbers and that the modest results actually achieved might point to a worrying and fundamental change in the tastes of the modern holiday maker. Although impossible to quantify, it was also suspected that the major construction work being carried out throughout 1958 and 1959 in connection with the new pavilion and theatre buildings on Bournemouth Pier may have contributed to keeping passengers away.

1959 was the last season for the oil barge *Melway* at Weymouth. She was by now in poor condition and it was felt that the difference between the cost of bulk oil and fuel delivered by road tanker was too small to justify her repair. With only *Consul* to be refuelled, use of a road tanker also represented a considerable saving in time and labour, so *Melway* was advertised for sale and towed away to Southampton where she was scrapped.

Another significant departure was that of Capt Philip St. Barbe Rawle, Cosens senior master and Commodore, who had served the company for 34 years. He retired on the day *Monarch* finished for the winter, with Capt Haines replacing him on the bridge of the *Embassy* for the last few days of the season and received a presentation from the board during their December meeting.

The winter of 1959-60 saw all three paddlers undergo their load line surveys. *Consul*, as usual, went onto the company's No 1 slip at Weymouth, but *Embassy* and *Monarch* broke with tradition and went to the Castletown Slipway at Portland Dockyard. This proved to be £700 cheaper than the normal drydock at Southampton, and was repeated for the rest of *Embassy*'s career. The cost of work resulting from the surveys more or less wiped out the increased profit made by the steamers during 1959, but the healthier results from the works and cold store departments allowed a 10% dividend to be declared.

In view of the uncertain future of the marine department, every effort had been made since the 1957 financial crisis to ensure the long-term profitability of the company by boosting the income from the works department. To reflect the increasing importance of engineering work for the company's future Mr Brookes, the Works Manager, was promoted to Assistant General Manager under Mr Kaile and promptly set about seeking new work. An attempt to obtain some sub-contracts from Thornycrofts of Southampton confirmed that Cosens' machine shops were too outdated to cope with such specialist work, and forced the board to agree to a substantial programme of modernisation. Several new machines were installed during the summer of 1957.

Ship repairing was quiet throughout 1957, but suddenly increased in January 1958 when contracts were obtained to construct a number of transducer testing stations for the AUWE and some steel pontoons and tanks to be used by the parent company at Cowes. The latter were constructed on No 2 slipway and led to several repeat orders for Southampton and Cowes. The first pontoon was completed and delivered in May 1959, to be followed by several others during the following twelve months.

In May 1958 a number of BP and Shell oil tankers arrived to lay up at the buoys in Portland Harbour and Cosens obtained the contract to decommission them and then undertake routine repair and maintenance. Similar duties were also carried out for the Stanhope Shipping Company during 1958 and 1959 and for the laid up troopship *Empire Fowey* during 1960. Cosens were appointed agents for the owning companies and the contract provided a useful source of additional income until the last of the tankers finally departed in December 1960. Cosens worked intermittently on the government vessel *Choctaw* which was laid up at Weymouth between January 1957 and June 1959, repainted all the Weymouth Harbour cranes, and undertook a whole variety of shore-based engineering tasks from lift maintenance to repairing the machinery in the local bakery.

One evening in July 1958, the cradle of No 1 slipway jammed solid during the launching of the RAF vessel *Rafmoor* and *Consul* had to be summoned to try to tow her off. Strollers on the harbourside were treated to the unusual sight of the paddler churning furiously away at the end of a tow rope only yards from the quay wall. *Consul*'s efforts were eventually rewarded and, as the cradle was dragged free, she shot forward narrowly avoiding Cosens' launch *Pearl* which was also assisting with the refloating.

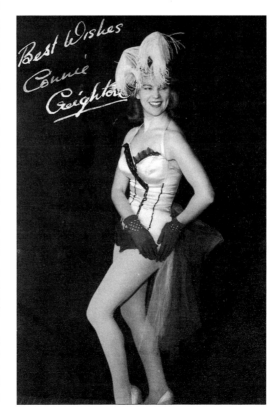

Connie Creighton, one of the regular cabaret artistes who appeared on the Showboat Cruises.
AUTHOR'S COLLECTION.

EMBASSY approaches Bournemouth Pier in August 1960. The removal of her deckhouse in 1957 greatly improved her appearance. B. COX.

The British Rail contract continued to provide the backbone of the works department's income, so serious concern was felt at the news that two new, far larger mail steamers were under construction at Cowes for the Weymouth-Channel Islands service. Would Cosens be able to cope with technical demands of the new ships? Would the all-important contract be renewed? Negotiations proceeded throughout 1959, introducing a sense of uncertainty into the workforce and inducing many valued staff to leave. It was a great relief therefore when a new five year contract was signed in May 1960. The old *St Helier* and *St Julien* departed for the breakers in December 1960 and April 1961 respectively, to be replaced by the smart new mailships *Caesarea* and *Sarnia*.

In January 1960 Cosens discovered that the Clyde paddle steamer *Jupiter* of 1937 was for sale, and considered her as a possible replacement for *Monarch*. On the surface this seems an odd idea for *Jupiter* at 642 tons and 230 ft long was a significantly larger vessel than *Monarch* and not at all what was needed at a time when passenger figures were dwindling. On the other hand she was newer, more modern in appearance, and was oil fired. This latter fact probably weighed most heavily with Cosens, as bunkering *Monarch* with coal at Poole was a dirty and inconvenient business, and was about to become even more expensive with the closure of the Poole Quay railway line. Delivery by lorry would add 2s 6d per ton to coal costs and, in addition, it was proving increasingly difficult to obtain good quality firemen for the ship.

Jupiter's running costs and condition were studied very thoroughly and, in May an offer was made through the brokers. Cosens, however, cannot have been very certain about the wisdom of the purchase, for they made an offer which was even lower than the shipbreaker's, and *Jupiter* was eventually broken up.

Bolsons, now trading under the name Crosons, opened their 1960 season at Easter and appeared to be doing well even with increased fares. Unfortunately, by the time the steamers arrived on station at the beginning of June the weather had begun to deteriorate and was particularly wet and windy during July and September. Fifteen days sailings were lost due to the weather and *Embassy* sustained serious damage to her port paddle box and sponson fender chocks whilst attempting to berth at Totland in poor conditions during July. Things were not helped by the withdrawal, at very short notice, of the booking kiosk at the pier entrance. To compensate, Bournemouth Corporation allowed more advertising placards near the pier, and Cosens placed a large advertising board on board *Monarch* which would be clearly visible when the ship was laying alongside.

The retirement of Capt Rawle led to a reshuffle of the company's masters. Capt E. S.Haines, previously of the *Monarch* replaced Capt Rawle on board *Embassy*. *Consul's* master, Harry Defrates moved to *Monarch* leaving his former chief officer, John Iliffe, to assume command of the Weymouth steamer.

The beginning of July saw a sudden influx of visitors to Bournemouth and for a while it seemed that things were looking up. On 18 June *Monarch* undertook her first long distance excursion for two years when she steamed to Portsmouth to witness the arrival of the Royal Yacht *Britannia* at the end of Princess Margaret's honeymoon cruise. Fog delayed her departure by an hour, but the rest of the day was completed in glorious sunshine.

Showboat cruises with a band on board were scheduled for each Thursday in August at 10s per ticket and during August *Embassy* ran additional trips

A selection of Cosen's tickets from the 1960s. The luggage ticket was a charming survival from the turn of the century when someone at Head Office must have seriously over-estimated the order from the printer. The bottom ticket has four parts, one for each stage of the popular combined steamer and coach tour of the Isle of Wight. AUTHOR'S COLLECTION

Passengers enjoy the sunshine on MONARCH's promenade deck P. MURRELL.

MONARCH's paddle box P. MURRELL

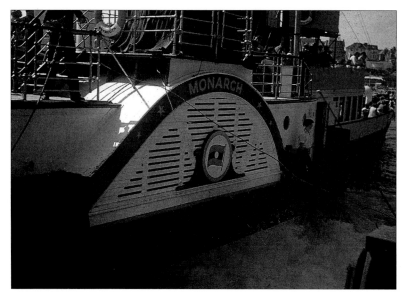

on Tuesday evenings billed as 'The Nightclub at Sea' and featuring cabaret-style entertainment including striptease. *Monarch*, meanwhile, introduced a number of evening cruises from Swanage which proved extremely popular. The Bournemouth season was further enlivened on 5 August when *Monarch* took 400 jazz fans on a 'Riverboat Shuffle' cruise with dancing to the Jerry Brown Jazzmen and on 2 and 3 August when *Embassy* ran special cruises to Cowes Week.

Consul's June and July visits to Bournemouth were restricted to once a week, increasing to twice during August and more Lulworth sailings were billed in their place. All in all 1960 turned out to be a dismal season. Financial analysis revealed a fall of over £15,000 in passenger revenue as compared with the previous year. Bournemouth, especially in July and September, had experienced a particularly dramatic fall. Once again the marine department had made a loss.

During the autumn the board carefully analysed all available statistics and at their December meeting the axe fell. It was announced that in view of the fact:

...the public is no longer pleasure steamer minded and that we cannot bank upon the weather... it would be in the best interests of the company that in future only one steamer, the *P.S. Embassy*, should operate from Bournemouth and the *P.S. Consul* should continue to operate from Weymouth.

Monarch's departure from Bournemouth on 8 September turned out to be her last voyage in steam. She was laid up in her usual berth in Weymouth Backwater until January when she was sold for £5,750. With her windows boarded up and looking a very dismal sight, she was moved from the Backwater on 31 January and moored at the Pleasure Pier. Bad weather prevented her departure and she had to be moved back up harbour to a sheltered berth to await the return of her tug, the *Salvonia*. Eventually, on 1 March, she left Weymouth bound for Passage West, Cork, and demolition in the yard of Haulbowline Industries Ltd.

Opposite:
MONARCH leaving Bournemouth Pier on another trip to Swanage. P. MURRELL

CHAPTER TWELVE

THE WHEEL TURNS FULL CIRCLE

1961 TO 1966

With *Monarch* gone and the fleet reduced to two ships, the company entered its final decade of steamer operation. It was a twilight period during which the decline of Cosens' dominance was paralleled by the emergence of a number of small, short-lived, single-ship companies whose limited capital forced them to experiment and grasp at every opportunity for trade. In a curious echo of the 1850s, stiff competition developed at both Bournemouth and Weymouth and to many it seemed that the wheel of history had, indeed, turned full circle.

It was obvious that *Embassy* alone could not offer the full programme of sailings to both the Isle of Wight and Swanage which had existed during 1960. The solution emerged in the form of an agreement to operate a joint service between Bournemouth and

Consul arriving at Weymouth

Swanage in cooperation with Crosons Ltd, whose small motor vessels would provide the bulk of the sailings whilst *Embassy* concentrated on the Island trade. The arrangement did not meet with universal approval amongst regular travellers, many of whom drew unflattering comparisons between the facilities and sea-keeping qualities of the motor vessels and the larger paddler. However, the agreement did enable both services to be maintained and, with minor variations, set the pattern for the remaining years of Cosen's operations at Bournemouth.

At the request of Bournemouth Corporation (and in return for a further reduction in pier dues) *Embassy* opened the 1961 season a little earlier than usual on Whit Sunday, 21 May. Her programme for the first six weeks saw her visiting Yarmouth or Totland on four days per week, and maintaining the Swanage

service on Tuesdays and Thursdays. Saturdays, as usual, were spent off-service at Poole. Indifferent weather caused several early season cancellations, but by mid-June things had settled down and passenger figures were encouraging.

News of *Monarch*'s disposal and the consequent downgrading of the Swanage service provided the trigger for the season's most significant development. During February it had been discovered that Mr Herbert Jennings' Brighton & South Coast Steamers Ltd, had approached Bournemouth Corporation for permission to operate the paddle steamer *Sussex Queen* between Bournemouth and Swanage for the 1961 season. *Sussex Queen* was the former railway paddler *Freshwater* which between 1927 and 1959 had maintained the Lymington to Yarmouth ferry service across the Solent. She had been sold to Mr Jennings who put her to work running excursions along the Sussex coast in 1960. The season was far from successful and Mr Jennings looked for a more profitable option for 1961.

The Swanage service seemed to provide a golden opportunity. At 152 feet in length *Sussex Queen* was smaller than *Embassy* but significantly larger and more comfortable that Croson's motor vessels and might be ideally suited to win the support of regular travellers and town councillors disgruntled by the loss of the regular steamer service. Her name was changed to *Swanage Queen*.

Cosens, of course, did everything possible to oppose the development. Their lobbying met with only limited success as both Swanage Council and Chamber of Trade gave their blessing to the new venture. It emerged that under their respective Pier Acts neither Bournemouth nor Swanage had the legal right to refuse to accept the newcomer at their piers, but it was possible to influence the timetable. Bournemouth Corporation's compromise position was therefore to leave the traditional, prime departure times in the hands of the Cosens/Croson's partnership whilst allowing *Swanage Queen* to operate the less popular, intermediate sailings.

Swanage Queen was originally intended to enter service on 11 June but this was postponed firstly until 25 June and then to 5 July when she made a short, late-afternoon introductory cruise from Swanage before commencing the regular ferry service on the following morning. Under the command of Capt F. Tasker, formerly of the Elder Dempster Line, and with Mr W. Crook (formerly of *Embassy*) as purser, she was advertised as 'The Blue Funnel Steamer'. Her sailing bills were a model of simplicity and clarity and forced a long-overdue improvement in the quality and quantity of Cosens' own advertising.

By the end of July *Embassy*'s appearances on the Swanage service had been reduced to Fridays only together with occasional evening calls. *Swanage Queen* cashed in on the consequent absence of sailings to the Isle of Wight by offering her own Friday day trip to Yarmouth. She departed later and returned earlier than the traditional Cosens timings and charged 12s 6d as compared with Cosens' 16s 0d. The fact that

these sailings attracted very substantial patronage did not escape the notice of Cosens who incorporated similar Friday excursions into their programmes in succeeding years.

1961 was *Embassy*'s Golden Jubilee season and with Capt E. S. Haines in command and Chief Engineer Alf Pover in the engineroom, the ship seemed to perform better than for many years. Mr Pover, who had previously earned a well-deserved reputation for *Monarch*'s immaculate and reliable engineroom, had transferred to *Embassy* at the start of the season and quickly set about achieving a similar transformation. From the level of the alleyway rails downwards the engineroom was 'scumbled' or painted and combed to give the effect of light, grained woodwork. Above this all was sparkling white. The engine frames were painted bright green, lined in yellow with detail picked out in scarlet. The large quantities of brasswork were kept polished to a mirror finish and, with the engineroom bathed in sunlight from the large skylight above, the whole effect was stunning. Mr Pover's influence was not simply cosmetic, for he quickly managed to eliminate

Passengers on board CONSUL *show great interest in an anchored warship during a Portland Harbour cruise, May 1961*
P. MURRELL

much of the troublesome smoke for which *Embassy* was renowned and achieved a consistent increase in speed.

On 26 May *Embassy* rescued two yachtsmen from their dismasted and waterlogged sailing dinghy in Poole Harbour. A month later she began a series of Tuesday night 'Showboat' evening cruises from Swanage together with a number of late night jazz cruises, but neither were particularly well supported. Her longest trips of the season took place on 1 and 2 August when she ran two extremely well-patronised sailings to Cowes for the regatta. On 27 August her 50th birthday was celebrated in style when members of the Paddle Steamer Preservation Society transformed a regular service run to Totland Bay into a Golden Jubilee Champagne Cruise. Speeches were made, toasts were drunk, and Capt Haines cut a magnificent cake encircled by a ribbon in Cosens' house colours and decorated with a model of the ship together with the dates 1911-61.

Consul meanwhile had spent nine weeks on the slipway at Weymouth having her entire port sponson renewed before entering service at Whitsun on an hourly shuttle service between Weymouth and Castletown Jetty at Portland in connection with Portland Navy Days. This service, which was faster than the bus, avoided parking problems and gave steamer ticket holders priority entry to the Dockyard, proved even more popular than usual. The old, wooden steamer pier on the western side of the jetty had fallen into disrepair some years before, and the steamer now berthed alongside the northern face of the stone jetty. *Consul* remained in service until 25 May when she was withdrawn until the main season began on 6 June.

Under the command of Capt Hollyoak, *Consul*'s

schedule was very much as before with short trips around Portland Harbour, morning and afternoon trips to Lulworth, Portland Bill and the Shambles Lightship, and evening cruises in the Bay. On Tuesdays and Thursdays she went to Swanage and Bournemouth, putting in an afternoon crossing on the Swanage ferry while her passengers enjoyed time ashore at Bournemouth.

The evening of 1 September saw both *Swanage Queen* and *Embassy* in difficulties with thick fog. *Swanage Queen* was returning from a day trip to Yarmouth, had called at Bournemouth and was *en route* to Swanage when she ran into a dense bank of fog. Her master, Capt George Carpenter, decided to drop anchor in deep water and wait for the weather to clear before proceeding. Some of the ninety passengers on board were critical of his decision, but there was nothing more to be done and the passengers settled down to make the best of the long night ahead. It was not until early next morning that the fog cleared sufficiently for *Swanage Queen* to creep into Swanage where she finally landed her weary cargo at 10.30am after 25 hours at sea.

Embassy meanwhile had completed her afternoon sailings, but cancelled her 6pm trip to Poole via Swanage and remained alongside Bournemouth Pier. At 9pm the fog lifted slightly and *Embassy* set off for Poole, but only got as far as the Bar Buoy at the entrance of Poole Harbour when she was forced to anchor again. As there were no passengers on board and the next day was 'off service' only her crew were inconvenienced and she remained at anchor until next morning.

CONSUL arrives at Weymouth Pleasure Pier, September 1961.
P. MURRELL

CONSUL's starboard paddle wheel, showing the feathering gear and the timber paddle floats. B. COX

The season closed at Weymouth on 14 September and at Bournemouth on Thursday 21 September with a single trip to Poole. *Embassy* returned to Weymouth next morning to lay up for the winter. Analysis of the season revealed that, due to her late start and unpopular sailing times, the competition

Down below, Chief Engineer Cyril Julian (right) and greaser 'Curly' Yates work on the main engine of the CONSUL. The bottom end bearings have been removed and are propped against the engine room bulkhead, while the two men work on the main bearing. B. COX

from *Swanage Queen* had had remarkably little effect on the Bournemouth station and that Cosens' steamer operations had broken even. Sadly, however, the works department made its first serious loss in many years due to an unfortunate hiccup in the arrangements for the British Transport Commission repair contract. Although the contract had been renewed for five years from May 1960 the timing of the departure of the old mailships *St Helier* and *St Julian* and the arrival of their brand new replacements *Caesarea* and *Sarnia* had meant that there were no passenger ships to refit during the winter of 1960-1. Despite the income of £2,462 obtained from the sale of the *Monarch*, this resulted in the company making a net loss of £3,794 for the year ending March 1961.

Both Cosens and the parent company had anticipated the loss and had, for some time, been seeking ways of extending their engineering trade into new areas. In May 1961 the parent company agreed to finance the reorganisation and re-equipping of the engineering shops and the conversion of the old joiner's shop into a precision machining shop capable of producing moulds and components for Government departments such as the AUWE.

Further contracts were obtained to build floating pontoons for Southampton Harbour Board and for use by the parent company at Cowes. Some difficulty was experienced when the land where the pontoons were constructed immediately outside the Backwater engineering works was reclaimed by the British Transport Commission. Frantic efforts were made to find a replacement building area and finally an agreement was reached to use the area between the two sets of railway lines in front of the works.

The British Transport Commission was lobbied hard throughout throughout the spring of 1962 with Cosens pointing out that if the Weymouth maintenance and repair facility was to survive, then BTC must find a way of sending more work in their direction. These efforts bore fruit in April when BTC agreed to send one or two extra ships to Cosens during the coming winter and to consider handing the day-to-day maintenance of the Weymouth cross channel fleet over to the company.

Although there was public talk of *Swanage Queen* returning to run again in 1962 it soon became clear that there were serious problems. At a creditors' meeting of Brighton & South Coast Steamers Ltd on 13 March 1962, Mr Jennings described a catalogue of disasters which had taken place during the previous season, even claiming 'sabotage in some form' on at least eighteen different occasions. Whatever the case, the company had made a loss of £6,629 during 1961 at Bournemouth. The ship was sold to Mr Townsend of Sandbanks and the company placed into liquidation. *Swanage Queen* did not re-enter service in 1962 but was sold again to Belgian shipbreakers.

While the events of 1960 and 1961 were unfolding in Dorset, other developments were taking place at Torquay which were to have considerable

effects on Cosens during 1962. When the parent company's last paddle steamer *Princess Elizabeth* was finally withdrawn and offered for sale it was widely assumed that she would go to the breaker's yard. To everyone's surprise, however, she was quickly purchased by Torbay Steamers Ltd and began running excursions from Torquay's Haldon Pier in May 1960. Her sailings to the River Dart, Exmouth, Sidmouth, Lyme Regis, Plymouth and Salcombe continued through the 1961 season until a legal dispute with Torquay Council forced the ship to beat a premature retreat to lay up in Weymouth Backwater.

Cosens immediately offered to undertake any refit work and sat back to watch developments with interest. The contract of sale to Torbay Steamers Ltd specified that the *Princess Elizabeth* was not allowed to run in opposition to the Southampton Company or Cosens, so there seemed little to be concerned about. Events in the Spring of 1962 were to prove otherwise.

During the winter of 1961-2 the parent company withdrew their pioneer motorship *Medina* from service and offered her to Cosens for use on the Swanage service or as a replacement for *Consul*. *Medina* was well known to Cosens, having received her annual refit at their yard since the late 1950s, but the offer was rejected, due to her unsuitability.

In April 1962 Cosens vacated their historic Head Office at 10 Custom House Quay and placed it on the market. Henceforth all of the company's activities would be conducted from the engineering works address at 50 Commercial Road, Weymouth.

Before going on to the slipway for routine overhaul and renewal of her starboard sponson, *Consul* received some major attention to her bridge structure. Famously, one day during the previous

season, the decking of the bridge wing had actually given way under Capt Hollyoak, leaving him suspended in a highly undignified position with his legs waving about in full view of the passengers on the deck below. The decking and the woodwork of the port wing were completely replaced and to disguise the new timber the front of her bridge was painted white. Although nobody knew it at the time, this was to be the last occasion on which a paddle steamer was ever slipped at Weymouth. During April *Embassy* went, as usual, to Castletown Slipway at Portland for slipping and load line survey.

Throughout the spring rumours were rife about the future employment of *Princess Elizabeth*. In view of the dispute with Torquay Council it seemed certain that she would not return to Devon, and this was confirmed when her owners announced that she would operate from Brighton on Sussex Coast cruises. Considerable coverage of the venture appeared in the Sussex and national press and during the third week in June the ship left her lay up berth at Weymouth and steamed to White's yard at Southampton for slipping and overhaul. Then, at the last moment, it was announced that the her ownership had been transferred to a new company, Coastal Steamers & Marine Services Ltd. This was in fact Torbay Steamers Ltd reconstituted under a new name, but the 'sale' allowed the company to circumvent the conditions of the contract of sale from the Southampton Company, and run in direct opposition to Cosens.

The transfer completed, Commander Rhodes announced that *Princess Elizabeth* would be taking advantage of the gap left by the demise of the *Swanage Queen* and operating on the Bournemouth-Swanage ferry. She entered service on 15 July, offering five

CONSUL departing from Castletown Jetty, Portland, during Navy Days, 1961. P. MURRELL

151

Engineer Brian Jackson on CONSUL'S *control platform The ship's engine room was so compact that the steam gauges were mounted on the forward bulkhead rather than above the control platform as was usual in the larger steamers.*

B. JACKSON COLLECTION

sailings daily in each direction, together with Wednesday evening cruises from Bournemouth. Still under the command of Harry Defrates, the ship was well turned out and reliable, and many older residents who remembered her from her period on the Swanage service during the 1930s and 1940s were delighted to see her back.

Embassy arrived on station on 3 June under the command of Capt Hollyoak and for the first two weeks operated a reduced service with off-service days on Fridays and Saturdays. Initially she operated to Swanage on Sundays and Tuesdays but after 15 July concentrated on the Isle of Wight run on six days a week. The company adopted *Swanage Queen*'s 12s 6d cut price Friday trips to Totland, and *Embassy* was regularly filled to capacity. A welcome innovation was the introduction of an onward cruise from Totland through the Solent to Cowes, giving passengers an hour and a half ashore. On one occasion over 300 passengers had to be turned away at Bournemouth and as a result the popular Friday excursion was offered on Mondays as well during September.

At Weymouth, *Consul* operated on a reduced certificate and, for the first time in many years, no longer went to Bournemouth or Swanage. Her only scheduled visit was to have been a charter sailing on 20 June but that was cancelled due to poor weather conditions. Restricted to Weymouth Bay, she was now able to offer a programme of local morning and afternoon cruises on six days a week. On two days a week she would go twice to Lulworth, offering the passengers the option of either a half or full day ashore. On the remaining days she offered either a morning cruise (Sundays excepted) around Portland Harbour or a Coffee Cruise in the Bay. 2pm each day saw her depart on the popular 4s one hour cruise around Portland Harbour to view the warships and laid up merchant shipping before setting off again at 3pm on her afternoon trips. These would take her

either on a long circuit of the Bay and Portland harbour; to Portland Bill or the Shambles Lightship. The latter was always a fascinating trip with a unique element of excitement. On the outward leg a member of the crew would tour the decks collecting newspapers, magazines and other gifts from the passengers. On arrival the steamer would lay as close to the lightship as the weather conditions permitted and a heaving line was thrown. A bucket was then attached and the gifts hauled across to the lightship's crew who would frequently respond by sending back a bucket full of fresh fish.

The season suffered from persistent poor weather with many days of fresh to gale force south west winds which caused cancellations and missed piers. Bournemouth was particularly exposed and on several occasions *Embassy* was forced to return direct to Poole from the Isle of Wight with her passengers transferring to Bournemouth by bus. On 3 and 23 August the weather was so severe that the homeward sailing had to be abandoned altogether and passengers returned by ferry and train. At Weymouth *Consul* fared somewhat better, but a large number of her landing trips to Lulworth had to be converted into sea cruises when heavy seas made the narrow entrance to the Cove far too dangerous to attempt.

Fortunately for Cosens *Princess Elizabeth*'s short season combined with poor weather and the unpopular sailing times inherited from *Swanage Queen* meant that she had little impact on the joint Cosens/Crosons trade. This was as well since, by the time *Consul* finished on 13 September and *Embassy* on 21 September, the financial situation was already dire. On 17 December a meeting of the board confirmed that there had been little improvement in the performance of the works department and that the marine department was very far from healthy. The Chairman, Mr Thatcher, expressed his extreme irritation that the individual ship's accounts had not been made available in recent years making detailed analysis difficult. He had sent a team from the parent company to look into the matter and their findings revealed that *Consul* had, in fact, been making a loss for the past three seasons. In view of this, combined with her heavy maintenance costs in recent years, the fact that she was due for a load line survey during the coming winter, and that there was little realistic hope that the Weymouth passenger figures would improve in the foreseeable future, an immediate decision was made to withdraw *Consul* from service.

The news of this bitter blow was announced to the public by the *Dorset Evening Echo* on 30 January 1963 at a time when, ironically, Weymouth Harbour had been playing host to the widest variety of paddle steamers for many years. Cosens's lobbying of the British Transport Commission had born fruit in the form of the large Portsmouth-Isle of Wight ferry steamer *Sandown* which had arrived for overhaul on 15 October. A month later, on 13 November, she was followed by P & A Campbell Ltd's flagship, the magnificent *Bristol Queen*. For a few days, therefore, four paddle steamers belonging to three different

With the Needles ahead, EMBASSY heads towards the Isle of Wight from Bournemouth. Note the wheel for the bow rudder. The anchor davit was more or less redundant as, unlike the rest of the fleet, EMBASSY carried her anchor permanently stowed in her port hawsepipe. This was positioned close to the waterline and when the ship was pitching in a head sea, a jet of water would frequently erupt from the hawsepipe to soak unsuspecting passengers.
A. E. BENNETT

EMBASSY going astern from Swanage Pier, with Ballard Down and Old Harry Rocks in the background.
K.ABRAHAM

PRINCESS ELIZABETH at Weymouth, 4 August, 1964
A. E. BENNETT

companies lay together in Weymouth.

Bristol Queen remained in the Backwater until April undergoing a substantial mechanical overhaul, together with the fitting of new inner funnels, sponson repairs and some redecking. Much was made in the local press of the size and splendour of the Bristol steamer, as well as the fact that Cosens was one of the few firms still capable of undertaking such specialised work. Added to their regular contract work on the Channel Islands cargo steamers *Roebuck* and *Sambur*, a spring refit of the parent company's *Vecta* and preparation of *Embassy* for the new season, the two visiting paddlers ensured that the engineering works was kept fully employed for the first time in several winters.

For some years the company's No1 slipway had been in poor condition and it was known that satisfactory repairs would involve the construction of a cofferdam and the expenditure of about £25,000. In view of the fact that *Consul* was their only ship small enough to use the slipway, and that demand for commercial slippings had fallen steeply, Cosens decided that it would better to cut their losses and attempt to sell both slipway sites.

In October 1962 an offer of £15,000 was received from Burness & Co, the promoters of a plan to operate a car ferry service between Weymouth and the Continent. The No 1 slip was to become the main ferry link-span while No 2 slip would provide the

marshalling area. Quite how the scheme would have worked without demolishing most of Weymouth's picturesque, Georgian harbourside to provide access roads is hard to imagine. With hindsight it is a great relief that Weymouth Council refused planning permission for the scheme, but purchased the site themselves in August 1963.

The news that *Consul* was to be withdrawn came as a shock to many local people and on 30 March the Paddle Steamer Preservation Society called a public meeting at Weymouth Guildhall to discuss whether anything could be done to ensure a continuation of steamer sailings from the resort. Among those present was Commander Edmund Rhodes, managing director of Coastal Steamers & Marine Services Ltd, who surprised and delighted the meeting by offering to bring *Princess Elizabeth* to Weymouth for the 1963 season. In addition to local morning, afternoon and evening cruises to Portland Harbour, the Shambles Lightship, and along the Dorset coast, she offered full day excursions to Yarmouth and Swanage. Because *Princess Elizabeth* was not equipped for beach landing she was unable to land passengers at Lulworth and had to be content with passing close by the entrance to the cove during her Dorset coast cruises

Cosens, meanwhile, had assumed that *Consul* would inevitably go to the breakers yard. To their surprise, however, the ship was purchased in March 1963 by a London bookmaker, William Smythe, who

EMBASSY at Totland Bay Pier, 1962
A. E. BENNETT

quickly repented of his decision and resold her to a newly-formed company called South Coast & Continental Steamers Ltd, comprising two admirers of the old ship and their London backers.

The new company announced its intention of putting *Consul* back into passenger service. Her wartime chief engineer, Bob Wills, was engaged to re-assemble the engines and the ship was repainted in the colours of the Aberdeen & Commonwealth Line with green hull and plain yellow funnel. Cosens, having just withdrawn the ship as uneconomic, were less than enthusiastic about her revival and Weymouth, having just committed itself to *Princess Elizabeth*, seemed to offer little immediate promise either as a maintenance or operating base for the coming season. Despite the misgivings of her managing director, Tony McGinnity, the decision was therefore made to base her at Newhaven for operation from the Sussex piers. Under the command of Capt Harry Defrates she proceeded to the Dorset Lake Shipyard at Poole for slipping, and there the first of her problems began.

The Board of Trade immediately applied the 'change of ownership' policy and demanded that the ship comply with a number of safety, subdivision and fire fighting regulations from which she had been exempt whilst she remained in Cosens' ownership. The lower saloon was divided in half by a new bulkhead, stability information was demanded for which no data existed, the permanent ballast had to be removed and weighed, and her passenger certificate was reduced from 450 to 230, making her future earning ability extremely marginal.

Embassy, meanwhile, entered service on Whit Sunday 2 June under the command of Capt John Iliffe, formerly of *Consul*. Ably assisted by the ship's long-standing first officer Eric Plater, purser Frank Holloway and chief engineer Alf Pover, Capt Iliffe ran an efficient ship which, as many regular passengers commented, was as smart and happy as she had been for years.

During the 1950s the catering on board all of the Bournemouth steamers had been contracted out with varying degrees of success but in 1961, following assorted problems and complaints, had returned to the control of the parent company who, for the next two seasons, supplied the stewards and made all of the arrangements. In 1963 the catering was once again put out to contract, this time to a Mr Gruchy.

In an attempt to boost her catering returns certain alterations were also made below decks. The maindeck saloon which contained a bar and lounge was redecorated in brighter, more modern colours. In a move which would appall modern 'heritage' values, the wooden panelling was torn out and replaced by cream-painted peg board and the polished bar counter covered with formica. Helped, no doubt, by the installation of pumps for a well-known draught

Capt. Cyril Hollyoak on EMBASSY's bridge during his first trip in command, 10.45a.m., 3 June, 1962.
B. COX.

EMBASSY *at Swanage Pier, 2 August 1964. The bathers in the foreground are standing on the remains of the old pier, once used as an overnight and coaling berth by the Cosens steamers.*
A. E. BENNETT

bitter, the scheme had the desired effect and use of the saloon increased dramatically. The food available on board was still severely limited and continued to attract a degree of criticism but one welcome innovation was the availability of packed lunches for passengers going to Totland on Sundays, when most of the shore-side facilities were firmly closed.

Up until 20 July *Embassy* maintained the Swanage ferry on Sundays and Tuesdays, but thereafter concentrated all her efforts on the Isle of Wight sailings. The successful Friday cheap-day excursion arrangements were extended to Sundays, with the added attraction of a 5s non-landing afternoon cruise from Totland back to Bournemouth. Here, provided the steamer had not been full on her morning departure, more passengers could embark for a non-landing cruise to Totland where the ship would collect her morning load for the homeward run. Two special excursions were run to Cowes during 'the Week' and evening showboat cruises increased towards the peak of the season as usual

The return fare to the island was increased from 16s 0d to 18s 0d; the cheap day trips from 12s 6d to 14s 6d; and the Swanage ferry from 7s 0d to 9s 0d during the high season, but passenger numbers did not appear to suffer as a consequence. The weather, however, could take no credit. During the early season several days were lost to strong winds and twice during June Bournemouth Pier had to be closed part way through the day. Fine weather in early August gave way to another spell of gales at the start of September but, by way of recompense, the middle of the month produced the finest spell for many years. Day after day of sunshine and breathless calm boosted the late season passenger figures while *Embassy* reverted to early and late season habit of visiting Swanage on two days per week.

An incident occurred during August which throws amusing light on the health and safety

regulations of the time. An alarmed entry in the minute book records that the Pier Master at Bournemouth had suffered an accident and his temporary replacement had actually 'been observed counting the passengers embarking'. It emerged that hitherto it had been the company's practice to count two children as one adult and that consequently the ship had regularly sailed with well over her legal capacity of 622 on board. Now that someone was having the temerity to actually check, it was felt prudent to count children as whole people.

To take advantage of this unexpected Indian summer the season was extended until 26 September and, although the final day was lost due to a severe gale, *Embassy* was still able to return to Weymouth as scheduled for lay up during the following day. Although her earnings had been adversely affected by the variable weather, they were clearly not disastrous and, encouraged by a healthy profit from the works department, the company quickly announced that it was looking forward to operating *Embassy* again next season.

Princess Elizabeth appeared to enjoy a relatively successful season at Weymouth before she retreated to Weymouth Backwater for the winter to lay up. Her owners announced their intention of returning to the resort in 1964.

Consul's Sussex season, in stark contrast, had been fraught with difficulties. She suffered a fuel pump failure off the Isle of Wight whilst on passage to Newhaven, missed her inaugural cruise and press reception, and suffered a mysterious series of steering gear failures which caused her to miss the majority of her public sailings. The financial situation was helped somewhat by a very successful September charter to Mr Don Rose who, trading under the happy name of New Belle Steamers, brought the steamer to the Thames for a week of sailings from Tower Pier and Southend. At the end of the charter the ship sailed for

Weymouth but suffered a fire in her ageing induced-draft fan engine and was forced to put into Dover. By the time she reached Newhaven the fan engine had disintegrated completely and her former chief engineer, Bob Wills, was once again summoned to her assistance. Using incredible ingenuity and skill, he made some rapid modifications and proceeded to steam the ship, which had been oil fired and induced draft since 1949, on natural draught back to Weymouth where she arrived, under an impressive pall of black smoke, on 7 October.

The season had been a financial disaster, largely due to mechanical problems, and the management had learned the important lesson that the successful operation of a sixty-six year old paddle steamer required a particular breed of chief engineer, which was almost impossible to recruit away from her home port. But for the ministrations of Bob Wills it is unlikely that the ship would have survived the season at all. The management therefore found itself with a stark choice between putting the company into immediate voluntary liquidation or returning *Consul* to service at Weymouth where it should be possible to find engineers who knew her well.

During the winter of 1963-4, in preparation for her load line survey in the spring, a considerable amount of money was spent on *Embassy*. Her inner funnel was replaced and the induced draft fan-engine ducting on the forward side of the funnel was remodelled in an attempt to reduce turbulence and thereby eradicate her trademark problem of excess smoke. The wheelhouse was removed to allow redecking of the bridge and received considerable attention, the most visible of which was the replacement of the solid timber front with veneered panels of less robust appearance.

Balmoral and *Vecta* were sent for refit by the parent company, but news that the *Sambur* was to be scrapped meant that Cosens had only one cross channel cargo ship - the *Roebuck* - to maintain that winter. Cosens continued to seek a replacement for the BTC work and made vigorous approaches to both the Royal Fleet Auxiliary and the Atomic Energy Establishment at Winfrith. Long negotiations with P & A Campbell Ltd to undertake more work on *Bristol Queen* unfortunately came to nothing. The only glimmer of hope came in the form of news that the BTC workshops at Southampton were to close and that Cosens might therefore expect to attract the refit work for their Southampton-based cargo ships.

Embassy's 1964 season opened on 31 May and proved to be one of the best for many years. Extended good weather led to an encouraging increase in passengers, which reached a peak during the week commencing 17 July when on no less than five occasions a notice declaring 'Isle of Wight steamer full' appeared at the gates of Bournemouth pier - an event unheard of since the halcyon days of 1949. Her timetable was very much as before, with the Bournemouth - Swanage service on Sundays and Tuesdays and the Isle of Wight on Mondays (cheap day to Totland), Wednesdays (full day to Yarmouth), Thursdays (full day to Totland) and Fridays (cheap day to Totland and Yarmouth). From mid-July the Tuesday trips to Swanage were dropped in favour of an additional day on the Island service, and the evening cruises, which were not paying well, were cut to twice a week on Sundays and Mondays only.

The high spot of the season was a charter by the Paddle Steamer Preservation Society on 5 July which took *Embassy* round the Isle of Wight for the first time since 1958. All 500 tickets were sold well in advance

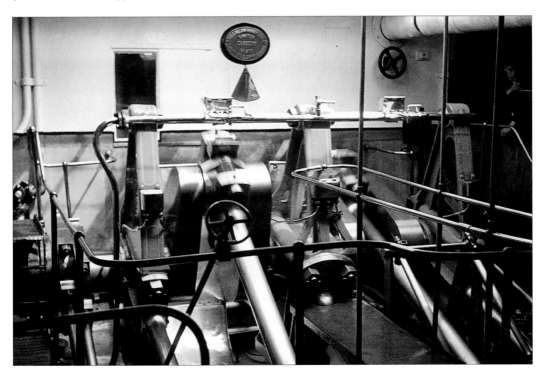

Bathed in sunlight from the skylight above, EMBASSY's highly polished engine room looks immaculate.
J. EDGINGTON

Cosens' days had been four-yearly, would henceforth be annual. Privately her owners knew that this represented the final nail in the old ship's coffin, but nonetheless decided to press ahead with their plans for the 1964 season.

Looking splendid in her new Ellerman Line colour scheme of black hull with red boot topping and yellow, black-topped funnel with narrow white stripe, *Consul* returned to Weymouth and entered service on 16 May. This of course brought her into direct competition with *Princess Elizabeth* and relations between the two companies became progressively more strained. Weymouth Council quite understandably decided to support the established operator and insisted that only *Princess Elizabeth* should be allowed a booking office at the pier entrance. *Consul*'s owners responded by launching an energetic advertising campaign on local buses and hoardings. Both companies distributed sailing bills along the seafront, engaged in spirited touting at the pier entrance and Tony Mc Ginnity was even seen marching up and down in sandwich boards! Nothing quite like this had been seen since the 1860s.

The return of *Consul* has often been blamed for the eventual demise of both ships and it is true that the presence of two ships must have split the potential market to some extent. On several occasions they were both to be seen departing, almost empty, on evening cruises. However, S C & C S Ltd decided to concentrate *Consul* on the job she did best, namely the revival of the landing cruises to Lulworth Cove. Landing rights were negotiated, the old wheeled landing stage reactivated and on most days of the week the ship was scheduled to operate both morning and afternoon return sailings to the Cove. This allowed Weymouth passengers the flexibility of half or full day landing trips or the option of a combined bus and steamer tour, whilst Lulworth residents could once again enjoy the convenience of a sailing giving two and a half hours ashore at Weymouth. The rest of *Consul*'s programme was made up of a variety of morning and evening cash bingo or coffee cruises, one hour early afternoon trips around Portland Harbour and occasional 'Rock & Dance Sea Cruises'.

Princess Elizabeth was not strengthened to land at the Cove so had to be content with passing close by the entrance before continuing towards Kimmeridge and St Aldhelm's Head. More ill-feeling was caused between the two companies by the fact that her sailing bills simply stated 'To Lulworth Cove' without making it clear that she did not land. *Consul*, of course, claimed that this was a deliberate attempt to mislead passengers, and certainly a good deal of confusion did arise. Her programme also included trips to the Shambles Lightship, Portland Bill, Portland Harbour and, on Wednesdays, the successful full day trip to Yarmouth. The latter proved so successful that, from the end of July, additional Friday sailings were provided. This benefited both ships since, whilst *Princess Elizabeth* carried good loads to the Island, *Consul* was left to mop up the local trade on two days a week.

and the day of the sailing was blessed with beautiful weather. Dressed overall the ship sailed from Bournemouth and proceeded clockwise around the Island, calling at Shanklin pier for just long enough to allow photographers to dash ashore and record the historic event. Such was the success of the sailing that Cosens repeated it on their own account twice more during the season. Other notable events were the two traditional sailings to Cowes week and an unusual Saturday charter in connection with Swiss National Day on 1 August. Once again the ship was noted for her happy atmosphere and immaculate condition, although her heavy loadings, which led to a slight loss in speed and delays at some piers, did prove a challenge to her normally impeccable time keeping. The season ended on 24 September.

Back at Weymouth the 1964 season proved to be the most exciting for years. In March *Consul*'s owners announced that they intended basing the ship at Weymouth and reviving the traditional service to land at Lulworth Cove. Cosens agreed to sell their landing stages at the Cove but, aware of the ship's financial situation and piqued that her owners should attempt to operate a service that they had so recently abandoned, refused to carry out any further work on the ship.

Two of *Consul*'s previous engineroom staff, Cyril Julian and 'Curly' Yates were appointed as chief engineer and greaser respectively. A replacement fan engine was located and fitted, and the ship set off for slipping at Poole on 28 April. Unfortunately, gale force winds forced her in to shelter at Swanage Pier where, much to the surprise of the pier master, she made the earliest steamer call for many years. By the time the weather had abated she had missed the suitable tides for getting onto the slipway and was hastily diverted to drydock in Southampton. At this point the BoT dropped another bombshell by announcing that her load line survey, which in

By the middle of August, although *Consul* was performing well under her local engineers, running reliably to time, covering her costs and making a small profit, it became clear that she would not be able to earn enough to pay off her creditors by the end of the season. Her owners also knew that the cost of getting the old ship through the annual load line survey would prove prohibitive and decided, very reluctantly, to put the company into voluntary liquidation. So it was, on the perfect summer afternoon of 28 August 1964, that *Consul* paid her last, sad call at Lulworth and retreated to her berth at Trinity Quay where she was once again advertised for sale.

Tony McGinnity, the managing director of South Coast & Continental Steamers Ltd, was also a marine surveyor and director of a shipbroking firm so was able to handle the ship's sale himself. Resisting an early offer from Haulbowline Industries Ltd to take her for scrap, he managed to find a more suitable buyer in the shape the Sailing & Travel Club of Dartmouth, who purchased her for use as an accommodations ship and clubhouse for their Sail-A-Boat sailing school on the Dart.

Early on the still, misty morning of 4 February 1965, *Consul* slipped quietly away from Weymouth for the very last time, bound for the waters of her youth and, appropriately perhaps, a return to her original name of *Duke of Devonshire*. Among the crew for her final voyage in steam were chief engineer Bob Wills, greaser Curly Yates and Bosun Alfie LePage all of whom had been on board the ship when she first arrived in Weymouth back in 1938.

Sadly Sail A Boat Holidays failed to prosper and *Duke of Devonshire* passed to Ferry Services and Supplies of Southampton, where she was broken up in October 1968. For many months the after part of her hull, from the engine room to the bulkhead back, lay on the mud at the breaker's yard and is believed to have been eventually buried as part of the infil for a new wharf extension.

During January 1965 a meeting had taken place between Cosens and Crosons with a view to the latter purchasing *Embassy* and the goodwill of the Bournemouth station. In the event terms could not be agreed and instead it was decided to operate the season on the same co-operative basis as in previous years. Back at Weymouth, *Embassy* went to Portland for slipping at Easter 1965 and entered service on 5 June with her most unusual sailing for many years. This was a charter by the PSPS which took the ship directly from her winter berth at Weymouth around the Isle of Wight via Swanage, Bournemouth and Yarmouth, returning in the evening to Poole whence the Weymouth passengers were coached home. This was the first direct sailing from Weymouth around the Island since 1914, the first from Yarmouth since 1951, and *Embassy*'s first public sailing from Weymouth since 1956.

Embassy's sailing schedule was almost identical to 1964 and the ship ran with great reliability and her usual happy atmosphere. The trade in June proved

very quiet whilst July and early August were dogged with the kind of bad weather which proved beyond all doubt the superiority of the paddler over Croson's smaller motor vessels. Crosons reported having to cancel trips on no less than thirty days whilst *Embassy* soldiered on, substituting a Bournemouth - Swanage service in place of the motor vessels on the one day that gales prevented her from sailing to the Island. The popular Round the Isle of Wight excursion was offered once again on 18 July but attracted less custom than usual, probably due to the fact that it was scheduled for a Sunday morning which had never been a popular departure time from Bournemouth.

August was blessed with better weather and saw the ship sail full on several occasions. The end of the season, however, was marred by more freak weather. On 17 September hurricane 'Betsy' passed by bringing force 9-10 winds and preventing *Embassy* from leaving Poole Quay at all. The next few days were calm but by 20 September a heavy swell developed close inshore and caused *Embassy* to part five ropes at Bournemouth and leave behind 20 intending passengers for the 2 pm Island sailing when it became too dangerous to remain alongside any longer. Berthing at Totland was accomplished with some difficulty, but she was prevented from attempting Bournemouth Pier on her return sailing and had to sail onwards via Swanage to Poole where her passengers were landed and returned to Bournemouth by bus.

On the following two days all sailings were cancelled due to dense fog but conditions improved sufficiently for her to operate on the last day of the season, 23 September. After completing a return run from Bournemouth to Totland she lay at the pier until 7pm when she departed direct for Weymouth. Having spent the night at the pleasure pier, she moved up harbour and passed through the Town Bridge next morning and was soon safely moored in her winter berth outside Cosens' offices.

When *Princess Elizabeth* emerged to open her 1965 season at Weymouth, she was under the new ownership of Coastal Steamers (Weymouth) Ltd, although Commander Rhodes, her previous managing director, remained centrally involved.

Fog delayed EMBASSY's departure from Weymouth on her historic Round the Isle of Wight sailing on 5 June 1965. Great trouble was experienced locating Swanage Pier and the ship was eventually guided in by the ringing of the pierhead bell. A little later, while on passage to Bournemouth, EMBASSY strayed off course and came perilously close to stranding on the cliffs at Ballard Point. The cliffs were spotted in the nick of time and the ship, with her helm hard over and engines full astern, came to rest with her port paddle box only yards from the rocks. This photograph, taken as she backed away from the cliffs, shows how close she came to disaster.
AUTHOR'S COLLECTION

EMBASSY, complete with her new mainmast, makes a wonderful sight as, fresh paint glittering, she backs out of Weymouth to begin her final season at Bournemouth, Whit Saturday 28 May, 1966.
AUTHOR

Shortly afterwards it was revealed that the mortgagees of the vessel were pressing for her to be sold. Her programme was very similar to the previous two seasons and ended on Wednesday 22 September. On the following morning she retired to Weymouth Backwater to lay up. Although nobody realised it at the time, this was to be her last trip in steam.

In June 1966 it was announced that she was for sale, but she remained steadily deteriorating in Weymouth Backwater until 1967 when she was sold for scrap to Metric Ltd of Newhaven. She was quickly resold, however, and after passing through a number of hands was eventually established as a floating restaurant on the Thames in London during 1969. She subsequently moved to Paris and is currently enjoying a new lease of life as a university conference centre at Dunkirk.

With the poor weather - heavy rain was recorded on no less than 47 days during the season - it was no surprise to discover that Cosens' 1965 passenger figures were down on the previous year. However, the company's overall situation was saved by better returns from the engineering department. During the winter of 1964-5 they had undertaken refit work on the cross channel vessels *Caesarea* and *Elk* and the

parent company's *Balmoral*, and had kept the workforce fully occupied during the summer months with overhauling transducer stations for the Admiralty, constructing more pontoons for use at East Cowes and assorted smaller contracts.

In September 1965 the parent company at Southampton announced the sale of their motor vessel *Vecta* to Townsend Car Ferries Ltd for use on the Bristol Channel by their subsidiary company, P & A Campbell Ltd. An unexpected but very welcome condition of the sale was that Cosens should undertake the annual refit of the vessel for the next two years. *Vecta* duly arrived in Weymouth during October and remained in Cosens' hands until March when *Balmoral* arrived for a five- week refit. Thus, despite the disappointing season at Bournemouth, the company was able to declare a 15% dividend for 1965.

In January 1966, Commander Johnson, the company's Bournemouth agent, moved to Southampton as the parent company's deputy berthing master and was replaced by Commander J. Lapage. At Weymouth the annual bustle of the pre-season mechanical overhaul and repainting started aboard *Embassy*. Since regulations had been changed in 1954 *Embassy*, in common with the other Cosens vessels, had been fitted with a bracket on her funnel from which a second masthead light could be hoisted when the vessel was operating after dark. Now a further alteration in the lighting regulations made it necessary to fit her with a mainmast for the first time in her career. The new mast, which was made of tubular metal and of a very considerable height, rather spoilt the ship's familiar profile and appeared to make her sit lower in the water. To support it a metal beam was inserted across the engine room deckhead and for the first time in her history the ship's navigation lights were powered by electricity.

EMBASSY's ornate paddle box.
AUTHOR

No longer would passengers be treated to the timeless sight of the deck crew lighting and hoisting the large oil-powered lanterns as darkness fell.

Cosens had given close consideration to reducing the ship's passenger certificate to cover only the area between Yarmouth and Swanage, but were eventually dissuaded by strong representations from the Paddle Steamer Preservation Society who argued that such a move would put an end to their own and other potential charterers' plans for the coming season. Their argument won, the PSPS duly chartered the ship for Sunday 24 July for an unusual sailing from Poole Quay and Bournemouth around the Isle of Wight, calling at Ventnor. Although Ventnor was a regular call for the parent company's Southampton-based motor ships, no Bournemouth steamer had called there since *Embassy*'s last visit on 30 June 1954.

Embassy left Weymouth for Poole on Whit Saturday 1966 and opened her season on the Sunday morning 29 May with her usual Swanage service. The season then settled into its regular rhythm except that the Tuesday Swanage sailings were replaced by an additional service to the Isle of Wight. Thus, Mondays, Tuesdays, Thursdays and Fridays saw the steamer leaving Bournemouth at 10.30am for Totland and on Wednesdays for Yarmouth. Passengers could choose between a full day trip with optional coach tour or a non-landing morning cruise. *Embassy* left the island at noon, offering Totland and Yarmouth passengers a trip to Bournemouth with 1 hour ashore, before departing again on a non-landing afternoon trip at 2.30pm On Mondays and Fridays she left the island at 4pm arriving at Bournemouth at 5.30pm, and on other days at

5.15pm arriving home at 6.45pm On Thursdays a one hour coastal cruise was offered from Bournemouth at 2pm between the ship's Isle of Wight runs.

On Sundays *Embassy* maintained the Swanage ferry with departures from Bournemouth at 10.45am, 2.30pm and 4.30pm returning from Swanage at 11.30am, 3.30pm and 5.15pm. On other days the service was maintained by Croson's motor vessels. On Sunday evenings at 7.45pm *Embassy* cruised towards the Needles with musical entertainment in the bar by 'Chris and his Accordians' and on the remaining evenings offered a one way cruise to Poole Quay, via Swanage on Mondays, Tuesdays and Fridays, with bus return.

1966 will be remembered, amongst other things, for the crippling national seamen's strike. As the dispute developed more and more shipping was laid up at Southampton and a remarkable collection of the world's major liners and cargo ships were to be seen crowded into docks. *Embassy*'s crew, who were unaffected by the dispute, suggested that trips might profitably be run to view this unique spectacle. Trips took place on Tuesdays 14, 21 and 28 June and Wednesday 6 July and, despite very limited advertising, were a great success. It was generally felt that under Commander Lapage's management the advertising at Bournemouth had taken a step backwards and there was much criticism of the company's inconspicuous newspaper adverts and the lack of advanced sailing details at the piers. Indeed, although *Embassy* called at Yarmouth on her 6 July docks cruise, no advanced advertising had taken place so only a handful of passengers were embarked.

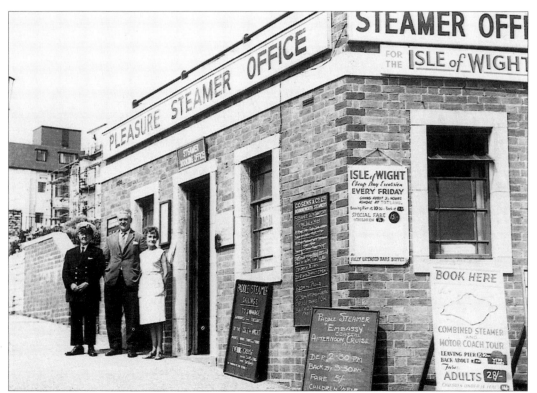

Commander Johnson, Cosens' Bournemouth agent, with his two assistants outside the steamer office on Pier Approach, June 1965. Tickets for showboat cruises, combined steamer and coach tours and special excursions were sold at the office, but the bulk of ordinary tickets were sold on board the steamer after sailing. If the ship was full this threw a considerable strain on the purser who, especially on the short crossing to Swanage, would be hard pressed to complete his task in the time available. Cosens vessels had no ticket offices so the purser would tour the decks, his uniform pockets bulging with the collected fares, selling tickets from a selection of perforated books.
B. Cox

Her season was further enlivened by a number of charters and special trips. On 24 June she operated an evening trip from Poole Quay for Plessey Ltd and on 4 July was billed as the Bournemouth Colleges Students' Union 'Ragboat' for a late-night jazz cruise. Sadly, the call at Ventnor on the PSPS Round the Island charter on 24 July had to be abandoned due to a very heavy swell which made berthing at the pier impossible, and a call at Yarmouth was made instead.

Behind the scenes, however, all was not well. As early as June the general manager had reported to the board that *Embassy* was 'causing him some concern in respect of her general condition' and that 'full consideration of the future prospects of the ship' would need to be given at the end of the season. As if to prove his point a series of boiler tube problems were experienced towards the end of the month which prevented *Embassy* from sailing on 26 and 30 June. Then, on Thursday 28 July, the ship suffered her first-ever major breakdown at sea.

Returning from Totland Bay to Bournemouth on her afternoon sailing, *Embassy* had just passed Hurst Castle and was taking the narrow, inshore channel parallel to the spit when a float broke loose from the port paddle wheel. A worse position for an accident to occur could scarcely be imagined, for the combination of swift tide, onshore wind and lee shore made it impossible for the ship to anchor in safety. Instead, Capt Iliffe was forced to continue until the ship was off Milford-on-Sea where she eventually came to anchor. By this time the flailing wreckage had caused further serious damage to both the paddle wheel and box, and the beautiful, decorative paddle box crest had been lost overboard.

A radio message was sent for assistance and at 8.45pm the tug *Wendy Ann* arrived to tow *Embassy* back to Poole. At the Poole Bar buoy the *Wendy Ann II* took a stern rope to allow the steamer to be steered through the harbour and berthed at Poole Quay,

which was finally reached at 2am the following morning. *Embassy* was subsequently off service until 7 August and all trips were cancelled, including two cruises to view the Cowes Week yacht racing on 1 and 3 August.

As it happened the weather was very poor during the time she was under repair and several days would probably have been cancelled due to high winds. The poor weather continued during August with several more days lost to wind or fog and, combined with the well-publicised disasters to the smaller excursion vessels *Prince of Wales* and *Darwin* elsewhere in the UK, conspired to keep passengers away. On 16 and 17 August spirits were lifted somewhat by the presence of BBC cameras on board to film all aspects of the ship's operation for inclusion in a TV documentary entitled 'The Paddlers'. September, however, offered little respite with sailings cancelled on four days and abandoned on 6 September after several ropes were broken and the ship was unable to land her morning cruise passenger on her return to Bournemouth Pier from Totland. Frequently she sailed almost empty.

If things appeared gloomy to the travelling public, they were even worse behind the scenes. Chief Engineer Pover continued to struggle to keep a series of minor mechanical problems in check until the end of the season, and it became apparent that a complete retubing of the boiler and some major work on the main engine would be required if the ship was to run again in 1967. In granting the previous load line certificate the Board of Trade surveyor had made a clear condition that all internal cement would have to be removed from the ship's bottom and all the hull shot-blasted externally for full survey during the coming winter. A meeting with the surveyor during September made it abundantly clear that major expenditure must be expected before any further certificates could be granted.

Thus, although the Cosens board resolved to investigate ways of keeping her in service for a further season and issued a press release stating that *Embassy* would be back as usual in 1967, the ship's fate was effectively sealed before she made her last sailing of 1966 on the afternoon of Thursday 22 September. Having departed from Totland for the last time at 5.15pm she landed her passengers at Bournemouth at 6.45pm and, with the customary long, farewell blast on her whistle set sail for Weymouth. Although none of the onlookers on the pier knew it at the time, *Embassy* had just completed her last passenger sailing and the era of the Cosens paddle steamers at Bournemouth was over.

Embassy arrived at Weymouth at 9.30pm and moored for the night at Custom House Quay. Next day she was due to pass through the bridge at 1.30pm but, symbolically perhaps, it suffered a breakdown and refused to open until 2.15pm *Embassy* passed safely through to her winter mooring in the backwater and a few moments later Capt Iliffe rang down 'finished with engines' for the very last time.

On 13 December Mr H. Bolson, Managing Director of Croson Ltd, attended a Cosens board meeting at Weymouth to discuss the future of the Bournemouth service. He expressed the strong view that a service to the Isle of Wight should be continued and offered, provided he could locate a suitable vessel, to take over from Cosens in 1967. His offer was immediately accepted and the rest of the meeting was spent in making arrangements to inform all interested parties. Messrs H. E. Moss & Co, shipbrokers, were instructed to negotiate for the sale of *Embassy* and both the Bournemouth Manager and Capt Iliffe were issued with redundancy notices. On 19 December the news was released to the press together with an explanation that the service had been making a heavy loss and the statement that 'This is a sad day for us, but the day of the paddle steamer is over.'

Embassy languished in Weymouth Backwater until 4 May 1967 when, with her windows and hatches boarded up, she was moved through the Town Bridge, turned in the Cove and moored outside the company's old head office at Custom House Quay. She lay there for a number of days awaiting the arrival of the German tug *Fairplay II* and on 25 May, watched by a small group of her former crew, was finally towed away to be broken up by Van Heyghen Freres of Ghent. By a curious and touching coincidence, Mr F. Thatcher who had resigned as Cosens' Chairman in December due to ill health, passed away in Southampton Hospital at the very time *Embassy* was beginning her own final voyage.

Embassy's departure marked the end of Cosens' distinguished 119 year history as excursion steamer operators which had begun back in 1848 when Capt Cosens introduced the little *Highland Maid* on the ferry service between Weymouth and Portland, and the continuous thread of local paddle steamer ownership which had lasted since the arrival of the *Rose* in 1840 was finally severed.

EMBASSY is towed away from Weymouth harbour on 25 May 1967 by the tug FAIRPLAY II, on her last journey to the Dutch breakers. AUTHOR'S COLLECTION.

CHAPTER THIRTEEN

AFTER THE PADDLE STEAMERS

With the steamer service withdrawn and the marine department closed, the parent company immediately commissioned a full report on the trading position and prospects of Cosens' remaining activities - cold storage, general engineering and ship repairing.

The report was presented to the board in April 1967 and painted a thoroughly gloomy picture. The cold store had been losing in excess of £1,000 per annum for several years and had only been retained as a bargaining chip in negotiations with Weymouth Corporation regarding the freehold of the company's main engineering works on Commercial Road. This facility was housed in a jumble of elderly buildings which contained a variety of machinery much of which was still belt-driven from overhead shafts and was too inaccurate to be used for precision work. Ship repairing, despite being the activity to which the company's workforce and machinery were best suited, was also predicted to make a loss in 1967. Expected earnings from refits of the parent

company's *Balmoral*, P.& A. Campbell Ltd's *Westward Ho*, the Channel Islands vessels and assorted other work was offset by the loss of income normally derived from the refit of the *Embassy*, resulting in a overall predicted trading loss for the company of £6000.

In view of these facts immediate closure would have be inevitable had it not been for the existence of £18,000 of past tax losses which could be recovered by the parent company if Cosens continued to trade. Accordingly it was decided to grant the company a three year reprieve during which period every effort would be made to cut costs and seek additional work. The parent company agreed to assist by sending a selection of their tugs to Weymouth for their annual refits, guaranteeing an increased income of approximately £15,000 per annum and tipping Cosens' accounts back into profit.

In truth, whereas in the past Cosens had relinquished a trade if it proved unsuccessful and seized the opportunity of another offering promise,

The historic engineering works on Commercial Road showing the wooden office building, machine shop and the tall, brick fitting shop.
R. B. GRICE

P .& A. Campbell Ltd's
BALMORAL refitting at
Cosens' yard during the
winter of 1969/70.
R. B. GRICE

these options were fast running out. Until the 1960s Cosens had been the sole general engineering company in the area, but this started to change with the opening of Universal Engineering Ltd, who represented the first serious challenge to Cosens' position.

Likewise, many of the institutions and businesses who were Cosens' customers were in decline. The gasworks, power station, waterworks, breweries, local dairies, bakeries and other small businesses had provided both regular work and the variety of small jobs -usually breakdowns - which required the urgent miracle cure which Cosens always seemed able to provide. Now, as some of these customers closed down and others replaced their old equipment with new technology, the maintenance contracts went to specialist firms. The growth of plant hire businesses also meant that Cosens' 6 ton Ransomes mobile crane, which since its purchase in 1946 had been the only decent crane available for general work around the town, was now seriously outclassed and trade was lost.

The lease of the main engineering works was due to expire on 16 August 1968 but an agreement was finally reached with Weymouth Corporation during the winter of 1967 for Cosens to obtain the freehold of the site in exchange for a cash payment and the cold stores which the council intended to demolish in order to create a short term car park.

With the long-term future of the site secured the parent company was persuaded to invest heavily in new buildings and equipment in the hope of attracting a much wider range of work from further afield. During 1968 and 1969 the warren of Dickensian offices and workshops was demolished to be replaced by modern 6,000 sq ft industrial units with adjoining single story office accommodation. New machinery enabled the workforce of 25 to offer

a comprehensive range of steel and aluminium fabrication, general engineering and ship repairing services and a far higher degree of precision than had previously been the case.

In March 1969 the Works Manager, Mr Gill, retired at the age of nearly 71 to be replaced by Mr A. W. 'Micky' Prowse. Mr Prowse had joined the firm in September 1937 as an apprentice boilermaker and always maintained that he owed his appointment to his skill as a footballer. Mr Mark Frowde, the company's long-standing managing director at that time was an important figure in local and national football and one-time President of the Football Association. When the young Prowse attended for

Mr. A.W. 'Micky' Prowse,
works manager from 1969,
General Manager from
1973 and Director from
1977 makes a retirement
presentation to Cosens' chief
clerk Miss Sylvia Lane, on
Christmas Eve 1985. Also
pictured are Works Manager
Mr. David Willshire, (left)
and clerks Mrs. Liz Davis
and Mrs. Veronica Garlick.
DORSET EVENING ECHO,
COURTESY MRS .M.
PROWSE.

interview Frowde recognised him from a local football competition and appointed him without further question.

The new workshops were officially opened on 24 November 1971 by the mayor of Weymouth, Mr A. D. W. Biles, who expressed the town's gratitude for the decision to retain Cosens' facilities at Weymouth. New marketing material was produced, describing Cosens as 'The old established firm with its eye on the future' and as a member of the parent company's 'Red Funnel Group'. Significantly, Cosens' familiar steamer house flag was now replaced on all advertising material by the Red Funnel Group's new corporate logo.

In 1973 'Micky' Prowse took over as General Manager in place of Mr Donald Brookes and Mr Alf Pover, formerly Chief Engineer of the *Embassy*, became Works Manager. Over the next decade the new management team worked successfully to expand their customer base. On the ship repairing front, regular refit work on the Channel Islands vessels and Red Funnel Group tugs was boosted by contracts to undertake repairs on board Royal Fleet Auxiliary tankers and supply ships. Steel and alloy fabrication work was undertaken for the Admiralty Underwater Research Establishment at Portland, the Ministry of Defence, the Atomic Energy Research Establishment at Winfrith and a host of smaller customers. Boiler maintenance, heating and ventilation contracts were obtained at Portland Dockyard, Bovington and Blandford Camps, Unigate Dairies and elsewhere and a vital contract was signed with the Ministry of Defence for the repair and refurbishment of the Mexeflote pontoons and catamarans used in naval dockyards and during the Falklands campaign.

On 10 June 1976 the company celebrated the centenary of its incorporation as a limited company with a staff visit to the parent company's Southampton headquarters and a four hour cruise on board their tug tender *Calshot*. A feature of the company throughout its history had been the length of service of many of its employees and the 1970s and 1980s were no exception. The local press was peppered with accounts of long service awards and retirements, notable amongst which were the departures of works manager Mr Alf Pover in 1978 and chief clerk Miss Sylvia Lane in 1986. Continuity was ensured by the appointment as Works Manager of Mr David Willshire who had been with the company all his working life and whose father, Mr Reg Willshire, also served his apprenticeship with Cosens and appeared earlier in this history as wartime engineer on board *Consul*. Finally, in April 1986, 'Micky' Prowse himself retired as General Manager after 49 years service, to be replaced by Mr Brian Verity.

A year later the somewhat surprising decision was made to close the Commercial Road workshops and relocate the firm on the top of Portland at the former Perryfield Stone Works. The site, which is located close to Pennsylvania Castle and Church Ope Cove, offered generous undercover workshop space, the historic Perryfield House which could be converted into spacious office accommodation, and plenty of space for open air storage and expansion. Most importantly it was relatively cheap. In contrast, plans for a town centre redevelopment and the construction of a marina in Weymouth Backwater had led to a dramatic increase in the value of Commercial Road site. The Red Funnel Group were not slow to identify the financial gain to be made from the move which took place during 1987. By July of the following year most of the Commercial Road buildings were demolished. Mr Verity resigned in September 1988. In January 1989 Mr Michael Hughes took over as director and General Manager but had only been in post for a few months when the parent company's Red Funnel Group was taken over by the giant Associated British Ports Holdings PLC. A minor engineering firm on the top of Portland did not fit into ABP's plans and Cosens was quickly offered for sale. Convinced of the company's potential, Michael Hughes headed a management buy-out and by 1990 Cosens & Co Ltd was once again an independent company.

Under Mr Hughes' management the firm set out to build on its existing customer base and diversify into new areas of engineering. In addition to the engineering division which continued to produce items as diverse as pontoons, link-spans, lead lined containers for nuclear waste, and specialised equipment for the Ministry of Defence, the company developed a property services division and a field services division. The former offered plant installation and maintenance to a wide range of government and private establishments. The latter undertook on-site fabrication, erection and refurbishment, which included work on pipelines, oil rigs, tanks and buildings. Both divisions were, of necessity, highly mobile and Cosens vans were to be seen in many unlikely parts of the country. Michael Hughes took a great interest in the company's history and went to considerable lengths to recover and display records and artifacts relating to the company in the offices at Perryfield House. Company advertising material once again emphasised Cosens' illustrious place in local maritime history.

One of the first major jobs undertaken at the Perryfields site was the construction of the 36m ferry *Tom Casey*, designed to carry eight cars and 100 passengers on the short Lower Ferry crossing between Dartmouth and Kingswear in Devon. Cosens won the £150,000 contract from South Hams District Council against stiff opposition and there was considerable satisfaction that the firm had returned to shipbuilding for the first time in many years. Manoeuvring the 54 ton ferry on a low loader through the narrow streets and steep hills of Fortuneswell vividly illustrated the disadvantages of the Portland site, but the task was accomplished safely and the ferry was launched at Castletown Jetty, Portland, on 7 July 1989.

Cosens also obtained the licence to build a series

of small oil pollution control vessels known as Pollcats, the first of which, *Sea Sweep* and *Sea Mop*, were delivered for use at Milford Haven late in 1991. Each of these vessels had to endure the tortuous road journey from the top of Portland before being launched and completed at Castletown. Sea trials were held in Portland Harbour and Weymouth Bay and those who knew the company's long history derived considerable pleasure from seeing the Cosens houseflag fluttering proudly above locally-built vessels once again. Other similar vessels followed including *Scapa Lass* in August 1992, *Vortex* in July 1993 and a general purpose vessel called *Tarambola* for the Port of Lisbon Port Authority.

The early 1990s were, however, a period of serious recession in British industry. Faced with a buyers' market, and cut-throat competition from other metalworking firms, Cosens had little option but to cut their margins to the bone in order to survive. The company undertook a wide range of work, from repairs on the jack-up rigs *Karissa A* and *Karissa B*, through conversion and repairs to various Ministry of Defence vessels, pontoon construction and work on oil tanks and power stations, to the construction of steel bridges for Brighton Marina. The costs involved in transporting finished boats from Perryfields to the sea undoubtedly reduced their competitiveness at this difficult time as well as creating marketing problems and leading to several lost orders. Nonetheless a major contract was obtained in 1992 to build the workboats *Sabrina* and *Diana* and modify a huge barge called *Sar III* at Avonmouth for use in the construction of the Second Severn Crossing near Bristol. Sadly, however, the

margins proved too tight and the completion of the contract saw the company in difficulties. These were compounded by the closure of the Portland Naval base with the loss of important associated maintenance contracts and the fact that some anticipated major orders failed to materialise. In late 1993 a number of staff were laid off.

The SCAPA LASS on sea trials in Portland Harbour.
AUTHOR'S COLLECTION

Michael Hughes, Cosens' last Managing Director.
DORSET EVENING ECHO

For the next three years, despite the difficult economic situation, the company continued to trade but, on Tuesday 30 April 1996 news broke that it had been placed in the hands of the receivers. Half of the workforce was immediately made redundant in an attempt to keep the company operating while a new buyer was sought. Michael Hughes thus had the melancholy honour of being the last in a long line of managing directors of Cosens & Co Ltd which could be traced back to Joseph Drew in 1876. After 120 years the thread was finally broken..

By July 1996 a buyer had been located and the company was reborn as Cosens Engineering Ltd under Managing Director Trevor Primett and Operational Director David Willshire. The latter had worked with Cosens for 28 years and provided not only a wealth of experience but also the last link with what had gone before. The property maintenance activities were abandoned, and the new company concentrated on the core business of metal fabrication, boat building and mechanical engineering. As orders continued to flow in for catamaran workboats, the workforce expanded again, and a general air of optimism pervaded the Perryfield Works.

Sadly, however, all was not well and in November 1999 Cosens Engineering Ltd called in the receivers. Once again the business was sold and at the time of writing continues to trade from the Perryfields Works as Castle Engineering Ltd.

All of the vessels which followed the demise of the Cosens steamers were small, screw-driven motor vessels of a completely different class to their illustrious predecessors. During the 1960s paddle steamers had become an endangered species as one famous name followed another to the breaker's yard and it seemed impossible to suppose that the sound of churning paddle wheels would ever again be heard in the waters of Weymouth or Bournemouth Bay.

Maintaining the tradition: having just arrived from Weymouth and Swanage, the magnificent WAVERLEY, fresh from her £4m rebuild, basks in the evening sunshine at Bournemouth Pier on 3 September, 2000. MIKE TEDSTONE

Then, in November 1973, the impossible happened. Caledonian MacBrayne, who had withdrawn their last Clyde paddle steamer *Waverley* at the end of that season, offered to gift her for a nominal £1 to the Paddle Steamer Preservation Society. The offer was accepted and, against all the odds, the Society returned the steamer to service on the Clyde during 1975. As confidence grew the steamer ventured further afield until, in the spring of 1978, she rounded Lands End and arrived on the south coast for her first ever visit. Bournemouth, Poole and Southampton were all ports of call during that historic few weeks and, on a number of occasions, *Waverley* sailed round the Isle of Wight. In 1979 Weymouth was added to the programme and for a few weeks each summer since then the magnificent *Waverley* has been a welcome visitor to the area.

In December 1984 the Waverley organisation purchased the motor vessel *Balmoral* to act as a running mate for *Waverley*. Readers will recall that *Balmoral* had been built to the order of Red Funnel Steamers of Southampton, Cosens' parent company from 1947, and was a frequent visitor to Cosens' Weymouth shipyard for refits. Withdrawn by the Southampton Company in 1968, she moved to the Bristol Channel where she was operated by P. & A. Campbell Ltd between 1969 and 1980 before becoming a floating pub in Dundee. Rescued from this ignominious role she received a massive refit before re-entering passenger service in April 1986. She spends her summer seasons on the Bristol Channel but in spring and autumn regularly circumnavigates the British Isles and is a frequent visitor to the Dorset coast. On 17 September 1987 she was the first major excursion steamer for many years

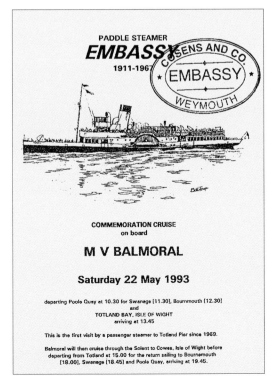

PADDLE STEAMER

EMBASSY

1911-1967

COSENS AND CO.
EMBASSY
WEYMOUTH

COMMEMORATION CRUISE
on board

M V BALMORAL

Saturday 22 May 1993

departing Poole Quay at 10.30 for Swanage [11.30], Bournemouth [12.30]
and
TOTLAND BAY, ISLE OF WIGHT
arriving at 13.45

This is the first visit by a passenger steamer to Totland Pier since 1969.

Balmoral will then cruise through the Solent to Cowes, Isle of Wight before
departing from Totland at 15.00 for the return sailing to Bournemouth
[18.00], Swanage [18.45] and Poole Quay, arriving at 19.45.

to sail right into Lulworth Cove and 22 May 1993 retraced *Embassy*'s regular route from Poole Quay, Swanage and Bournemouth to make the first landing call at Totland Bay Pier since 1989.

Balmoral and *Waverley* are Britain's very last traditional sea going excursion steamers and survive only because of the dedication of their operating charities, Waverley Excursions Ltd and the Paddle Steamer Preservation Society. Both ships are over fifty years old and it is an enormous privilege and pleasure to tread their decks as they retrace one or other of the traditional steamer routes and offer a new generation a flavour of what it was like to voyage along the Dorset, Devon and Hampshire coasts in the great days of Cosens' Buff Funnel Fleet.

EMBASSY's name pennant and housflag fly proudly at BALMORAL's mast, 22 May, 1993. BALMORAL retraced EMBASSY's traditional route from Poole Quay to Swanage, Bournemouth and Totland, and was the first large passenger vessel to call there since EMBASSY's last departure in 1966. EMBASSY's final master, Capt John Illiffe, was guest of honour for the occasion. AUTHOR

Souvenir brochure AUTHOR'S COLLECTION.

ACKNOWLEGEMENTS

This history is the culmination of almost thirty years research. During that period the author has benefited from the unstinting generosity and encouragement of a large number of friends, correspondents and institutions who have given freely of their time and knowledge, as well as allowing access to their photographic collections and archives. Without them the book could not have been completed.

Brian Jackson, well-known Weymouth transport historian and ex-Cosens apprentice, has been a tower of strength and friendship, sharing his extensive knowledge and enthusiasm for the subject at every step along the way. Victor Gray, acknowledged expert on Cosens' Bournemouth activities, has shared his remarkable knowledge of the company's day-to-day workings and I have drawn extensively on his numerous published articles. I am grateful to them both, together with John Megoran for their meticulous reading of my final manuscript.

Many fascinating hours have been spent talking with former Cosens employees. Their memories (many of which have been recorded on tape) have added an authenticity and colour to this history which could not have been achieved by the use of printed sources alone. It is a source of deep regret that many of them have not lived to see the publication of a book they did so much to encourage. My thanks are due to Captains John Iliffe and Harry Defrates; Michael Hughes and David Willshire (respectively the company's last managing director and works manager); managers and workshop staff Sidney Davis, Micky Prowse, Brian Jackson and Reginald Fry; stewards George Morris, Peter Lloydworth and Hector Lowman; deck crew Sandy Rashleigh, Desmond Palmer and Ken Moore; and engineers Alf Pover, Reg Willshire, and Bob Wills. The latter was one of Weymouth's great quayside characters – chief engineer, publican, and motorboat operator. The author owes him a great debt, not only for the hours of entertainment he provided with his detailed but irreverent stories of 'the old days' at Cosens, but also for introducing me to the intricacies of the *Consul*'s engine room.

I am grateful to the following friends, collectors and historians for their assistance with this work: Keith Adams, Maureen Attwool, Tony Bennett, Rev Norman Bird, Chris Collard, Nigel Coombes, Bernard Cox, R.B. 'Bob' Grice, David Haysom, Alan Kittridge, Martin Langley, Bill Macey, John Megoran , Shiela Morris, Stewart Morris, Ken Moore, George Owen, the late Eric Payne, Geoffrey Pritchard, Geoffrey Poole, Trevor Primett, Ken Saunders, Mike Tedstone, the late George Thomas, the late Jack West and Chris Woods. A special mention is due to A. M. C. 'Tony' Mc.Ginnity who, as managing owner of the *Consul* from 1963 to 1965 allowed the author to become a sort of unofficial 'ship's boy' and somehow found time to encourage my interest in the old ship. Since then he has always been willing to share his unique, practical knowledge of the twilight years of the British excursion steamers, and has been a keen advocate of the publication of this history.

I am also indebted to the following organisations and institutions: Dorset County Records Office, Dorset Library Service (in particular the local studies departments at Weymouth and Dorchester Libraries), Dorset County Museum, Imperial War Museum, National Maritime Museum, Nothe Fort Museum at Weymouth, Public Records Office, The Royal Navy Submarine Museum at Gosport, The Tythe Barn Museum at Swanage, Weymouth & Portland Museum Services.

Finally, I thank my wife Carol for her boundless patience, encouragement and advice during this project.

A NOTE ON THE PHOTOGRAPHS:

The author and publisher have made every effort to establish the provenance of each photograph used in the book and apologise if any copyright has been inadvertently infringed.

Many of the photographs have been drawn from a small number of key collections. Keith Abraham, Tony Bennett, Richard Danielson, John Edgington, Brian Jackson, Victor Gray, Ken Saunders, John Megoran, Geoff Pritchard and David Haysom have all allowed me access to their personal collections, while Keith Adams has made available the Cosens albums and sailing bills from the H. A. Allen collection, of which he is a trustee. The late Eric Payne of Ryde always supplied copies, accompanied by meticulous historical notes, of any treasures he unearthed, while the late George Thomas could always be relied upon to identify and date a photograph from the top six inches of a steamer's mast. Bernard Cox, the well-known Bournemouth steamer historian and photographer has loaned his unique collection of 1960s negatives and his former collection of historical photographs is now available to the public in Dorchester Library. The local studies collection at Weymouth Library contains many unique shots, including the King Collection, recently returned to the town by the former Cosens draughtsman who rescued a great deal of valuable material during his years with the company. Finally, the extensive archives of the Paddle Steamer Preservation Society have been made available through the kindness of the society's museums officer, Andrew Gladwell.

The author's own collection of photos, plans and ephemera has been built up over the years partly through chance finds and purchases, but largely as a result of the kindness of others who have been happy to contribute to this project. I am grateful to Miss Shiela Morris for the gift of her late father's stewarding pictures and to Mrs M. Prowse who passed on a large amount of material accumulated by her late husband, Micky Prowse, during his long career with the company. Wherever possible I have acknowledged the original owner. A number of photos credited 'Author's collection/Seward' were taken by the famous Weymouth postcard photographer E. N. Seward. Upon his death his unique collection of glass plates passed to local collector Eric Latcham who in turn left the Cosens plates to the author.

SOURCES

COMPANY ARCHIVES AND PUBLICATIONS:

For many years the author had been led to understand that the Cosens' official records had been destroyed during the war but in 1990, when the company was sold by the Red Funnel Group, a truly amazing collection of documents emerged from the parent company's archive room in Southampton. Their discovery led to complete re-appraisal of the research which had previously taken place. Thanks to the generosity of Michael Hughes, Cosens' Managing Director at the time and David Willshire, the author was allowed free access to the archive, which has provided the backbone around which this history has been written. The archive is extensive, but includes:

Minute Books, 1868-1966
Share transfer, dividend, and mortgage records.
Accounting records 1876-1968, including ledgers, journals, day books and assorted accounts.
Articles of Association
Correspondence files and assorted ephemera.

Reference has also been made to company guide books:
Cosens & Co's Official Guide, 1923
The Buff Funnel Book, 1959, by Bernard Cox

Newspapers and Magazines:
Bridport News
Bournemouth Daily Echo
Dorset, the County Magazine
Dorset County Chronicle
Dorset Daily Echo
Dorset Evening Echo
Paddle Wheels, Quarterly Journal of the Paddle Steamer Preservation Society, 1960 to date
Sea Breezes
Ship Ahoy, Journal of the South Wales Branch of the World Ship Society
Ships Monthly
Southern Times
Abstracts relating to the steamer services compiled by the late Eric Payne of Ryde from :
Isle of Wight Observer
Isle of Wight County Press
Isle of Wight Mercury
Portsmouth Evening News

Articles:
Anon. 'If It's Contraband It Won't Get to Germany', *The War Illustrated*, 28 October, 1939.
Bird, N. & Abrahams K. 'The Cosens Story', *Ship Ahoy*, Vol. 14, No 4, 1967
Boddy, M. 'Dorset Shipwrecks', *Dorset*, No 48-50, 1975-6
Clammer, R. 'Swansong of the Weymouth Paddlers', *Ships Monthly*, Vol.29, No.9 & 10, 1994
Gray, G.V.W. 'Bournemouth Excursion Steamers', *Paddle Wheels*, Nos. 81-86, 1980-81
Grice, R.B. 'Cosens of Weymouth', *Ships Monthly*, Vol5. No.2-7, April-July 1970
Kittridge, A. 'Coastal Cruising out of Plymouth' *Paddle Wheels*, No 94-97, 1983-84
Kittridge, A. 'The Duke, The Duchess and Campbells', *Paddle Wheels*, No 116, 1989

Taped Interviews:
Copies of taped interviews conducted by the author with Brian Jackson, Martin Langley, Hector Lowman, Peter Lloydworth, George Morris, Sandy Rashleigh, Bob Wills and Reg Willshire are lodged with the National Maritime Museum at Greenwich. Additional interviews with Reginald Fry and Desmond Palmer are in the author's collection.

Public Record Office:
ADM 179/374 Weymouth and Portland Defence Scheme
ADM 199/369,404,420,629,1395 and 1443, Portland War Diaries, 1940-45.
ADM208 Admiralty Red Lists Weekly movements of minor war vessels
ADM 199/334,328,331,335, Examination Service and Contraband Control Records.
ADM 53/113587-113589 Log Books of HMS AMBASSADOR (EMBASSY) 26.8.41. - 5.12.41.
BT 336 Registrar General of Shipping and Seamen: Registers of Changes of Master.

Miscellaneous Documents:
Weymouth Shipping registers, held at the Dorset County Record Office, Dorchester
Weymouth Harbour Bridge Books, courtesy of Weymouth & Portland Borough Council.

BIBLIOGRAPHY

Adams, R.B. *Red Funnel and Before*, Kingfisher Railway Publications, 1986.
Attwooll, M. & Harrison, D. *Weymouth & Portland at War*, Dovecote Press, 1993
Boddy, M. & West, J. *Weymouth, An illustrated History*, Dovecote Press, 1983
Burtt, F. *Steamers of the Thames and Medway*, Richard Tilling, 1949.
Burtt, F. *Cross Channel and Coastal Paddle Steamers*, Richard Tilling, 1934.
Carter, G. *The Royal Navy at Portland since 1845*, Maritime Books, 1987
Chalk, D. *Any More for the Skylark?*, David Chalk, 1980.
Collard, C. *Special Excursions, The story of P .& A. Campbell's steamers 1919-1939*, Wheelhouse Books, 1998.
Collard, C. *White Funnels, The story of P. & A. Campbell's steamers, 1946-68*, 1996.
Coombes, N. *Passenger Steamers of the Bristol Channel*, Twelveheads Press, 1990.
Coombes, N. *White Funnel Magic*, Twelveheads Press, 1995.
Cox, B. *Paddling Across the Bay*, Paddle Steamer Preservation Society, 1981.
Cox, B. *The Development and Decline of Cross Channel Excursions from Bournemouth*, Unpublished historical study, King Alfred's College Winchester, 1972
Danielson, R. *The Honourable Balmoral, her Peers and Piers*, Maritime Publications, 1999.
Durrant, J.S. & M.S. *Sunlit Seas, Vols. 1 & 2*, Unpublished personal scrapbooks describing the Bournemouth Steamers during the seasons of 1937 - 1939, courtesy of Victor Gray.

Eccott, P. *Allied Minesweeping in World War II*, Patrick Stevens Ltd., 1979.
Farr, G. *Wreck and Rescue on the Dorset Coast*, D. Bradford Barton Ltd., 1971.
Farr, G. *West Country Passenger Steamers*, Richard Tilling, 1956.
Grimshaw, G. *British Pleasure Steamers 1920-1939*, Richard Tilling, 1944.
Hill, R. *Weymouth at War*, Dorset Publishing Company, 1990.
Lane, M. *Piers of the Isle of Wight*, Isle of Wight Council, 1996.
Langley, M. *A Pageantry of Steam & Paddle*, Unpublished manuscript, courtesy of the author.
Leigh-Bennett, E.P. *Red Funnel Stuff*, Official Guide of Red Funnel Steamers, 1939.
Lucking J. H. *The Great Western at Weymouth*, David & Charles, 1971.
Lund, P. & Ludlam, H. *Out Sweeps*, W. Foulsham & Co. Ltd., 1978.
Morris, S. *Portland, An Illustrated History*, Dovecote Press, 1985.
O'Connor, G.W. *The First Hundred Years*, Red Funnel Steamers Ltd., 1961.
Plummer, R. *The Ships that Saved an Army*, Patrick Stevens Ltd., 1978.
Plummer, R. *Paddle Steamers at War*, GMS Enterprises, 1995.
Pushman, D. *The Loss of the S.S. Treveal*, Downsway Books, 1999.
Read, W. C. *The Journal of Capt. William Carey Read*, Unpublished manuscript, Weymouth Library, ref. L.921.REA.1.
Shovelar, S. *Dorset Shipwrecks*, Freestyle Publications, 1996.
Taffrail (Capt T. Dorling), *Swept Channels*, Hodder & Stoughton, 1935.
Thornton, E.C.B. *South Coast Pleasure Steamers*, T. Stephenson & Sons Ltd., 1962.
Thornton, E.C.B. *Thames Coast Pleasure Steamers*, T. Stephenson & Sons Ltd., 1972.

APPENDIX ONE

PASSENGER FIGURES, 1931 TO 1961

	EXCURSIONS FROM BOURNEMOUTH	EXCURSIONS FROM WEYMOUTH	TO & FROM PORTLAND	TO & FROM LULWORTH	TO WARSHIPS	MOTORBOATS FROM BEACH	IN SPEEDBOATS	TOTAL
1931	106,273	7,272	18,343	19,149	4,949	16,724	10,458	183,168
1932	111,005	15,679	17,737	19,945	12,419	28,061	11,589	220,435
1933	125,385	13,012	20,914	23,653	8,673	20,872	9,190	221,699
1934	117,225	12,649	21,829	22,766	7,571	20,615	7,893	210,548
1935	121,355	23,155	23,497	23,953	7,476	23,147	7,054	229,637
1936	123,999	20,776	24,953	21,475	4,386	19,085	7,687	222,360
1937	139,396	29,754	30,072	27,997	2,612	20,408	7,626	257,865
1938	127,658	34,825	26,567	24,265	7,240	19,662	6,360	246,577
1939	111,505	45,287	25,117	17,865	6,819	24,960	6,053	237,605
1946	29,646	49,850	0	32,478	50,034	0	2,817	164,824
1947	193,757	48,291	0	35,325	29,906	35,813	17,847	360,939
1948	202,298	36,184	0	26,939	21,725	38,637	12,303	338,086
1949	167,562	57,787	0	30,420	19,211	36,651	11,359	322,990
1950	110,725	38,763	0	22,287	13,599	30,556	7,428	223,358
1951	186,528	29,928	0	21,494	15,603	29,481	5,288	288,322
1952	219,958	41,532	3,231	21,880	12,392	29,763	7,847	336,604
1953	202,968*	43,132*	1,891	18,870	6,798	28,304	0	301,963
1954	175,700	34,839	5,168	15,018	8,264	26,254	0	265,343
1955	199,561	34,676	4,553	21,420	7,616	29,077	0	296,903
1956	133,429	19,497	8,008	8,647	0	19,239	0	188,820

	BOURNEMOUTH DAY TRIPS	BOURNEMOUTH EVENING TRIPS	BOURNEMOUTH TO SWANAGE	POOLE	MOTOR COACH	WEYMOUTH DAY TRIPS & CRUISES	WEYMOUTH TO LULWORTH	PORTLAND HARBOUR	
1957	46,569	2,491**	56,513	7,155**	13,989**	16,692	6,196	12,546	138,516
1958	45,763	698**	63,359	8,505**	13,861**	15,146	5,506	21,069	152,880
1959	46,317	2,928**	66,773	10,780**	15,571**	18,592	6,618	18,367	156,668
1960	35,356	3,735**	47,702	6,139**	12,205**	15,997	5,828	13,591	118,475
1961	19,003	19,003	12,936	1,788	11,838	17,199	5,831	11,776	84,873

* Includes 9,789 by Bournemouth steamers and 4,987 by Weymouth steamers carried from Southampton during naval review.
** The figures for Bournemouth evening trips, Poole and motor coaches were also included within the Bournemouth day trips total from 1957 to 1960, but not in 1961.

APPENDIX TWO

Cosens & Co Ltd Passenger Steamer Fleet List

Name	Official Number	Acquired Built Displaced Scrapped	Tons	Length Breadth Depth	Engines — Type	Cylinders Diameter	Stroke	Nominal HP	Builder Hull Type Engine Builder	Notes
Highland Maid (on charter)	9072	1848 1846 1848 1874		66.2 ft 13 ft 8 ft				22	P. Legg Wood J. Harrison	Tug, Reg. Newcastle 1846, London 1847
Princess	21528	1848 1847? 1853 1882	60.9 burthen	112.5 ft 13.5 ft 7.7 ft	Oscillating 2 cylinders			2 x 20 1849 2 x 16	Ditchburn & Mare Iron John Penn	Owned by John Penn 1847-9 New engines 1849 Sold J. T. Leather 1853 Sold Plymouth 1857. Scrapped 1882
Wave Queen (on charter)		1852 1852 1852		220 ft 18 ft -				80	Robinson Russel & Co, Millwall	
Prince	21519	1852 1852 1888 1897	60.8 burthen	120.5 ft 13.3 ft 7.6 ft					John Scott Russell Iron John Penn	Bow and rig altered 1878-9 1888 Sold to Ellet & Matthews, Exmouth
Contractor	13941	1858 1847 1863 -		84.4 ft 15.8 ft 8.9 ft					J Jackson Wood	Tug/passenger bought P. Dodson 1852 To Cosens 1858 To Plymouth 1863
Ocean Bride	6228	1858 1844 1865 1867?	29.2 grt 18.4 rt	72 ft 12.6 ft 5.8 ft				18	? East Wood	Tug at Newcastle. Bought Dodson 1856 To Cosens 1858 Sold to J. T. Leather 1865 Sold to Crown 1867
Bannockburn	2102	1860 1847 1869 1869	53.2 grt 10.5 rt	69.6 ft 16 ft 8.4 ft				28	E. Oliver Wood	T. Brewis Newcastle Sold to J. Tizard, Weymouth 1859 To Cosens 1860 Converted to barge 1865
Premier	6387	1860 1846 1938 1938	98.4 grt / 62 rt FROM 1878: 115.2 grt / 72.6 rt	240.2 x 17 x 6.5 ft FROM 1878: 148.5 x 17.3 x 6.7 ft	Steeple FROM 1878: Oscillating, 2 cylinders	25 ins & 29 ins	33 ins	65 50	Denny Iron Tullock & Denny FROM 1878: Penn	1846 Dumbarton Steambot Co 1859 To Tizard, Weymouth 1860 To Cosens 1878 Rebuilt, new engines
Commodore	28012	1863 1863 1890 1894	96.3 grt 26.2 rt	93 ft 18.6 ft 9.6 ft	Side lever			60	A. Woodhouse	1890 to J. Campbell, Ho;yhead
Empress	63915	1879 1879 1958 1958	163.5 grt 98 rt	160.1 ft 18.5 ft 8.3 ft	Oscillating, 2 cylinders	30 ins	33 ins	52	Samunda Iron Penn	1884 Reboilered 1906 Reboilered, mainmast removed.
Queen	88126	1883 1883 1920 1923	146.1 grt 77 rt	110.2 ft 19.7 ft 8.9 ft	2 Side lever	26 ins	48 ins	70	Smit & Zoon Iron Vulcan Ironworks	1920 To Ardrossan Harbour Board.
Victoria	82355	1884 1884 1953 1953	191.7 grt 99.8 rt	166 ft 19.2 ft 8.7 ft	Oscillating, 2 cylinders	35 ins	36 ins	75	S & K Smit Steel Penn	
Monarch	82358	1888 1888 1950 1950	309 grt 92.7 rt	210 ft 22.2 ft 9 ft	Diagonal, direct acting, condensing, 2 cylinders	41 ins	48 ins	130 850 IHP	R & H Green Steel Penn	1889 Foc's'le lengthened 1912 Forward lifeboats fitted 1929-30 Reboilered and larger funnels and wheelhouse fitted
Albert Victor (ex-Lass O'Gowrie)	86379	1889 1883 1928 1928	128.4 grt 32.7 rt	106 ft 19.8 ft 9.7 ft	Side lever, 2 cylinders	37 ins	54 ins	70	Eltringham & Co Iron Reynoldson & Sons	1897 Engines converted to condensing and new boilers fitted 192? Wheelhouse fitted
Prince George	104425	1898 1898 1928 1928	27.2 grt 8.5 rt	67.7 ft 10.5 ft 6.9 ft	Screw, compound inverted, surface condensing, 2 cylinders	7.75 ins 14.25 ins	12 ins	9 7.5 IHP	Cosens Steel Cosens	
Majestic	104427	1901 1901 1916 1916	408.4 grt 93 rt	215.5 ft 27.1 ft 8.9 ft	Triple expansion, diagonal, 3 cylinders	21 ins 35 ins 54 ins	60 ins	200 1300 IHP	A & J Inglis Steel A & J Inglis	1906 mainmast removed 1910 converted to barge and foundered off Portland
Brodick Castle	78614	1901 1878 1910 1910	283 grt 134 rt	207.6 ft 21.7 ft 7.5 ft	Simple diagonal, surface condensing 2 cylinders	38.25 ins	66 ins	96	McIntyre & Co Iron King & Co	1951 From Portsmouth
Emperor of India (ex-Princess Royal)	119739	1908 1906 1957 1957	487 grt / 191rt FROM 1948: 533 grt / 210 rt	217.2 ft FROM 1907 25.1 ft 8.4 ft	Compound diagonal surface condensing, 2 cylinders	30 ins 57 ins	60 ins	138 1450 IHP	Thornycroft Steel Thornycroft	1907 Lengthened by 21ft 8ins. 1909 Plated up to bow. 1948 Rebuilt.
Lord Roberts (on charter)		1911 1900 1912 1934	235 grt	135 ft 21.4 ft 9.7 ft	Simple diagonal, 2 cylinders	30 ins	48 ins	80	W. Allsup	
Audrey (on charter)		1911	203 grt	126 ft 21.1 ft 8 ft	Compound diagonal, 2 cylinders	17 ins 34 ins	42 ins	60	Armstrong Whitworth Steel	From Cork, Blackrock & Passage Ferry Co.
Helper (ex-Sir Francis Drake)	68324	1910 1873 1920 1929	172.5 grt 58.8 rt	131.3 ft 25.1 ft 8.4 ft	Simple diaginal, 2 cylinders	30 ins	48 ins	80	Allsup Iron Allsup	1910 From GWR (Plymouth) 1920 Sold to Guernsey
Melcombe Regis (ex-Lune)	89706	1913 1892 1923 1923	252.9 grt 55.8 rt	129 ft 24.1 ft 9.5 ft	Compound diagonal, 2 cylinders	24 ins 48 ins	54 ins	96	Thomas Seath Steel Thomas Seath	
Alexandra (ex-)	81004	1915 1879 1931 1934	234.7 grt 98 rt	171 ft 20.2 ft 8.5 ft	Compound diagonal surface condensing, 2 cylinders	25 ins 50 ins	54 ins	120	Scott & Co Iron Scott & Co	1915 From Portsmouth 1931 sold to breakers (resold as 'Showboat') 1934 Scrapped
Embassy (ex-Duchess of Norfolk)	131994	1937 1911 1967 1967	380.7 grt / 154.2 rt FROM 1948: 446.1 grt / 184.4 rt	190 ft 26.1 ft 8.7 ft	Compound diagonal, 2 cylinders	27 ins 51 ins	54 ins	180 1000 IHP	D & W Henderson Steel D & W Henderson	1937 From Portsmouth 1947 Rebuilt
Consul (ex-Duke of Devonshire)	194431	1937 1896 1963 1968	256.5 grt 106.6 rt	175 ft 20.6 ft 8.2 ft	Compound diagonal, 2 cylinders	23 ins 46 ins	36 ins	100 500 IHP	R & H Green Steel Penn	1937 From Torquay 1938 New funnel 1949 Rebuilt
Monarch (ex-Shanklin)	147994	1951 1824 1961 1961	399 grt 181.2 rt	190 ft 26.1 ft 8.7 ft	Compound diagonal, 2 cylinders	27 ins 51 ins	54 ins	187 1100 IHP	D & W Henderson Steel D & W Henderson	1951 From Portsmouth

Ship's Masters, 1918 to 1966

Year	Premier	Empress	Queen	Victoria	Monarch (1)	Albert Victor	Emperor of India	Helper	Melcombe Regis	Alexandra	Embassy	Consul	Monarch(2)
1918	Hollyoak	J J Marshallsay	H A Garnett	War service?	Janman RNR	H A Garnett	War service	Laid up	War service	W C Read			
1919		H J Hardy	H A Garnett	War service?	?	H A Garnett	War service		War service	W C Read			
1920	A Cox?	J Cox?		J J Marshallsay	H J Hardy	H A Garnett	War service/ refit		Laid up	W C Read			
1921	A Cox?	J Cox?		J J Marshallsay	H A Garnett	W C King	W C Read		Laid up	Read / Hardy			
1922	A Cox?	J Cox?		J J Marshallsay	H A Garnett	W C King	W C Read		Laid up	H J Hardy			
1923	W C King	J Cox		J J Marshallsay	H A Garnett	King / Rawle	W C Read		Marshallsay (scrap)	H J Hardy			
1924	W C King	J Cox		J J Marshallsay	H A Garnett	St Barbe Rawle	W C Read			W J Carter			
1925	W C King	J Cox		J J Marshallsay	H A Garnett	Rawle / Hardy	W C Read			W J Carter			
1926	W C King	J Cox		J J Marshallsay	H A Garnett	St Barbe Rawle	W C Read			W J Carter			
1927	W C King	J Cox		J J Marshallsay	H A Garnett	St Barbe Rawle	W C Read			W J Carter			
1928	W C King	J J Marshallsay?		W J Carter	H A Garnett	St Barbe Rawle	W C Read			W J Carter			
1929	W C King	St Barbe Rawle		W J Carter	H A Garnett		W C Read			St Barbe Rawle			
1930	W C King	W E Leddy		W J Carter	H A Garnett		W C Read			St Barbe Rawle			
1931	W C King	W E Leddy		W J Carter	H A Garnett		W C Read			A E G Hawkes			
1932	A R Moore	W E Leddy		W J Carter	H A Garnett		W C Read			H F Defrates			
1933	A R Moore	W E Leddy		St Barbe Rawle	W J Carter		W C Read						
1934	A R Moore	W E Leddy		St Barbe Rawle	W J Carter		W C Read						
1935	A R Moore	W E Leddy		St Barbe Rawle	W J Carter		W C Read						
1936	A R Moore	W E Leddy		R Bowering	St Barbe Rawle		W J Carter						
1937	J W Knight	Leddy (retired)		A R Moore	St Barbe Rawle		W J Carter				R Bowering	A R Moore	
1938		E F J Cook		J W Knight	St Barbe Rawle		W J Carter				R Bowering	A R Moore	
1939		E F J Cook		Knight / Carter	St Barbe Rawle		W J Carter				R Bowering	A R Moore	
1940		E F J Cook		W J Carter	St Barbe Rawle		War service				R Bowering	A R Moore	
1941		Laid up		Laid up	St Barbe Rawle		War service				War service	Moore/Laid up	
1942		Laid up		Laid up	St Barbe Rawle		War service				War service	Laid up	
1943		Laid up		Laid up	St Barbe Rawle		War service				War service	Laid up	
1944		Laid up/Palmer		Laid up / Rousell	St Barbe Rawle		War service				War service	W J Carter	
1945				Refiting	Refiting		War service				Refiting	Laid up	
1946		A R Moore		Moore / Cooke	A R Moore		Laid up				St Barbe Rawle	Laid up	
1947		Cook / Carter		A R Moore	E F J Cook		Refiting				St Barbe Rawle	Laid up	
1948		Hollyoak / Rousell		Merryweather/Hollyoak	E F J Cook		St Barbe Rawle				A R Moore	Refiting	
1949		F Merryweather		A E Hollyoak?	E F J Cook		St Barbe Rawle				E S Haines	Refiting	
1950		F Merryweather		E J Haines	E F J Cook		St Barbe Rawle				A R Moore	E S Haines	
1951		F Merryweather		Haines/Defrates			St Barbe Rawle				A R Moore	E F J Cook	E F J Cook
1952		F Merryweather		A R Moore			St Barbe Rawle				E F J Cook	Cook/Haines	E S Haines
1953		F Merryweather		Moore (to scrap)			Rawle / Moore				E F J Cook	H F Defrates	E S Haines
1954		F Merryweather					St Barbe Rawle				E S Haines	A R Moore	H F Defrates
1955		F Merryweather					St Barbe Rawle				E S Haines	A R Moore	H F Defrates
1956		F Merryweather					St Barbe Rawle				E S Haines	A R Moore	H F Defrates
1957											St Barbe Rawle	H F Defrates	E S Haines
1958											St Barbe Rawle	H F Defrates	E S Haines
1959											St Barbe Rawle	H F Defrates	E S Haines
1960											E S Haines	H F Defrates	H F Defrates
1961											E S Haines	J Iliffe	H F Defrates
1962											C Hollyoak	C Hollyoak	
1963											J Iliffe	J Iliffe	
1964											J Iliffe	H F Defrates	
1965											J Iliffe	C Hollyoak	
1966											J Iliffe	H F Defrates	

INDEX